# MILITARY INTERVENTION AND SECESSION IN SOUTH ASIA

# MILITARY INTERVENTION AND SECESSION IN SOUTH ASIA

*The Cases of Bangladesh, Sri Lanka, Kashmir, and Punjab*

**Anne Noronha Dos Santos**

PRAEGER SECURITY INTERNATIONAL
Westport, Connecticut • London

**Library of Congress Cataloging-in-Publication Data**

Santos, Anne Noronha dos.
Military intervention and secession in South Asia: the cases of Bangladesh, Sri Lanka, Kashmir, and Punjab / Anne Noronha Dos Santos.
p. cm.
Includes bibliographical references and index.
ISBN 978-0-275-99949-0 (alk. paper)
1. National security—South Asia—Case studies. 2. South Asia—Military relations—Case studies. 3. Intervention (International law) 4. South Asia—Politics and government. I. Title.
UA832.7.S36 2007
341.5'840954—dc22 2007028085

British Library Cataloguing in Publication Data is available.



Library of Congress Catalog Card Number: 2007028085
ISBN: 978-0-275-99949-0

First published in 2007

Praeger Security International, 88 Post Road West, Westport, CT 06881
An imprint of Greenwood Publishing Group, Inc.
www.praeger.com

Printed in the United States of America

The paper used in this book complies with the Permanent Paper Standard issued by the National Information Standards Organization (Z39.48-1984).

10 9 8 7 6 5 4 3 2 1

This book is dedicated to my family
Clyde, Earl, Bruce, and Brittany, with love.

# Contents

# Acknowledgments

THIS BOOK BEGAN as a dissertation, under the astute guidance of Prof. Andrew Kydd, while I was getting my PhD at the University of California, Riverside (UCR). His scholarly advice and substantive comments encouraged me to keep thinking. I felt privileged when he agreed to continue advising me after he moved to Harvard University in 2001. His unwavering patience and belief in me motivated me to get this manuscript published. I am ever grateful to him. I am also grateful to Prof. Juliann Emmons Allison of UCR whose insightful ideas, enthusiasm, and friendship made my years as a graduate student a happy experience. I thank Prof. Ronald Chiclote of UCR whose interest in my work kept my level of confidence high.

I am especially indebted to a number of good friends without whom this book would not have been possible. My sincere thanks go to Arvind D'Souza, who inspired me to pursue higher studies. My thanks also go to Gerard Tellis, whose comments on several initial drafts showed me how to organize my writing. I appreciate all the support and words of encouragement, throughout the long writing process, from Patricia D'Souza, Norma Lopez-Perez, Lillian Pereira, Cheryl Tellis, and George Viegas. My nephew, Carlyle D'Costa's computer skills helped me meet the deadline to turn in the manuscript.

I would like to acknowledge with deep gratitude the help I received from UCR Library's Document Delivery Service. Maria Mendoza, Kimberly Noon, and Janet Moores spared no effort in tracking down hundreds of documents, journals, and books from around the country. Their untiring smiles, patience, and cooperation in providing my research needs were outstanding. Kelly Donovan, graphic artist at California State University, Fullerton, deserves a special mention.

The figures in the book were carefully and skillfully drawn by her. Thank you, Kelly.

Last but not the least, my husband Clyde, and children, Earl, Bruce, and Brittany, deserve special thanks for their love, patience, and understanding. They allowed me to devote a great amount of time to this project—time that I would normally have spent with them. For their love, this work is dedicated to them.

# 1

# Introduction

MAJOR SECESSIONIST MOVEMENTS are currently ongoing in Russia, Turkey, Thailand, Nigeria, Spain, India, Pakistan, and Sri Lanka, among others, and these movements have had a strong impact on international security. The ongoing secessionist movement in Kashmir, for example, is a major threat to security in South Asia and may eventually bring about international military intervention.[1] Despite the importance of this issue, theories of international relations have not adequately addressed the link between secessionist sentiment and international intervention. Exploring this link raises the following research question: How, when, and why do secessionist movements increase both intrastate and interstate security competition and increase the risk of international military intervention?

This study develops a conceptual framework that identifies the conditions that make international military intervention more or less likely. It seeks to delineate a causal sequence that explains the processes by which a secessionist movement becomes a secessionist war, expands, internationalizes, and either succeeds, fails, or results in a stalemate. Exploring the range of outcomes from stalemates to full-scale military intervention can help contribute to the management and resolution of secessionist conflict. The thoughts presented here are generalizations based on hypotheses that are tested by historical evidence. In other words, patterns of behavior associated with secession have been analyzed in order to build a theory of secessionist war and international intervention with a view toward guiding future policy choices. The theory is then tested by an in-depth historical analysis of four case studies of secessionist war drawn from South Asia: the Kashmir and Punjab movements in India, the Tamil movement in Sri Lanka, and the East Pakistan movement that resulted in the creation of Bangladesh.

A secessionist movement is one that tries to establish a separate sovereign state. The very act of secession has been defined as "an attempt by an ethnic group claiming a homeland to withdraw with its territory from the authority of a larger state of which it is a part."[2] In other words, it is "the unilateral withdrawal of territory and people from a state."[3] A secessionist movement is "directed at the state, though indirectly challenging the dominant ethnic group's tight grip on political and economic power, together with its cultural dominance in the state."[4] Secessionist movements usually begin as demands for regional autonomy but often escalate into full-fledged attempts to form separate internationally recognized states out of existing sovereign states. The term secession does not apply to independence movements from colonial powers.

This study uses neorealist[5] concepts such as balance of power, alliances, and preventive war, among others. However, it goes beyond neorealism,[6] the dominant paradigm in international relations. It combines unit-level variables such as secessionist sentiments, nationalistic beliefs of secessionist groups with system-level variables like states to form one cohesive theory that explains phenomena such as international intervention in a secessionist war. By including domestic or internal factors within states, this analysis differs from the Waltzian state-centric approach to international relations and draws attention to the internal structures of states.

My primary thesis is that a shift in the balance of power between a secessionist group and the host state (the state that a group wants to secede from) will lead to a preventive war[7] on the secessionists by the central government of the host state. A preventive war increases the chances of an alliance[8] between the secessionist group and an external power. A preventive war on the secessionists is also likely to lead to an explosive growth of the movement. My supporting theses are that rivalry between the host state and an external power and/or religious or ethnic kinship between the external power and the secessionists will exacerbate this risk of an alliance being formed. My ultimate thesis is that the stronger the alliance, the greater the chances of international military intervention in the secessionist war.

Developing a theory of secessionist war and international intervention is important for several reasons. First, secessionist movements in so many parts of the world remain a big threat to international security. From Chechnya in Russia to Kashmir in India, these movements have incurred huge human, social, and economic losses. For example, there have been as least 30,000 deaths in Kashmir since 1989 (*The Indian Express,* August 8, 2000) and more than 62,000 people have died in Sri Lanka since the Tamil uprising began in 1983 (Anti-Defamation League, 2001). Although these movements usually originate in one state, they can quickly become internationalized. The dynamic process by which secessionist movements become internationalized is largely understudied.

Second, understanding the conditions under which secessionist wars take place, expand, and invite international military intervention has strong policy implications. It can go a long way toward guiding policy makers who may want to mitigate or avoid these conditions in their states. Speaking of foreign military intervention, Tillema states, "It is the ultimate instrument of forceful foreign policy. It is the most awesome threat, the most grievous form of punishment, and the culminating reward of alliance. Its prevention is the first object of deterrent security policy."[9]

Third, discussing the link between secessionist movements and international security allows us to link the internal structures of states (nationalistic beliefs, and social and economic factors) with the structure of the international system.

## LITERATURE

There is a large literature on the internationalization of ethnic conflict—the effects of ethnic conflict on neighboring states and the reactions of neighboring states with respect to these conflicts.[10] However, this literature has hardly accorded adequate attention to secessionist conflict as a type of ethnic conflict. In fact, secessionist conflict "has been considered fit only for the antechambers of the discipline and then only if clothed in the procrustean attire of 'the ethnic': ethnic conflict, ethnic separatism, and so on."[11] One can argue that since secessionist conflict is a type of ethnic conflict, it can be dealt with within the confines of ethnic conflict. However, secessionist conflicts are different in that they challenge the territorial integrity of the state and therefore, the state plays an important role in these conflicts.

Studies that have dealt exclusively with secession have focused largely on the causes of secession. Some studies have analyzed secession using a rational choice approach. Stephane Dion's rational choice approach to secession proposes a causal explanation of secession based on fear and confidence. He claims that "secessionist movements are rooted in two types of perceptions: the fear inspired by the union and the confidence inspired by secession."[12] Speaking of Quebec, he refers to the French Quebecers' fear of the disappearing French language and culture and the confidence in them that they will survive well as a separate state.

Another rational choice approach by Michael Hechter sees secession as the result of a number of collective decisions made by people who want to secede on the one hand, and the host state on the other.[13] Secession is said to occur when the host state feels that it is less expensive to cede the territory than to maintain it.[14]

Ralph Premdas's framework of secessionist movements emphasizes the "psychological collective factor of group consciousness"[15] that triggers the movement. He distinguishes between primordial and secondary factors that cause secession. Primordial causes such as religion, race, language, and territory, among others, define the identity of a group and are deeply embedded in a society. Premdas describes secondary factors as those that have been recently experienced like exploitation, repression, neglect, and domination that "serve as the triggering mechanism of collective consciousness felt by a group as it proceeds to define its demands."[16]

Some studies have dealt with the complexity of the secession process. John R. Wood's analysis of secession[17] deals with the stages of the secession process from the preconditions of the secessionist movement to its resolution through armed conflict. Wood's framework emphasizes the complexity of the secession process but does not specify any causative links. He assembles the different aspects of a secessionist movement but does not pinpoint related variables with predictive power.

Rupen Cetinyan's "perfect information strategic interaction model"[18] shows how bargaining between an ethnic group and its host state takes place amidst prospective intervention by an external party. Unlike my framework, which specifically focuses on situations where power is shifting, Cetinyan's model assumes that power is fixed. Therefore, in my model, commitment problems and preventive war occurs, whereas in Cetinyan's, neither rebellion nor outside intervention takes place.

A number of studies have examined separate cases of secessionist movements[19] and explained them in ad hoc ways, but the field of International Relations has yet to come up with general theories that explain why different outcomes occur: some secessionist movements bring on international military intervention and others do not; those that do bring on international military intervention have different outcomes: some succeed, some fail, and some result in a stalemate. Although several cases of secessionist activity in Sudan, Nigeria, Spain, India, Pakistan, and Sri Lanka, among others, have been examined, none provides a framework showing the causal links between secessionist sentiment and international intervention. None of the above studies has applied the concepts of International Relations such as balance of power, alliances, and preventive war to a theory that explains how, why, and when secessionist movements increase the security competition within and between states and thereby increase the probability of international military intervention.

It is important to note that my use of these International Relations concepts differs from neorealism. Unlike neorealism, which focuses exclusively on states as primary actors, my study also includes secessionists groups as primary actors. Unlike structural balance-of-power theory, my analysis is not entirely based on the distribution of aggregate capabilities or power among states. I include in my analysis the distribution of power between central governments and groups within states. Unlike Walt's definition of an alliance, my definition is not limited to "two or more sovereign states."[20] I explore how a secessionist group forms an alliance with an external state to balance against its own central government. Drawing on the literature on preventive war,[21] I apply the concept of preventive war to the actions of states on secessionist groups.

## RESEARCH DESIGN

This study uses "the method of comparative historical *analysis*"[22] to answer the research question: How, when, and why do secessionist movements affect international security and increase the risk of international military intervention? Four secessionist movements from South Asia are analyzed: East Pakistan (now Bangladesh), Kashmir, Sri Lanka, and Punjab. The "structured, focused comparison"[23] of these cases tests and refines a theory of secessionist war and international intervention. The study is structured in the sense that the same information will be collected (the same questions will be asked) on each case in order to draw valid causal inferences. "This standardized set of questions or hypotheses insures the comparability of results."[24] The study will be focused in that the case studies will focus on the causal mechanisms rather than on just a broad description of events.[25] The case studies will focus on the research problem being examined, which in this case deals with how, when, and why secessionist movements bring on international military intervention.

The method of focused comparison is an offshoot of the case study method. However, instead of delving into one case study in depth, this method uses a small number of cases "and then compares the pattern of events from one to another."[26] The researcher "looks for similarities among the patterns of course; but he also looks for significant differences."[27] Therefore, in this study, I examine similar aspects of each secessionist movement in order to "come up with variables and relationships that are similar enough to permit realistic comparisons."[28]

This comparative analysis thus concentrates on similar cases in South Asia. Most of these movements have tried to balance with an external power against their own central governments; most have received military aid from external powers. By allying with external powers, these movements have intensified the security competition within and between states. However, the outcomes of these movements have been different. By choosing a set of cases with different outcomes I have employed J.S. Mill's method of difference design.[29] This method compares cases where the outcomes are different in order to pinpoint the causal factor that is responsible for the change.

I have chosen to focus on South Asia (see figure 1.1) because the region being fraught with separatist movements provides an ideal laboratory for the examination of my research problem. Besides the four cases I examine, South Asia is also home to other separatist movements such as the Muhajir movement in the southern province of Pakistan, the Chakma (Chittagong) Hill tribal movement in Bangladesh, and the movement in Assam, among others. Although the case studies are drawn from South Asia, the model on which they are based is applicable to other regions as well.

In order to test whether a shift in the balance of power in favor of a secessionist group leads to suppression of the secessionists by the central government, I compare the behavior of the central government toward the group before and after the shift in the balance of power took place. This procedure uses the old relationship as a control case so as to assess the impact of the shift in balance of power on the relations between the secessionist group and the central government.

In order to test whether a preventive war on the secessionist group by the central government causes an alliance between the secessionists and an external

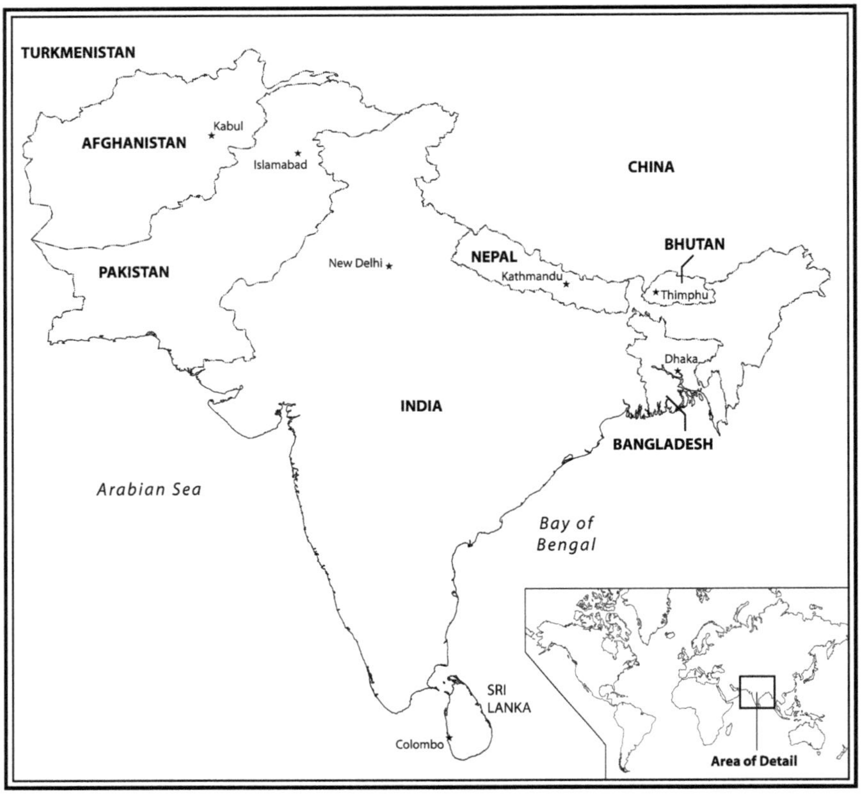


**Figure 1.1 Map of South Asia**

*Source*: *South Asia Intelligence Review*, Weekly Assesments and Briefings, 1.47 (June 9, 2003).

power, I compare the relations of the secessionist group, in each case, with the respective external power before and after the suppression began. Other things being equal, was the propensity to form an alliance lower or higher before the suppression began? If it was "lower," then the suppression plausibly had an independent causal effect on the formation of an alliance.

To explain whether the preventive war on the secessionists results in an explosive growth of the movement, I compare the movement before and after the preventive war took place. Was the movement strengthened, larger, and more radicalized after the preventive war?

To test whether an alliance increases the risk of international military intervention in a secessionist war, I compare the situations before and after the formation of an alliance. Did the alliance increase the security competition between states in the region? I compare the relationship between states in the region before and after the alliance was formed. Once again, the old relationship is used as a control case to assess the impact of the alliance on the security competition between the states.

To explain if rivalries lead to an alliance and eventually increase the risk of external military intervention in a secessionist war, I compare the Sri Lankan case with the other secessionist conflicts. Rivalry between India and Pakistan formed alliances between the secessionist group and an external power in the case of Kashmir, Punjab, and East Pakistan. In the case of Sri Lanka, there is no rivalry between India and Sri Lanka, so it was not rivalry but ethnic/religious ties between the secessionists and an external power that led to the alliance.

To explain whether ethnic/religious ties lead to an alliance between the secessionists and an external power, I compare the Punjab case with the other three cases. Ethnic/religious kinship contributed to the alliances in the East Pakistan, Sri Lanka, and Kashmir cases. In the Punjab case, religious ties between the secessionists and the external power were absent and other cultural bonds were not strong.

The rest of this book is as follows: Chapter 2 elaborates my theoretical argument examining in detail the causal propositions I have put forth. Chapters 3–6 deal with the case studies of the secessionist movements in East Pakistan, Sri Lanka, Kashmir, and Punjab, respectively. Chapter 7 summarizes the findings of the cases, comparing the results and discussing their future relevance and implications for policy making.

# 2

# A Theory of International Intervention in a Secessionist War

WHY, WHEN, AND HOW do secessionist movements become secessionist wars and increase the risk of international military intervention? I present a theoretical framework or model that lays out a causal sequence that precedes external military intervention in a secessionist war. Doing so provides a method of explaining why some secessionist wars bring about external military intervention whereas others do not. My explanation begins with the interaction that takes place between a state and a secessionist group in that state. I then analyze the interaction that takes place when an external party gets involved. Finally, I show how these processes increase the risk of military intervention. Therefore, in order to explain international military intervention in a secessionist war, I uncover the causal dynamics that bring it about. Specifically, what factors intensify security competition and lead to military intervention?

The analytical framework presented here is based on the following assumptions regarding the behavior of states and groups within the states:

First, domestic politics and international politics are closely related. In other words, politics that takes place within states affects politics that occurs outsides states.

Second, states are not the only important actors in the international system. Groups within states are also important actors. Robert Gilpin has appropriately stated, "The argument that the state . . . is the principal actor in international relations does not deny the existence of other individual and collective actors."[1] According to Ernst Haas, any entity that is able to express its demands effectively is an actor in international relations.[2]

Third, a sovereign state wants to preserve its territorial integrity. For this reason, it will fight any group wanting to secede from it. Describing the state, Naomi Chazan writes, "The state, a legal-territorial concept, refers to that set of structures and institutions that seek to maintain effective control over a given population within a specifically defined geographical area."[3] In other words, a state's primary goal is to control its territory and population. A state possesses military capabilities that enable it to fight not only external challenges but also internal uprisings within its territory. In the words of Ishtiaq Ahmed, "as the state possesses organized power it has greater advantage in acting in a deliberate and specific way upon society. On the other hand, society consisting of various autonomous units cannot ordinarily act upon the state in a similar fashion."[4]

Fourth, survival is the main goal of a secessionist group within a state. It tries to enhance its security by increasing its power. A secessionist group will try to alter the balance of power within a state by acquiring an increase in power at the expense of the state. Just like "the security and power dilemma"[5] of John Herz, a secessionist group's increase in power is a loss in power for the state.

Fifth, besides security, a secessionist group has other goals—economic, political, or cultural. It strives to preserve its language or religion and wants the same economic and political status as other groups. For this reason, a secessionist group will want to increase its power to enable it to fight any discrimination it may face at the hands of a majority group/state.

Sixth, a state can never be sure about the intentions of a secessionist group. Since a secessionist group is constantly trying to increase its capabilities, a state is always suspicious of the group's actions. Although the domestic political structure of a state "is characterized by a hierarchical order based on authority"[6] the distribution of power between a state and groups within a state can shift over time.

Seventh, states and secessionist groups are rational actors. States think strategically about how to maintain their territorial integrity and secessionist groups develop their strategy for survival.

## DEFINITION OF CONCEPTS

Before laying out the conceptual framework, it is important to define the concepts at hand. Vasquez has noted that "since everyday language is robust and living, most words have more than one meaning, and this can lead to ambiguity and a lack of conceptual rigor if an analyst fails to stipulate in what sense a concept is being used."[7] Adopting a working definition of a concept identifies the "defining criteria"[8] that decide which phenomena should be included in the "empirical domain of an enquiry."[9]

### Balance of Power

Just as in neorealism, the balance of power is a central concept in my analysis. In the words of Robert Gilpin:

> Realist writers from Thucydides and Mackinder to present-day scholars have attributed the dynamics of international relations to the fact that the distribution of power in

> an international system shifts over a period of time; this shift results in profound changes in the relationships among states and eventually changes in the nature of the international system itself.[10]

But what is the balance of power? Morgenthau has defined balance of power as "an actual state of affairs in which power is distributed among several nations with approximate equality."[11] In fact, Morgenthau has listed four ways in which the term has been used:

> [A]s a policy aimed at bringing about a certain power distribution; as a description of an actual state of affairs in international politics; as an approximately equal distribution of power internationally; and as a term describing any distribution of political power in international relations.[12]

Dina Zinnes has noted that a balance of power is "a particular distribution of power among the states of that system such that no single state and no existing alliance has an 'overwhelming' or 'preponderant' amount of power."[13]

My conceptualization of the balance of power refers to the "existing distribution of power"[14] or "the prevailing political situation."[15] "Here all sense of a genuine balance or equilibrium has been lost and the phrase has become simply a synonym for the distribution of power at a particular time."[16] More importantly, in my analysis, the distribution of power is between the state and a secessionist group. So, when I speak of balance of power, I refer to the "existing distribution of power" between the central government of a state and a secessionist group within that state.

How do we define power? Although power is a very important concept in political science, the discipline lacks a universal definition and measurement of the concept. For this reason, the "nature of our theory of international politics determines how we conceptualize power."[17] In my study, I conceptualize an entity's power in terms of its ability "to recruit, extract, and organize human and material resources, then use them coherently (efficiently over time)"[18] in the pursuit its objectives.

## Preventive War

Preventive war[19] "generally refers to a war fought *now* in order to avoid the risks of war under worsening conditions *later*."[20] It has been defined as a war that is "motivated by the fear that one's military power and potential are declining relative to that of a rising adversary."[21] The concept flows from "the phenomenon of changing power differentials"[22] or "decline in relative power capabilities"[23] and is traced back to the fifth century BC writings of Thucydides and the Peloponnesian War. The idea that "the dominant power initiates preventive action to block the rising challenger while the latter is still too weak to mount a serious threat"[24] is applied to my analysis. In my study, however, the rising challenger is the secessionist group and the declining power is the state.

### Rivalry

"Rivalry is . . . a term that characterizes a competitive relationship between two actors over an issue that is of the highest salience to them."[25] But competitiveness alone is not enough. Rivalries have a temporal component: some last for a short time, whereas others are long term.[26] They also have a spatial component: "rivalries include a consistent set of states in their domain."[27] An enduring rivalry has been defined as "a long-term hate affair between nations"[28] or specifically as "repeated militarized interstate disputes between the same set of states over time."[29]

Paul Diehl has operationally defined rivalry as one in which two states have experienced two militarized disputes over a span of 15 years.[30] Wayman and Jones have operationally defined an enduring rivalry as any two states that have had five militarized disputes over a span of 25 years.[31]

Rather than emphasizing the number of militarized disputes between two states, my study conceptualizes rivalry as a constant hate relationship between two states over an issue that is very important to both of them.

### Transnational Ethnic or Religious Ties

A secessionist group often shares strong ethnocultural or ethnoreligious ties with co-nationals in a neighboring state. These "transnational kin groups"[32] serve as an important variable in a secessionist war.

### Alliance

"It is impossible to speak of international relations without referring to alliances; the two often merge in all but name."[33] Rather than defining an alliance "as a formal or informal arrangement for security cooperation between two or more sovereign states"[34] or as "a promise of mutual military assistance between two or more sovereign states,"[35] I use the term loosely to refer to an agreement between a secessionist group and an external power for the latter's help in military training, supply of arms, monetary assistance, and protection. It includes covert aid granted to the secessionist group by the external power and excludes overt military operations undertaken by the external power to assist the secessionist group. In this study, I distinguish between alliance and intervention. Whereas the former refers to an informal, generally covert arrangement for assistance, the latter refers to an actual military operation in another state designed to accomplish a certain goal.

### International Military Intervention

The term "intervention" has been used in international relations in many different ways. Intervention has been defined as "the dictatorial interference by a state in the affairs of another state for the purpose of maintaining or altering the actual condition of things."[36] "From gunboat diplomacy to humanitarian intervention,"[37] it has been used as an instrument of foreign policy and is a "built-in feature of our present international arrangements."[38] Intervention can also take the form of economic sanctions and military force.

In this study, I use intervention to mean "foreign overt military intervention" as operationalized by Herbert K. Tillema. In Tillema's words.

> "Foreign overt military intervention" represents overt military operations undertaken directly by a state's regular military forces within foreign lands in such a manner as to risk immediate combat, hence war, if they encounter armed resistance. It includes all combat-ready deployments of conventional ground forces, air and commando raids, and naval and artillery shelling, whether or not such operations result in direct bloodshed. It excludes less blatant forms of international interference that do not necessarily risk international war immediately, including covert operations, military alerts, shows of force, pacific military deployments, incidental incursions, cross border small arms fire, aerial or naval encounters, and actions of irregular forces, police units, diplomatic personnel, and international peace forces or international observation groups that do not include overt military operations.[39]

## THEORY

My theory, which brings together internal and external actors, is laid out as follows. I want to emphasize that my intent is not to take a position against or for secession but to delineate the dynamic causal sequence that leads to external military intervention in a secessionist war. Delineating the causal path helps us understand why some secessionist wars bring about military intervention whereas others do not. I want to identify the conditions that make intervention more likely. Military intervention results in more violence and more deaths. Knowing the conditions that bring about international military intervention in a secessionist war can go a long way in mitigating these conditions in an attempt to avoid more hostility and bloodshed.

### The State and the Secessionist Group

A secessionist group usually exerts pressure on the central government of the state to meet its demand for a separate state. The main demand of such a group may not start with secession, but some degree of autonomy. The reason that a group demands autonomy or secession is the discrimination that it experiences at the hands of the central government. Central governments oppose secession because it is antithetical to the concept of the modern state. "Territorial withdrawal by a disaffected group not only risks weakening a state economically and politically but also redefines the very meaning and identity of the state in question."[40] Yet, "from the Canadian glaciers across to the moors of Britain and to the high Pyrenees, down through the broad belt of Africa, the arid hills of Turkey, Iraq . . . to the riverbanks and deltas of South Asia, peoples are challenging nation-states."[41]

It is hardly necessary to stress the importance of the state vis-à-vis a secessionist group. Describing nationalism, John Breuilly maintains that it "is, above all about politics, and that politics is about power. Power, in the modern world, is primarily about control of the state"[42] Speaking of South Asia, Ishtiaq Ahmed has said that "the state is the central actor—and in the perceptions of the separatists the arch villain—in all separatist dramas being enacted in South Asia."[43]

A strong state will resist the demands of a secessionist group. This is because a group's demands, "based on the principles of self-determination and articulated in the rhetoric of popular sovereignty, may challenge the legitimacy and integrity of the state."[44] Therefore, when a state is strong, the secessionists will have no success in achieving their demands.

### Shift in the Balance of Power

The desire to survive is the principal motive that encourages a secessionist group to mobilize and increase its strength. Also, a secessionist group will fight any economic, political, or cultural discrimination it may face at the hands of the government. For this reason, a secessionist group will make a great effort to increase its power in order to alter the balance of power between the state and the group. What happens if the balance of power shifts? As a secessionist group mobilizes (recruits more people, increases its funds and arms) and increases its power, the central government of the host state (the state from which a group wants to secede) may find that its own power is declining relative to the secessionists. For example, when the Awami League, the Bengali nationalist party of East Pakistan, won a landslide victory in the 1970 general elections of Pakistan, and thereby increased its political power, there was a shift in the balance of power in its favor. The central government of Pakistan found that its power had declined relative to the Awami League, the party that was demanding autonomy.

### Preventive War on the Secessionists

When the central government of a state perceives a shift in the balance of power in favor of the secessionists, it is likely to resort to a preventive war on the secessionists. The central government wants to "fight a war under relatively favorable circumstances now in order to block or retard the further rise of an adversary and to avoid both the worsening of the status quo over time and the risk of war under less favorable circumstances later."[45] As Gilpin concludes, "By launching a preventive war, the declining power destroys or weakens the rising challenger while the military advantage is still with the declining power."[46] So while the military capabilities of the host state are still high it decides to wage war on the secessionists in order to crush them before they accumulate too much power. Thus, when the Indian government perceived a shift in the balance of power after the Kashmiri uprising of 1989, it resorted to a preventive war on the Kashmir secessionists. New Delhi sent in thousands of troops and security personnel to destroy the movement before it could become more powerful. Similarly, a shift in the balance of power in favor of the Sikh secessionists led the Indian government to launch a preventive war, in June 1984, to crush the secessionists before they increased their power.

Why is it that the two parties do not negotiate? Since a preventive war is risky and very costly, it would be in the interests of the central government to avoid war and arrive at a negotiated settlement with the secessionists. Similarly, in order to avoid being crushed by the central government, the secessionists would have the incentive to construct a bargain with the central government. However, the parties do not negotiate because a shift in the balance of power creates problems of credible commitment, "situations in which mutually preferable bargains are unattainable because one or more states would have an incentive to renege on the terms."[47] In other words, as the power of the central government declines relative to the secessionists, previously enforceable agreements or bargains become unenforceable. Drawing on James Fearon's theory and applying it to ethnic groups, David Lake and Donald Rothchild have said:

> [O]ne group cannot effectively reassure the other that it will not renege on an agreement and exploit it at some future date. . . . As the influence of one side declines, previously enforceable ethnic contracts become unenforceable. The checks and balances that safeguard the agreement today become insufficient tomorrow.[48]

Applying Fearon's "commitment problems" to my study, I believe that without a third party to guarantee agreements, the central government fears that today's contracts with the secessionists may be unenforceable in the future. Therefore, it is likely that the central government will choose to suppress the secessionists today rather than later when contracts will not be honored and the risk of being exploited by the secessionists is high. For instance, fearing that the Bengali secessionists would not honor any contracts in the future, the Pakistan government waged a massive preventive war on them to wipe them out in 1971. Though the power of the Pakistan government was still high, it decided to suppress the secessionists rather than be exploited by them in the future.

## Explosive Growth of Movement

A preventive war on the secessionists is likely to strengthen the resolve of the secessionists and lead to an explosive growth of the movement. Secessionist movements are identity-based movements that "derive their collective identity from conflicting and confrontational interaction with other groups."[49] When the central government tries to crush a secessionist movement, the collective identity of the secessionists is strengthened. A strengthened collective identity will provoke rather than discourage mobilization and will radicalize rather than restrain the range of action.[50] After the 1990 preventive war on the Kashmiris by the Indian government, thousands of Kashmiri youth, who were previously not involved in the secessionist movement or who were against it, became radicalized and joined secessionist groups demanding secession from India. Simultaneously, several new secessionist groups came into existence and strengthened the resolve of the Kashmir secessionists.

In his study on ethnicity and the state, Ishtiaq Ahmed has noted:

> [S]eparatist movements tend to acquire a lasting and unbending character only when the state resorts to massive repression against them. For it is from the experience of repression that alienated cultural groups acquire a lasting memory of hatred and vengeance against the state, providing them with a cause strong enough to justify their own acts of terrorism.[51]

The character of the repression has an effect on the direction the movement will take. Jack Goldstone has shown that "where government responds with unfocused repression that terrorizes a wide range of civilians and groups either unconnected or only loosely connected to the movement supporters, or where repression is inconsistent and arbitrary . . . the movement is likely to attract supporters while becoming more radicalized in its goals and actions."[52] Thus, movements that start out as autonomous movements generally become secessionist movements after a preventive war. This is exactly what happened in East Pakistan after the preventive war on the Bengalis in March 1971. The East Pakistan movement had begun as a movement for regional autonomy within a united Pakistan but after the preventive war, it was transformed into a full-fledged secessionist movement for an independent state of Bangladesh.

Sabine Karstedt-Henke has argued that when a movement's actions become radicalized, the authorities respond with further repression, resulting in a spiral of violence and counterviolence and a growth of terrorist organizations.[53] In keeping with these findings, I believe that once a secessionist movement grows and more secessionist groups come into existence, there will be a feedback effect on the shift in the balance of power, which in turn will lead to a preventive war and so on. Interactive dynamics are set in motion.

Thus, in Sri Lanka, waves of repression took place on the Tamils by the Sri Lankan government in 1977, 1981, and 1983. Each time, the movement's actions became further radicalized and it responded with violence against the Sri Lankan government leading to a spiral of violence and counterviolence. After each preventive war, the Tamil movement grew and many new Tamil secessionist groups came into existence resulting in a further shift in the balance of power in favor of the Tamils.

## Alliance of Secessionists and External Power

In order to survive the preventive war, the secessionists will want to increase their military capabilities. For this reason, in an effort to increase their power, they will try to form an alliance with an external power for arms, military training, and monetary assistance. Here I apply Morgenthau's basic rule of realism[54] that when a state's security is threatened, it will form an alliance in order to shift the balance of power in its favor and increase its military strength. In my study, a group allies to balance not only against power but also against the threats[55] from the central government. In Walt's words, "Although power is an important part of the equation, it is not the only one."[56] For example, in order to survive the preventive war in 1990, the Kashmiris acquired arms, military training, financial assistance, and moral and logistical support from Pakistan. Training camps for the Kashmir secessionists were created in Pakistan in order to help them achieve their goal of secession.

### Rivalry Between Host State and External Power

However, a preventive war on the secessionists is not sufficient to explain the formation of an alliance. Rivalry between the host state and an external power plays a very important role in the formation of an alliance. "Rivalry, by definition . . . embodies a considerable amount of negative interaction and hostility stemming from persistent disagreement over a fundamental issue."[57] Rivals are usually suspicious of each other based on historical experience and are keen on ironing out past grievances. Therefore, an external power that is a rival of the host state may see certain benefits from helping the secessionist group. Preventive war creates a window of opportunity for both the secessionists and the external power. It was Indo-Pak rivalry that led Pakistan to ally with the Sikhs after the preventive war on the Sikhs by the Indian government in 1984. Pakistan wanted to pay India back for helping the Bengalis secede from Pakistan and form Bangladesh. India and Pakistan have been rivals for well over fifty years and are still locked in a power struggle over the disputed territory of Kashmir.

Rivals have private information and competing interests that can lead to information failures. They tend to misrepresent private information in order to trick the other. Misperceptions of each other and competing interests lead to increased tension between rivals and information failures make negotiations and bargaining difficult to achieve.[58] For this reason, an external power that is a rival of a host state will be very willing to form an alliance with the secessionists.

### Transnational Ethnic or Religious Ties Between Secessionists and External Power

Besides rivalry, transnational ethnic/religious ties between the secessionist group and the external power is an important factor that influences the formation of an alliance. Will Moore and David Davis refer to such an alliance as an "ethnic alliance."[59] They contend "ethnic ties among peoples across state borders in the international system act as unstated alliances among those people."[60] After a preventive war, secessionists look for military, financial, or logistical help and they often find it in their ethnic brethren in a neighboring state. The ethnic kinship between the Tamils of Sri Lanka and the Tamils of India led to an alliance between India and the Tamil secessionists of Sri Lanka. After the massive preventive war on the Sri Lankan Tamils by the government of Sri Lanka in 1983, the Tamils of India reached out to help their ethnic brethren in Sri Lanka. India trained thousands of Tamil secessionists in training camps located on Indian soil.

## International Military Intervention by External Power

Once an alliance is formed between a secessionist group and an external power, it is seen as a threat to the host state that takes steps to diminish the security of the alliance. The creation of a security dilemma[61] and the ensuing spirals of suspicion, hostility, and arms racing increase the security competition between the host state and the alliance. The security dilemma increases the risk of military intervention by the external power.

However, military intervention takes place only if the alliance between the secessionists and the external power is a strong one. A strong alliance will be perceived as a threat by the host state. For the alliance to be strong, both variables—rivalry and ethnic kinship—have to be present. If only one of these exists, the resulting alliance will be weak and no military intervention will take place. For example, in 1971, India's alliance with the Bengali secessionists was a strong one because rivalry between India (the external power) and Pakistan (the host state) and ethnic ties between the East Pakistan Bengalis (the secessionists) and Indian Bengalis were both present. That is why Indian intervention took place on behalf of the Bengali secessionists in 1971. Likewise, the alliance between Pakistan and the Kashmiri secessionists in 1990 was strong enough to be seen as potentially threatening by India. Rivalry and ethnic kinship were responsible for the strong alliance. The ensuing security dilemma increased tensions between Indian and Pakistan leading to military intervention by Pakistan in 1999. On the other hand, the alliance between the Tamil secessionists and India was not strong enough to lead to military intervention by India because the alliance was built on ethnic ties alone. India and Sri Lanka are not rivals and it was not in India's interest to intervene militarily and break up Sri Lanka. Similarly in Punjab, the alliance between the Sikhs and Pakistan was weak because the cultural bonds between them are weak. The Sikhs and Pakistanis belong to different religions. Rivalry between India and Pakistan was the only variable present. Therefore, no military intervention took place by Pakistan on behalf of the Sikhs.

Thus, by contributing to the security dilemma, an alliance between the external power and the secessionist group leaves the host state insecure. Alliance formation acts as "a catalyst to arms racing"[62] thereby increasing the security competition between the host state and the alliance between the secessionists and the external power. The result is an increase in the risk of military intervention by the external power. Thus, in the 1990s, the alliance between the Kashmir secessionists and Pakistan led to a nuclear arms race between India and Pakistan culminating in both countries conducting nuclear tests and becoming nuclear powers. On the effects of arms racing, Lord Grey has said:

> The increase of armaments, that is intended in each nation to produce consciousness of strength, and a sense of security, does not produce these effects. On the contrary, it produces a consciousness of the strength of other nations and a sense of fear. Fear begets suspicion and distrust and evil imaginings of all sorts, till each Government feels it would be criminal and a betrayal of its own country not to take every precaution,

> while every Government regards every precaution of every other Government as evidence of hostile intent.[63]

Robert Bates and Barry Weingast[64] (1995) and Weingast[65] (1997) have demonstrated that uncertainty by one side (in this analysis the host state) over the intentions of the other side (the alliance) creates problems of credible commitment that can undermine any contracts between two sides. Applying their findings to my study, once the alliance is formed, especially if information is incomplete, the host state is uncertain about the intentions of the alliance. The ensuing security dilemma provokes military intervention. Thus, in 1971, India's alliance with the Bengali secessionists made Pakistan uncertain about the alliance's intentions and led Pakistan to send its troops and tanks to the Indo-Pak border in preparation for war. In the words of Lake and Rothchild, "[t]he dilemma follows from the inability of the two sides to observe each other's intentions directly; if each party knew that the other was arming strictly for defensive purposes the potential spiral would be cut short."[66]

Another reason the two parties are unable to reach a negotiated settlement is "*private information* about relative capabilities or resolve and *incentives to misrepresent* such information."[67] When parties misrepresent private information "[b]y exaggerating their strengths, minimizing their weaknesses, and misstating their preferences"[68] negotiations are likely to fail and war will not be avoided. The chances for miscalculation are high. For example, miscalculating Indian strength in May 1999, Pakistan forces allied with Kashmir secessionists invaded the Kargil sector of Kashmir in an attempt to wrest Kashmir from India. Misinformation and misperception had led Pakistan to exaggerate its recently acquired nuclear capability and to underestimate India's military expertise.

There is evidence of a positive association between alliance membership and war participation. R.M. Siverson and J. King (1979) studied the role that alliances play in the expansion of an existing war and found that "nations with alliances are more war-prone than nations without alliances."[69] Paul Huth and Bruce Russett (1984) found that the existence of an alliance would make it likely that a defender state would fight to protect its weaker ally or protégé from its attacker.[70] G. Modelski[71] (1964) and C.R. Mitchell[72] (1970) have found that "cooperative linkages between internal and external political groups are an important prerequisite for foreign intervention."[73]

## HYPOTHESES AND MODEL

The theory outlined above leads to the following hypotheses and can be summed up in: Figure 2.1

H1: The more the balance of power between a secessionist group and the host state shifts in favor of the former, the greater the risk of a preventive war on the secessionists by the central government.

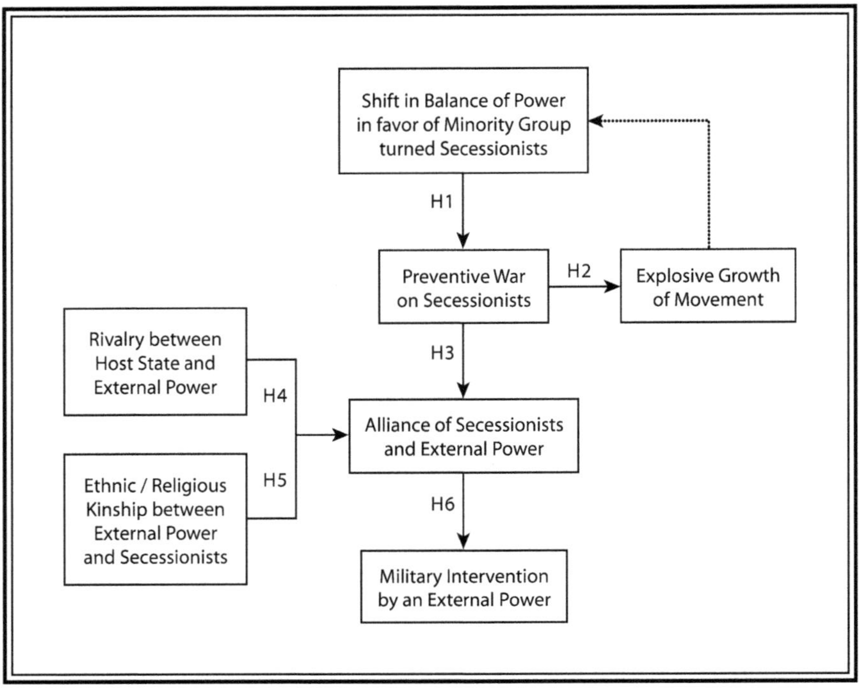


**Figure 2.1 The Theory**

H2: A preventive war on the secessionists by the central government will result in an explosive growth of the secessionist movement.
H3: A preventive war on the secessionists by the central government increases the chances that the secessionists will ally with an external power for its support and assistance.
H4: Rivalry between the host state and an external power increases the likelihood of an alliance being formed between the secessionists and an external power.
H5: A strong ethnic or religious kinship between the external power and the secessionists will increase the chances of an alliance being formed between them.
H6: The stronger the alliance between the secessionists and an external power the greater the risk of military intervention in the secessionist war by the external power.

## TESTING THE THEORY

Figure 2.1 outlines the various causal mechanisms leading to foreign military intervention in a secessionist war. It predicts that secessionist movements will eventually increase security competition between states and increase the chances of foreign military intervention in an ongoing secessionist war.

In the four case studies that follow this chapter, I explore whether these different mechanisms took place and had the predicted effects. I can consider the theory supported if, first, military intervention took place for the reasons outlined in the theory; second, military intervention did not occur because one of the causal mechanisms specified in the theory was muted or absent; and third, the predicted security competition between the states was present but other factors prevented military intervention from occurring.

The theory laid out in this chapter explains why secessionist movements eventually increase security competition between states and increase the probability of military intervention. A secessionist movement produces dangerous conditions, which make the outcome of military intervention very likely. To find out whether my theory is supported, I begin by examining the Bengali secessionist movement in the former East Pakistan.

# 3

# Bangladesh

AN ANALYSIS OF the events leading to the successful East Pakistani secessionist movement of 1971 throws light on how, when, and why secessionist activity in East Pakistan (formerly East Bengal and now known as Bangladesh)[1] increased the security competition between India and Pakistan and eventually led to India's intervention on behalf of the secessionists. The case study delineates the causal links between secessionist sentiment and international military intervention and provides strong support for the theory outlined in the previous chapter.

First, as the theory suggests, the East Pakistani secessionist movement made preventive war by the host state (Pakistan) on the secessionists (Bengalis) more likely by creating a shift in the balance of power in favor of the Bengalis. Second, an alliance between the Bengalis and the external power (India) was fueled by Pakistan's preventive war. Third, the chances of an alliance being formed were exacerbated by rivalry between Pakistan and India, and ethnic kinship between the Bengalis of East Pakistan and the Bengalis of India. Finally, the risk of external/international military intervention was increased by a strong alliance between the Bengali secessionists and India.

The chapter begins with a historical background that describes the discrimination experienced by the East Pakistanis at the hands of the West Pakistanis. It goes on to explain how the East Pakistanis mobilized into action. Finally, each hypothesis described in chapter 2 is evaluated in the order presented there.

## BACKGROUND

When Pakistan became a state in 1947, it consisted of two parts that had little in common except for the religion of Islam. West Pakistan was approximately

1,200 miles away from East Pakistan (with India in between) and the two parts differed with respect to language, culture, ethnic origin, and economy. West Pakistan had four main ethnic groups: Punjabis, Pakhtuns, Sindhis, and Baluchis, each with a language of its own. East Pakistan, on the other hand, was more homogeneous in character with 98 percent of its population speaking Bengali.[2] East Pakistan consisted of 14.8 percent of Pakistan's total land area but had 55.5 percent of her total population.[3] According to the 1951 Census of Pakistan, East Pakistan's population was 42 million and West Pakistan's was 33 million.[4] This meant that the density of the population in the east wing was very high. The physical separation of East and West Pakistan by more than 1,000 miles made administration of the country difficult. Mobility of resources and people from one part to the other was hard, and the absence of a common language hampered communication between the two wings.

It was the religion of Islam that had brought these two parts together in 1947 to form the state of Pakistan partitioned from India, whose main religion was Hinduism. "Simply stated, the raison d'être for the creation of Pakistan was the desire of the Muslims of the Indian sub-continent for a separate homeland to avoid domination by the Hindus, who constituted the majority community, when the British withdrew."[5] However, cultural and linguistic differences between the two wings of Pakistan far outweighed the unity that religion could provide. "The East Pakistanis who spoke Bengali were intensely conscious of their Bengali heritage and revealed a sense of linguistic nationalism. They were very proud of their language and guarded it zealously against displacement."[6] On the other hand, "[t]he elite in West Pakistan was . . . convinced that Bengali, with a script based on Devnagari and with a Sanskrit vocabulary, smacked too much of Hindu culture and had to be given up in favor of Urdu, which was more 'Islamic' in origin."[7] Moreover, Urdu's script is similar to the Arabic script of the Koran.

Problems between the east and the west started to emerge as early as 1948 and it was said: "A feeling is growing among the East Pakistanis that East Pakistan is being neglected and treated merely as a 'colony' of Western Pakistan."[8]

## Discrimination Against Bengalis

ECONOMIC AND POLITICAL DISPARITIES Despite their majority, the political and economic interests of the people of East Pakistan were subordinated to those of West Pakistan. An abundance of evidence supports this claim. The central government was located in West Pakistan and West Pakistanis held almost all the important posts. According to 1960 data, all senior military officers and 87 percent of senior members of the civil services were West Pakistanis.[9] Since the West Pakistanis or rather, the "Punjabi-dominated bureaucratic-military oligarchy"[10] formulated economic policy for the country, more resources were spent on the development of West Pakistan at the expense of the East.

According to reports by the Pakistan Planning Commission, a mere 20 percent of the total central government development expenditure was spent on East Pakistan during the period 1950/1951 to 1954/55 reaching a maximum of 36 percent during the period 1965/66 to 1969/70.[11] This disparity in development expenditure resulted in a much slower rate of growth of the private sector in East Pakistan than that in West Pakistan. From the time of its inception, the government of Pakistan adopted a policy of industrialization in West Pakistan. The Pakistan Industrial Development Corporation, which was established in 1952 in Karachi, encouraged the growth of private enterprise in West Pakistan at the expense of East Pakistan.[12]

There were disparities in the distribution of foreign exchange earnings and foreign aid between the two wings. Typically, 50–70 percent of Pakistan's total export earnings were earned by East Pakistan through its export of raw materials such as jute, hides, and skin.[13] However, East Pakistan received only 25–30 percent of all foreign imports into Pakistan.[14] East Pakistan's trade surplus was used to finance the industries of West Pakistan leading to a net transfer of resources of approximately $2.6 billion over the period 1948–49 to 1968–69.[15]

The transfer of resources from the east to the west resulted in a big gap in the per capita income of the two wings. The per capita income in West Pakistan in 1959–60 was 32 percent higher than that in East Pakistan. With continued exploitation of the east, this income gap doubled in 10 years. By 1969–70, the per capita income in the west was 61 percent higher than in the east.[16] To make matters worse, the Bengalis of East Pakistan paid a much higher price for food than their counterparts in the west. Table 3.1[17] compares the prices of rice (the staple food of East Pakistan) and wheat (the staple food of West Pakistan) in the two wings.

Although West Pakistan was poor, their poverty was nothing like the dumbfounding poverty of East Pakistan. In the words of Anthony Mascarenhas:

> Unlike West Pakistan, the poverty in the east is manifest in equal measure in the towns and in the countryside. The wheezing cycle-rickshaw man in Dacca who sleeps in the shelter of his rickety vehicle at night and looks 40 but is probably only in his early twenties is as haggard and worn-out as the fisherman in Barisal, the dockworker in Chittagong, the farmer in the rice fields of Comilla and the man selling pineapple by the roadside in Sylhet. Malnutrition is endemic. So are tuberculosis and other respiratory diseases and stomach complaints.[18]

**Table 3.1 Price Discrimination (in rupees)**

| | West Pakistan | East Pakistan |
|---|---|---|
| Rice per mound (82 lbs) | 18 | 50 |
| Wheat per mound (82 lbs) | 10 | 35 |

*Source*: Bangla Desh documents, vol. I, 21.

In short, Pakistan's economic policy of import controls, tariffs, and industrial licensing favored West Pakistan and led to increasing economic disparities between the east and the west. East Pakistan received goods that were made in West Pakistan from East Pakistan raw materials. In fact, East Pakistan was a market for 47 percent of finished goods made by West Pakistani industries.[19] East Pakistan was "used as a dumping ground for shoddy, high-priced goods produced by inefficient industrial units in West Pakistan."[20]

These economic and political disparities between the two wings of Pakistan made it apparent that West Pakistan treated East Pakistan like a colonial power would treat its colony. It was as if "East Pakistan existed only for the benefit of West Pakistan capitalist merchants, industrialists and contractors, for the militarists and civil bureaucrats."[21] This colonial-style relationship between the west and the east wings of Pakistan prompted Chowdhury to state, "If the whole of Pakistan was subjected to the bizarre experiments of political adventurists, it was the lot of the East Bengal people to play, in the name of Islam, the role of a loyal but subordinate colony."[22]

CULTURAL DISCRIMINATION The seeds of nationalism were sown in East Pakistan in the early 1950s soon after the government of Pakistan tried to enforce Urdu as the national language of the state. Although only a minority of the population (7.2 percent)[23] of Pakistan spoke Urdu, the language was "closely associated with the Muslim politics of the sub-continent"[24] and "was considered to be the principal language of Muslim India."[25] For this reason, as early as 1948, Prime Minister Liaquat Ali Khan of Pakistan stated: "Pakistan is a Muslim state and it must have as its *lingua franca* the language of the Muslim nation."[26] He further reiterated: "It is necessary for a nation to have one common language and that language can only be Urdu and no other language"[27]

This enraged the Bengalis who were extremely attached to the Bengali language. They viewed the language policy of the central government "as an attempt at cultural intrusion, to destroy the cultural heritage of Bengal."[28] They felt that Bengali, rather than Urdu alone, should be recognized as one of the official languages of Pakistan. The language issue united the Bengalis from all walks of life. It brought together diverse political parties, students, rich and poor, onto a common platform. The Bengalis wanted to preserve their rich cultural heritage and were determined not to allow anyone to destroy it. "In fact the demand for Bengali became the focal point of an emerging national identity in East Bengal."[29]

## Mobilization of Bengalis

Increasing disparities between East and West Pakistan in terms of allocation of funds for development, and distribution of foreign exchange and foreign aid between the two wings led to mounting Bengali opposition to the central government. The language policy of the government added fuel to the fire. The Bengalis decided to mobilize in order to increase their strength and power as a group.

The national movement of the Bengalis in East Pakistan began with a demand for Bengali to be recognized as a state language of Pakistan along with Urdu. On February 21, 1952, Bengali students protested against the government with a mass demonstration. The police, in an attempt to quell the demonstration, killed 26 people and injured 400. This incident "triggered off . . . a wide-spread movement, both political and cultural, which was momentous in its consequences. The genesis of Bangladesh must ultimately be traced to this movement."[30] Thus, "what was initially a movement for recognition of Bengali as one of the state languages, soon developed into a national movement for the protection of civil liberties and the attainment of provincial autonomy."[31]

In response to the demands and protests of the Bengalis, the Pakistani Constitutions of 1956 and 1962 recognized both Urdu and Bengali as national languages of Pakistan. However, "in spite of the constitutional provision, the government of Pakistan and the Islamic parties refused to accord the same status to Urdu and Bengali. Bengali was not given the same position in West Pakistan as Urdu was given in the East."[32]

In 1966, the Awami (people's) League, the Bengali nationalist party under the leadership of Sheikh Mujibur (Mujib) Rahman, demanded provincial autonomy for East Pakistan. Mujib's six-point economic and political program demanding regional autonomy "lighted the fuse of a national time bomb."[33] It demanded, among other things, that control over foreign aid allocation, taxation, and foreign trade be transferred to the provinces in order to end the disproportionate control of the central government over resource allocation.[34] In other words, the plan sought to even out the disparities between the two wings. The six-point plan,[35] in a nutshell, is as follows:

First, Pakistan should be a federation with a parliamentary form of government and a legislature elected through the system of universal adult franchise. Second, the federal government should deal only with defense and foreign affairs and all other matters should be in the hands of the federating states. Third, two separate and freely convertible currencies were recommended; however, in case one currency was maintained, safeguards to prevent the flight of capital from the east wing to the west would be in place. Fourth, as stated earlier, power over taxation would be vested with the federating states; the central government would receive a fixed share of the state's taxes. Fifth, two separate accounts would be maintained for foreign exchange earnings of the two wings. The federal government would receive its share of foreign exchange earnings from each of the federating units according to a fixed ratio. Sixth, a paramilitary force would be set up for East Pakistan.

Mujib's six-point plan "became the platform of Bengali politics and the rallying cry of the league's opposition to the government."[36] Pakistan's President Ayub denounced the program as a call for complete independence of East Pakistan. He even threatened the autonomists with the "language of weapons." However, the Bengali demands for autonomy continued unabated. Mujib firmly believed that his plan "truly reflected the mind and correctly represented the demands of

55 million East Pakistanis of their right to live."[37] Elaborating on the plight of the Bengalis, Mujib has stated:

> Our present experience has only brought into sharp focus and underlines the basic truth that every Bengali has felt in his bones, that we have been treated so long as a colony and a market. We have been denied our birthrights as the free citizens of an independent state. All decisions of consequence are made in Rawalpindi or Islamabad. All powers vest in the Central Government and its bureaucrats. It is they who I accuse today of criminal neglect and discrimination.[38]

## SHIFT IN BALANCE OF POWER

When Yahya Khan became president of Pakistan in March 1969, he promised to hold "the country's first-ever free and democratic elections,"[39] in December 1970, based on universal adult franchise. He did this in response to the "countrywide anti-Ayub agitation for political freedoms."[40] The National Assembly that was to be elected would draft a constitution for Pakistan. In an address to the nation a few days before the election, President Yahya Khan stated:

> For the first time in our national existence you have a chance to vote for the security of the country. . . . The elections are only the first phase of our plan. The next phase will be the framing of the Constitution and the final phase would be the transfer of power to the elected representatives. Sovereignty would pass to the National Assembly on conclusion of this last phase and on lifting of Martial Law.[41]

In the elections that were held on December 7, 1970, Mujib's Awami League of East Pakistan won an absolute majority in Parliament. Out of a total of 313 seats in the National Constitutional Assembly, the Awami League won 167 out of 169 seats allotted to East Pakistan.[42] Zulfikar Ali Bhutto's Pakistani People's Party in the west won 88 out of 140 seats.[43] The Awami League became the largest party in the National Assembly, which was scheduled to have its first session on March 3, 1971. It had been decided that the National Assembly would draft a constitution within 120 days of its first session.[44]

The balance of power had clearly shifted in favor of the Awami League. The landslide victory gave a strong boost to the six-point program on which the Awami League ran. The elections in East Bengal turned out to be a "historic verdict"[45] and a referendum on the league's six-point program of autonomy. Mujib now demanded that Pakistan's constitution be based on his program of regional autonomy. "There can be no constitution except one which is based on the six-point programme."[46]

The sweeping Awami League victory gave Sheikh Mujib the mandate to become prime minister of Pakistan. The Bengalis now wanted full autonomy under the rule of the Awami League. "We have emerged as the absolute majority party in the elections not only in Bangladesh but also in the whole country. So the right to rule the country is ours."[47] There was certainly a decline in the power of the central government of Pakistan relative to the Awami League.

The West Pakistanis, "particularly the military whose budget was threatened, and large businesses who stood both to lose markets and the foreign exchange earnings of the East, opposed autonomy for the East."[48] Zulfikar Ali Bhutto, leader of the West Pakistani People's Party insisted that control of foreign trade and foreign aid should remain with the central government.[49] When a compromise could not be reached on the six-point autonomy mandate, Bhutto decided he was going to boycott the National Assembly that was to meet on March 3 to draft the constitution.[50] President Yahya Khan took this opportunity to indefinitely postpone the National Assembly, which he did without even consulting Sheikh Mujib.[51] In this way, the government of Pakistan blatantly tried to frustrate the will of the people expressed unequivocally through the elections.[52] "The postponement of the National Assembly was a denial to the people of East Bengal of their legitimate democratic rights to rule according to their own wishes."[53]

## PREVENTIVE WAR ON THE BENGALI SECESSIONISTS

When the central government of Pakistan perceived a shift in the balance of power in favor of the Awami League, it decided to crush the movement for autonomy by fighting a preventive war on the people of East Pakistan. Due to problems of credible commitment, the government was unsuccessful in reaching a settlement with the Bengali secessionists. So, on the midnight of March 25–26, 1971, West Pakistani troops descended on East Pakistan with machine guns and tanks and in the first 24 hours of the army attack, 7,000 civilians were slaughtered in Dacca alone and the number of dead in the entire region including Chittagong, Jessore, and Comilla was put at 15,000.[54] The army units "carried lists of people to be liquidated. These included the Hindus and large numbers of Muslims; students, Awami leaguers, professors, journalists and those who had been prominent in Sheikh Mujib's movement."[55] In this way, the government of Pakistan tried to suppress the self-determination of the Bengalis by terrorizing the population into submission.[56] This suppression continued into the early days of December 1971. Estimates of the death toll of the Bengalis during eight months of preventive war were more than 1 million.[57]

There is extensive evidence to prove that the West Pakistan army wanted to destroy the Awami League before it formed a government based on its six-point plan. The objective of West Pakistan's military action on East Pakistan was to crush the Bengalis before they accumulated more power. Anthony Mascarenhas, a Pakistani journalist has revealed that military officers in the 16th Division Headquarters at Comilla told him, "We are determined to cleanse East Pakistan once and for all of the threat of secession, even if it means killing of two million people and ruling the province as a colony for 30 years."[58]

Simon Dring of the *Daily Telegraph* has reported how the military operation on the Bengalis was organized to kill the leaders of the Awami League: "The soldiers would fire a flare and the informer would point out the houses of staunch Awami League supporters. The house would then be destroyed—either with direct tank or recoilless rifle fire or with a can of petrol."[59]

It is evident from several eyewitness accounts that the military operation that began on the night of March 25, 1971, had as its targets, professors, students, and intellectuals—in short, anyone who could lead an autonomous East Pakistan. The University of Dacca, a hotbed of protests and campaigns, was one of the first targets of the preventive war led by the army. Dr. John Rhode, an American physician, who worked in Dacca under USAID at the time of the army crackdown and witnessed the massacre, had this to say in his report:

> It is clear that the law of the jungle prevails in East Bengal, where the mass killing of unarmed civilians, the systematic elimination of the intelligentsia and the annihilation of the Hindu population is in progress. . . . At the university area . . . we walked through the Jagannath Hall and Iqbal Hall, two of the student dormitories at Dacca University shelled by army tanks. All inmates were slaughtered. We saw the breach in the wall where the tank broke through, the tank tracks and the mass grave in front of the hall. A man, who was forced to drag the bodies outside, counted one hundred [and] three of the Hindu students buried there. Outside were the massive holes in the walls of the dormitory, while inside were the smoking remains of the rooms and the heavily bloodstained floors. . . . The two ensuing weeks have documented the planned killing of much of the intellectual community, including the majority of professors of Dacca University. . . . Many families of these professors were shot as well. . . . In Gushan, one of the suburban areas of Dacca, where we lived, we witnessed the disarming of the East Pakistan Rifles . . . and finally the execution of several EPR[60] as they were forced by Punjabi soldiers onto a truck to be "taken away." The mass execution of several thousands of Bengali policemen and East Pakistani Rifles is already documented.[61]

Mrs. Edward Sammel, another eyewitness, wrote about what she and her husband saw:

> We have been witness to what amounts to genocide. The West Pakistan army used tanks; heavy artillery and machine guns on unarmed civilians, killed 1,600 police while sleeping in their barracks (thus eliminating the only source of armed resistance), demolished the student dormitories at Dacca University and excavated a mass grave for the thousands of students; they've systematically eliminated the intelligentsia of the country, wiped out entire villages—I could go on and on. It's hard to believe it happened.[62]

Other eyewitnesses reported how the army attacked the office of *The People*, an English language newspaper that had supported Sheikh Mujib and the Awami League and condemned the army and the government.[63] Offices of the Bengali language newspaper were also destroyed on March 26. Simon Dring of the *Daily Telegraph* writes,

> One of the last targets was the daily Bengali language newspaper "Ittefaq." More than 400 people reportedly had taken shelter in its offices when the fighting started.

> At 4 o'clock Friday afternoon, four tanks appeared in the road outside. By 4-30, the building was an inferno, witnesses said. By Saturday morning only the charred remains of a lot of corpses huddled in the back room were left.[64]

The above evidence clearly shows that the government of Pakistan launched a preventive war against the East Pakistanis in an attempt to destroy them before they could assert their power. President Yahya Khan "reverted to the law of the jungle in his bid to crush the people of Bangla Desh."[65] In her address to the Lower House of Parliament on March 27, 1971, Prime Minister Indira Gandhi declared, "It is not merely the suppression of a movement, but it is meeting an unarmed people with tanks."[66]

When asked when the killing would stop, Major-General Shaukat Raza told Anthony Mascarenhas on April 16, 1971:

> You must be absolutely sure that we have not undertaken such a drastic and expensive operation—expensive both in men and money—for nothing. We've undertaken a job. We are going to finish it, not hand it over half done to the politicians so that they can mess it up again. The army can't keep coming back like this every three or four years. It has a more important task. I assure you that when we have got through with what we are doing there will never be need again for such an operation.[67]

On the night of the massacre, the Pakistani army arrested Mujib at his residence and imprisoned him on charges of treason. Before his arrest, Mujib issued a statement to his people:

> You are citizens of a free country . . . Today the West Pakistan's military force is engaged in genocide in Bangla Desh. . . . They have unleashed unparalleled barbarity on the golden Bengal. . . . You should not be misled by the false propaganda of the military rulers. Our struggle is more rewarding. Certain is our victory.[68]

The editorial of a newspaper in London sums up the reason for the preventive war:

> From the evidence available one must conclude that the aim was to wipe out the Awami League leadership so that it could no longer provide an effective leadership for any resistance movement. Sheikh Mujib was arrested and may have been taken to West Pakistan. How many of his lieutenants are gone is impossible to say. The slaughter of students in Dacca, as likely organizers of guerrilla operations, seems well attested. If some move to reverse the orders were now to be made, lest the slaughter go on spreading, leaders who might help to moderate the passions on the Bengali side would be lacking.[69]

## EXPLOSIVE GROWTH OF THE MOVEMENT

There is substantial evidence that the preventive war on the Bengalis by the central government of Pakistan led to an explosive growth of the movement. In response to the Pakistani massacre of Bengalis in March 1971, a Bengali liberation army or *Mukti Fauj* (later called *Mukti Bahini*)[70] came into existence almost overnight to fight the Pakistani government. By and large, the *Mukti Fauj* consisted of the student community, the East Pakistan Rifles (EPR), the police, members of the Awami League and basically, anyone who had the determination and courage to put up a strong resistance against the marauding Pakistan army.[71] The people of Bangladesh had to defend themselves against the ruthless West Pakistani soldiers who were determined to wipe them out.

In a radio broadcast to the region on April 11, 1971, Mr. Tajuddin Ahmed[72] stated:

> Today a mighty army is being formed around the nucleus of professional soldiers from the Bengal Regiment and E.P.R.[73] who have rallied to the cause of the liberation struggle. These have been joined by the Police, Ansars and Mujahids[74] and now by thousands of Awami League volunteers and are being trained into a fighting force.[75]

The *Mukti Fauj* caught the Pakistan military by surprise. The dedication and determination of the *Mukti Fauj* "succeeded in creating a forceful dent on the organized Pakistan Military Government."[76] The *Mukti Fauj* was a liberation army that wanted East Pakistan to be liberated from the rest of Pakistan.

Thus, what started as a movement for regional autonomy for East Pakistan within a united Pakistan turned into a secessionist movement for an independent East Pakistan, namely, Bangladesh. In fact, in November 1970 when Sheikh Mujibur Rehman was asked whether his six-point plan was a call for secession, his reply was, "We are demanding regional autonomy and not independence."[77] However, "through the strength of an awakened people"[78] and roused by the injustice and savagery of the central government, the movement for autonomy was transformed into a full-fledged secessionist movement for an independent state of Bangladesh. A group of scholars in Vienna wrote:

> The Bengalis' demand for independence had been forced upon the people of East Pakistan by the savage and atrocious action of the West Pakistani army government. What the Bengalis had really been wanting were regional autonomy and social and economic justice. Recent events have conclusively proved that there was no plan for secession and there was no armed preparation on the part of the Bengalis to achieve that. They were confidently expecting a good result from President Yahya Khan's democratic gesture. But the West Pakistani army, through its systematic butchery of unarmed civilians, forced the Bengalis to take the ultimate decision—to become a completely independent sovereign state.[79]

Therefore, the preventive war on the Bengalis only resulted in hardening their resistance to put up a strong fight against the Pakistani army. The resolve and determination of the Bengalis to defeat the Pakistani government were apparent in the burgeoning of the movement. On March 29, 1971, a newspaper appropriately commented that all the bayonets of West Pakistan would not be able to put "the genie of Bengali nationalism"[80] back into its bottle.

## ALLIANCE OF SECESSIONISTS AND EXTERNAL POWER

The preventive war on the Bengalis led to an alliance between India and the Bengali secessionists. In order to fight the suppression of the central government, the Bengalis turned to India for assistance. The secessionists wanted to increase their power by forming an alliance with India for arms, military training, and monetary help.

> Resistance operations such as the Mukti Bahini's can only hope to succeed if there is a very large degree of military support from a friendly power—or physical intervention. If the Mukti Bahini were to succeed in liberating Pakistan, it would require all the help that the Indian armed forces could give them—morally, materially, and, if the occasion arose, by physical intervention.[81]

In response to the preventive war on the Bengalis, the prime minister of India, Indira Gandhi, moved a resolution in Parliament assuring the people of East Pakistan "the whole hearted sympathy and support of the people of India."[82] With Gandhi's assurance of support, the general secretary of the Awami League, Mr. Tajuddin Ahmed and other Awami League leaders who had escaped from East Pakistan met in Calcutta, India, to form a Bangladesh government in exile. A Declaration of Independence[83] drawn up at this meeting elected Mujibur Rahman as president.

India began to provide guerrilla training to the *Mukti Fauj* and support "in the way of border sanctuaries, arms and ammunition, co-ordination and training."[84] Thus, an alliance was formed between the secessionists and India.

Conclusive evidence that India was aiding and abetting the secessionists with arms, military training, funds, and protection is available from several journalists who reported from India at the time of the crisis.

On April 2, 1971, *Amrita Bazaar Patrika*, a Calcutta newspaper reported:

> A powerful central organization to render all possible help and assistance to the freedom fighters of Bangla Desh was formed in Calcutta on Thursday with Mr. Ajoy Kumar Mukherji, the Chief Minister designate as its President. The organization was named the "Committee for Assistance to the Freedom struggle of Bangla Desh." The Committee intends to mobilize aid and assistance for the fighting people of East Pakistan and campaign for the recognition of the People's Republic of Bangla Desh and arms and ammunition to them by the Government of India.[85]

On April 14, 1971, London's *Daily Telegraph* wrote:

> A trainload of Indian weapons has apparently reached the secessionist forces near Madaripur, 70 miles east of the Indian border. At least one Indian army major was reported to be instructing Bangla Desh forces in the use of weapons.[86]

On April 29, 1971, *New York Times*' Sidney Schanberg reported from Calcutta:

> The Indian roads leading north from Calcutta to points along the border already look like supply route. Bengali trucks can be seen heading into Indian towns for fresh

supplies—carrying empty fuel drums and ammunition boxes. Bengali independence forces have set up camps near the Indian border posts which probably explains some of the brief shooting incidents recently between Indian and Pakistani troops. In Calcutta, capital of West Bengal state, there are many stories of new instances of Indian military assistance. One report is that Indian ammunitions factories are turning out weapons and ammunition without Indian markings. Another is that Indian officers accompanied a large guerrilla force on a raid last week on a Pakistani army garrison at Navaran on the road to Jessore.[87]

Reporting on the military training camps set up to train the secessionists, Peter Hazelhurst reported from Calcutta:

My informant said that three types of training camps have been set up in India. . . . According to him, the East Bengali volunteers are screened at these transit camps and if they pass a physical test they are sent on a six week training course conducted by the East Pakistan Rifles and Indian instructors. Potential officers are sent back to Indian military establishments on a six-month training course.[88]

Maurice Quaintance of *Reuters News Agency* reported on India's assistance to the Bengali rebels:

In Dacca, three Khaki-clad soldiers Friday confessed they were captured prisoners sent from India to Pakistan to help the dissident East Pakistan Rifle units supporting the secessionists. Speaking through an interpreter, one told six foreign correspondents at Dacca Army headquarters he came into Pakistan territory at night after being told with others of his platoon that they were moving to the border post. . . . The soldier gave his name as Lance Corporal Mamla Pati Singh, 23 of 104 BSF (Border Security Force). The Army said he was captured at Sylhet, about 15 miles inside the border. Two other captured prisoners presented to the press today identified themselves as Ram Raawesh Sharma, 23, a private from 104 BSF, and Pancha Ram, 25, a private of 108 BSF, normally based in Rajasthan. . . . Army Headquarters in Dacca Friday displayed a selection of captured weapons and ammunition said to be mainly of Indian origin. They included rifles, mortar bombs, and hand grenades all of which, the army said, bore markings proving they were manufactured in India.[89]

The *Daily Observer* of London carried an article written by its reporter Colin Smith in Calcutta. Smith had visited some of the armed rebels and reported:

Hidden in tented camps along East Pakistan's western border with India are the official armed forces of the Bangladesh government in exile, the Mukti Fauj. In some cases, regular Indian army units, ignoring the treaty in force since partition under which both sides would keep their forces five miles back from the border, have moved right in beside them. They are easy to find because their signalers have not had time to bury the field telephone cables that lead from divisional to battalion headquarters and you can follow them from tree to ditch right up to the border . . . Nearby, heavily camouflaged under trees, was the headquarters of a Sikh infantry company. . . . At the base I visited, the Mukti Fauj was entirely made up of East Pakistan Rifles who had simply walked over the border with most of their equipment intact. Tents were provided by

> the Indian government who made up any kit deficiencies. . . . Their tents were pitched around some trees about half a mile from the Indian side of the border.[90]

The guerrilla training that India provided to the Bengalis started to bear fruit in August when the *Mukti Bahini* attacked a number of supply ships to Pakistan.[91] Two ships were attacked and sunk in the Chittagong Harbor on August 23 and several more vessels were destroyed thereafter.[92] The guerrilla tactics of the Mukti Bahini "destroyed many bridges, culverts and disrupted communication in many places and made the movement of the Pak troops difficult. In opportune moments, they ambushed enemy convoys, inflicted casualty and kept the enemy under constant fear."[93] Thus, by allying with India and benefiting from all the training and military supplies, the secessionists were able to hold their own against the Pakistan government.

## RIVALRY BETWEEN HOST STATE AND EXTERNAL POWER

The rivalry between India and Pakistan that began with the partition of India in 1947 was an important factor that influenced the formation of an alliance between India and the secessionists. "The partition of British India was hastily devised and extremely sloppy, and it is not surprising that the new governments of India and Pakistan faced a host of complex territorial problems and disputes."[94] Indo-Pak rivalry has continued to fester over the disputed territory of Kashmir, which has been the major bone of contention between the two countries. Before 1971, India and Pakistan fought two wars over Kashmir—the first one in 1947–48 and the second in 1965. Being an enduring rival of Pakistan, it was in India's interest to ally with the Bengali secessionists and help them defend themselves against the Pakistan army. In view of the hostile relations between India and Pakistan, India had much to gain if Pakistan was broken up into two and a friendly Bangladesh emerged as its neighbor.

India's reasons for allying with the secessionists have been aptly summed up by J.N. Dixit, former Indian foreign secretary and ambassador to Pakistan:

> India was . . . getting a little tired of having to confront and possibly fight Pakistan on two fronts whenever a conflict situation arose, specially so when the eastern front would strategically attract a China-Pakistan nexus. So if the people of East Pakistan, because of their socio-ethnic and linguistic considerations and in the face of the obstinate negation of their aspirations, wished secession from Pakistan and independence, India had no objection. If Indian endorsement and support resulted in this new entity being friendly to India, it was all to the good. A non-hostile Bangladesh instead of a hostile East Pakistan was considered desirable. Given the encouragement being offered off and on to the centrifugal forces in India's north-eastern states from East Pakistan bases, it was natural for India to support the liberation movement, which, in addition, had powerful humanistic rationale in the context of Pakistan's denial of democratic rights to the Bengalis and their military crackdown.[95]

The rivalry between India and Pakistan is evident in President Yahya Khan's speech to his nation, on June 28, 1971. Referring to India, President Yahya Khan said:

> It is unfortunate that our neighbor, which has never missed an opportunity to weaken or cripple our country, rushed to help the secessionists with men and material to inflame the situation further. This was all preplanned. . . . The whole dark plan of collusion between the Awami League extremists, rebels and our hostile neighbor gradually unfolded itself.[96]

In another broadcast to his nation on October 12, 1971, President Yahya Khan reiterated his opinion of India:

> As you are aware, the hostile forces, which opposed the establishment of Pakistan, have never accepted its existence, and have constantly been on the lookout to weaken us and to ultimately destroy this country. . . . I regret to say that India has never missed an opportunity to bring harm to Pakistan. . . . India's latest efforts to disintegrate Pakistan are well-known. . . . She has tried to cut away East Pakistan from the rest of the country . . . by assisting the miscreants with arms, ammunition and funds and . . . [97]

A reporter from Calcutta summed up the situation in the *Wall Street Journal*:

> For many reasons, India has been openly sympathetic with the Bangla Desh cause. Pakistan is an enemy and half an enemy is better than a whole nation. An independent Bengal nation, under moderate leadership, might even be friendly to India.[98]

## ETHNIC KINSHIP BETWEEN SECESSIONISTS AND EXTERNAL POWER

Strong ethnic ties between the Bengalis of West Bengal in India and the Bengalis of East Pakistan led to the alliance between India and the Bengali secessionists. Originally, East and West Bengal were part of one state, Bengal. The people spoke the same language, Bengali, and shared the same culture. It was in 1905 that Bengal was split into two parts on the basis of religion. West Bengal was predominantly Hindu and East Bengal, Muslim. And in 1947, during the partition of India, East Bengal became part of Pakistan and was named East Pakistan. Although the people of East and West Bengal had different religions, their cultural bonds originating from a common language, Bengali, were very strong. Therefore, the Bengalis of West Bengal were very willing to help their ethnic brethren in East Pakistan. Thus, the ethnic kinship between the Bengalis of India and the Bengali secessionists of East Pakistan contributed to the formation of the alliance between India and the secessionists.

## INTERNATIONAL MILITARY INTERVENTION BY EXTERNAL POWER

India's alliance with the Bengali secessionists was very strong because both rivalry and ethnic ties led to its formation. It is evident that a strong alliance increased the risk of military intervention by India. The alliance was seen as a threat to Pakistan and it heightened tensions between India and Pakistan. Speaking to the people of Pakistan on June 28, 1971, President Yahya Khan said:

> Our plans for reconstruction of the economy and early resumption of political activity in East Pakistan are threatened by India's continued interference in our internal affairs. Armed infiltration and open encouragement and assistance to the secessionists have heightened tensions between the two countries.[99]

On July 19, 1971, UN Secretary General U. Thant summed up the tense relationship between India and Pakistan:

> Although there can be no question of deep desire of both Governments for peace, tensions between them show no sign of subsiding. The situation on the borders of East Pakistan is particularly disturbing. Border clashes, clandestine raids, and acts of sabotage appear to be becoming frequent, and this is all the more serious since the refugees must cross this disturbed border if repatriation is to become a reality.[100]

In order to diminish the security of the alliance between India and the Bengali secessionists, Pakistan threatened war against India and began to move its troops and tanks to its borders with India. Pakistani officials made a number of threatening statements: "Our army is fully prepared and now we do not need any notice for waging a war,"[101] and "The people of Pakistan have understood India's filthy and nefarious game. They have decided to crush her evil designs,"[102] and "Hostilities on the border with East Pakistan have created a warlike situation. This might well escalate . . . if no attempt is made to check it."[103] Uncertainty and the incentive to misrepresent private information led to misperceptions of each other, thereby increasing the security competition between India and Pakistan. The creation of the security dilemma increased the risk of military intervention by India.

By the middle of October 1971, India and Pakistan were in the throes of war fever.[104] Tensions continued to increase between the two countries with the build up of both Indian and Pakistani troops along the border. "In fact, it was learned on the 16th of October that five Pakistani divisions, on a war footing, had been massed along the western front of India, while defensive measures had been taken on the Indian side."[105] Reporting on the Pakistani build-up of troops on the eastern front, Sidney Schanberg wrote, "The border areas in East Pakistan, where it is believed there are four or five divisions, have also . . . been strengthened. . . . The Indians are also said to have four or five Divisions along their side of the border."[106]

Border violations and clashes between the two armies began in earnest on the East Pakistani border. In a statement to the Indian Parliament on November 24, 1971, Prime Minister Indira Gandhi accused Pakistan of creating an extremely volatile situation:

> Pakistan's armed forces have been shelling our border areas, inflicting damage on life and property. Their air force has wantonly violated our air space several times. . . . Since March 1971, we have lodged 66 protests for border violations covering 890 incidents. For air violations, we have lodged 17 protests covering 50 incidents. However, these protests have had no effect and to cover up their incessant violations, Pakistani propaganda media have been putting out the story that we are engaged in an

> undeclared war and have mounted massive attacks with tanks and troops. This is wholly untrue. In fact, it was Pakistan which threatened total war and moved its entire armed strength into operational positions on our borders, and . . . we had, therefore, to take appropriate measures and move our forces to defensive positions. . . . It has never been our intention to escalate the situation or to start a conflict. To this end, we have instructed our troops not to cross the borders except in self-defense.[107]

Uncertain over Pakistan's intentions, India made the following moves:

> From 21 to 25 November several Indian army divisions, divided into smaller tactical units, launched simultaneous military actions on all of the key border regions of East Pakistan, and from all directions, with both armored and air support. These were, as usual, described as "defensive" responses to Pakistan shellings of Indian (or in a couple of cases, Mukti Bahini-controlled East Pakistani) territory. . . . From 21 November to 3 December, Indian forces moved into key strategic areas around the principal Pakistani defensive positions on or near the Indian border with the objective of either capturing or neutralizing them.[108]

In a statement to the Lok Sabha on December 3, 1971, Indian Foreign Minister Swaran Singh spoke about the heightened security competition between India and Pakistan:

> The continuing presence of ten million refugees on our soil, and a daily influx of over ten thousand, together with the concentration of Pakistani troops all along our border, and hundreds of violations of our ground and air, and continuous shelling of our territory, endanger our security.[109]

On December 3, 1971, war officially began between India and Pakistan, when the Pakistan Air Force suddenly attacked the military airfields in western India. On December 4, India launched a combined air, ground, and naval attack on East Pakistan. Allying with the Mukti Bahini, the Indian army entered East Pakistan. "An Indian army superior in numbers and aircraft to the 90,000 Pakistanis fighting the Bengalis took only 12 days, from December 4 to December 16, to execute an elaborate pincer movement on Dacca, moving from points in West Bengal, Assam, and Tripura to force the Pakistanis to lay down their arms."[110]

Thus, India's alliance with the secessionists led to uncertainty, information failures, problems of credible commitment, and a security dilemma that culminated in the direct military intervention of Indian forces on Pakistani soil and eventually into a full-scale war between India and Pakistan.

## SUCCESS OF THE BENGALI SECESSIONIST MOVEMENT

On December 16, 1971, Indian Prime Minister Indira Gandhi made the following announcement in Parliament:

> The West Pakistani forces have unconditionally surrendered in Bangla Desh. . . . Dacca is now the free capital of a free country. . . . This House and the entire nation rejoice

> in this historic event. We hail the people of Bangla Desh in their hour of triumph. We hail the brave young men and boys of the Mukti Bahini for their valor and dedication. We are proud of our own Army, Navy, Air Force and the Border Security Force, who have so magnificently demonstrated their quality and capacity. . . . Our objectives were limited—to assist the gallant people of Bangla Desh and their Mukti Bahini to liberate their country from a reign of terror and to resist aggression on our own land.[111]

## CONCLUSION

The evidence laid out in this chapter supports the main hypotheses that are put forth in the previous chapter. As the theory predicted, the East Pakistani secessionist movement increased the security competition between India and Pakistan and eventually led to military intervention by India. Although conflict is a recurrent feature between India and Pakistan due to their enduring rivalry and some kind of war might have taken place between them even without the secessionist movement, yet, it was the East Pakistan movement that was responsible for the war that took place in 1971.

The dynamic causal mechanisms that led to the war also support the theory advanced in chapter 2. A shift in the balance of power in favor of the secessionists led to a preventive war on the secessionists by the host state. The preventive war led to an explosive growth of the movement and encouraged an alliance between the secessionists and an external power, and eventually led to military intervention by the external power. The formation of an alliance was aggravated by rivalry between the host state and an external power and ethnic kinship between the secessionists and an external power.

The East Pakistani movement altered the balance of power in its favor when the Awami League won the elections in December 1970 and secured the largest number of seats in the National Assembly. The landslide Awami League victory led to a decline in the power of the Pakistan government relative to the Bengalis (or East Pakistanis). When the Pakistan government perceived a shift in the balance of power in favor of the Bengalis, it resorted to a preventive war on them in order to wipe them out before they accumulated too much power. Although the military capabilities of the Pakistan government were still high, it decided to wage war on the Bengalis and suppress them rather than risk war later under less favorable circumstances.

Pakistan's preventive war led to an explosive growth of the East Pakistan movement. With the formation of the *Mukti Fauj,* the movement for autonomy of East Pakistan changed into a movement for complete independence of East Pakistan from the rest of Pakistan. The preventive war on the Bengalis also led to an alliance between the secessionists and India. India aided and abetted the Bengali secessionists and trained them in guerrilla warfare. India and the *Mukti Fauj* formed a strong alliance against Pakistan.

The enduring rivalry between India and Pakistan was an important factor that led India to ally with the Bengali secessionists. Ethnic kinship between the Bengalis of West Bengal in India and the Bengalis of East Pakistan led the latter to appeal to India for help. Finally, the strong alliance between the India and the Bengali secessionists increased the security competition between India and Pakistan and led to India's intervention on behalf of the secessionists.

4

# Sri Lanka

LIKE THE EAST PAKISTANI secessionist movement, the Tamil secessionist movement in Sri Lanka created a shift in the balance of power in favor of the secessionists (in this case the Tamils). A shift in the balance of power led to a preventive war on the Tamils by the Sri Lankan government. The preventive war, in turn, led to an alliance between the Tamil secessionists and India and also resulted in a massive explosion of the Tamil secessionist movement. Ethnic ties between the Tamils of the two countries—India and Sri Lanka—stimulated the alliance. Once the alliance was formed between India and the Tamil secessionists of Sri Lanka, the creation of a security dilemma and the ensuing spirals of suspicion, hostility, distrust, and arms racing raised the level of security competition between India and Sri Lanka. However, India did not resort to a "Bangladesh-style intervention" that Sri Lanka feared might happen. India intervened through mediation and diplomacy, humanitarian means, and peacekeeping efforts but not by military invasion. The absence of rivalry between India and Sri Lanka did not make external military intervention[1] (like in the case of Bangladesh) worthwhile.

The conflict in Sri Lanka between the Sinhalese-dominated central government and the secessionist group, the Liberation Tigers of Tamil Eelam (LTTE), has still not been resolved. The conflict began as a demand for greater autonomy by the Tamils in the northern and eastern part of the country and grew into a struggle for a separate state, Tamil Eelam,[2] by the mid-1970s. Despite the devastating effects of the insurgency in terms of lives lost, people displaced, human rights violations, and a shattered economy,[3] the conflict continues and there seems to be no solution in sight. In 2002 the Sri Lankan government and the LTTE signed a ceasefire agreement, brokered by Norway. Peace lasted only a few years until violence erupted once again in 2006 thus violating the peace process and reverting back to 2001. In order to comprehend this intractable conflict, one has to look at its historical and political background.

## BACKGROUND

Sri Lanka, a small teardrop-shaped island located in the Indian Ocean at the southern tip of India is separated from the Indian sub-continent by the Palk Strait. Only 22 nautical miles lie between the two countries at the narrowest point of the Palk Strait.[4] The country consists of several ethnic groups: Sinhalese, Sri Lankan Tamils, Indian Tamils, Sri Lankan Moors, Burghers and Eurasians, Malays, and others. Formerly known as Ceylon,[5] the island was once a peaceful tropical paradise until it began to be torn apart by ethnic conflict. Historically, the relationship between the two largest groups, the Sinhalese and the Tamils, has been marked by discord rooted in linguistic and religious differences. Most of the Sinhalese are Buddhists who speak the Sinhala language or Sinhalese. The Tamils, on the other hand, are mostly Hindu who speak Tamil.

Table 4.1 shows the ethnic composition of Sri Lanka in 1981[6] and 2001.[7] The table shows the Sinhalese as the dominant ethnic group, comprising 74 percent of the population in 1981 and in 2001. The Tamils are divided into two groups: The Indian Tamils or Estate Tamils are descendents of Tamils who were brought from India to Sri Lanka during the British colonial rule in the nineteenth and early twentieth centuries to work as laborers in the plantations.[8] The Sri Lankan Tamils are natives of the island.

The geographical distribution of Sri Lanka's population in terms of ethnicity is worth noting. The Indian Tamils occupy the central highlands around Kandy where they work in the tea plantations. The Sri Lankan Tamils live in the northern and eastern areas of the island. The Jaffna Peninsula in the Northern Province has a large concentration of Tamils (see figure 4.1). Outside the northern and eastern

**Table 4.1 Ethnic Composition of Sri Lanka**

| Ethnic Group | 1981 | Percentage | 2001 | Percentage |
|---|---|---|---|---|
| Total | 14,846,800 | 100 | 18,732,000 | 100 |
| Sinhalese | 10,979,400 | 74 | 13,815,500 | 74 |
| Sri Lanka Tamils | 1,886,900 | 12.6 | 730,200 | 4 |
| Indian Tamils | 818,700 | 5.5 | 855,900 | 4.6 |
| Sri Lankan Moors (Muslims) | 1,046,900 | 7.1 | 1,351,400 | 7.2 |
| Burghers and Eurasians | 39,400 | 0.3 | 34,600 | 0.2 |
| Malays | 47,000 | 0.3 | 47,600 | 0.3 |
| Others | 28,400 | 0.2 | 29,500 | 0.2 |

*Source*: Department of Census and Statistics, Colombo, Sri Lanka.

**Figure 4.1 Map of Sri Lanka Showing Tamil-speaking Areas**

*Source*: Edgar O'Ballance, *The Cyanide War: Tamil Insurrection in Sri Lanka 1973–1988* (London: Brassey's, 1989), 34.

parts of Sri Lanka, the Colombo area is home to over half a million Sri Lankan Tamils.[9] The Sinhalese live predominantly in the western, southern, and central parts of the country.

Thus, Sri Lanka has "one of the most complex plural societies in the world"[10] that includes three main ethnic groups, and as many as four major religions. The religious breakdown of the island is shown in table 4.2.

The Buddhists who constituted 69 percent of the total population in 1981 and 2001 are by far the largest religious group. The Hindus comprised 15.5 percent of the population in 1981 and 13.8 percent in 2001.

Ethnic competition over the scarce resources of Sri Lanka underlies the tension between the various ethnic groups, especially the two main groups: the Sinhalese and the Tamils. This competition dates back to the nineteenth-century British colonial period. Under British rule, the Sinhalese language and Buddhism were hardly given any importance. Instead, it was the English language and Christianity that dominated over other languages and religions.[11] Christian missionaries established many English schools in the Jaffna Peninsula, which provided the Tamils living there an educational advantage over the Sinhalese. An English education enabled the Tamils to obtain employment in the Colonial Civil Service.[12] Around 1920, "Tamils accounted for more than half of the English-educated Ceylonese and were well represented in the bureaucracy."[13] However, when Sri Lanka became independent from British colonial rule in 1948, the Sinhalese, by virtue of their majority, began to control the government. A multiparty democracy emerged with two main Sinhalese-dominated parties—"the center-right United National Party (UNP) and the center-left Sri Lanka Freedom Party (SLFP)—alternating in power at six successive parliamentary elections between 1956 and 1977."[14] Once in control of the government, the Sinhalese decided it was time to "settle scores" with the Tamils. The Tamils did not support the Sinhalese parties but backed the Tamil Congress initially, then the Federal Party in the 1950s, and eventually the Tamil United Liberation Front (TULF) in the 1970s.[15]

**Table 4.2 Religions of Sri Lanka**

| Religion | 1981 | Percentage | 2001 | Percentage |
|---|---|---|---|---|
| Buddhism | 10,288,300 | 69.3 | 13,085,435 | 69.3 |
| Hinduism | 2,297,800 | 15.5 | 2,600,890 | 13.8 |
| Islam | 1,121,700 | 7.6 | 1,747,428 | 9.3 |
| Roman Catholicism/ Christianity | 1,130,600 | 7.6 | 1,415,045 | 7.5 |
| Other | 8,300 | 0.1 | 10,197 | 0.1 |
| Total | 14,846,700 | 100 | 18,858,995 | 100 |

*Source*: Department of Census and Statistics, Sri Lanka.

### Discrimination Against the Tamils

The discrimination against the Tamil minority by the Sinhalese government began as early as the first year of independence. In 1948, the Sinhalese-dominated UNP government passed the Citizenship Act that denied citizenship to more than half a million Indian Tamils. Consequently, the Indian Tamils were rendered stateless and were disenfranchised.[16] The disenfranchisement of the Indian Tamils "enabled the Sinhalese, in general, to increase their share of elected seats in Parliament to close to 80 percent of the total. From 1952 onwards, the Sri Lankan Parliament would be more like an assembly of Sinhalese notables than anything else."[17]

In 1956 a coalition of parties, led by S.W.R.D. Bandaranaike of the SLFP, was "elected on a wave of Buddhist nationalism which demanded, amongst other things, that the Sinhala-Buddhist majority should receive its 'rightful' share of official employment."[18] The new government soon made Sinhalese the sole official language of Sri Lanka. The "Sinhala-only" language policy of the Bandaranaike government

> forced Tamil government employees to study and work in Sinhala or leave employment. Tamil officers were given three years to learn Sinhala or face dismissal. This discrimination was extended to the security services, public corporations and other services, and to the private sector, where proficiency in the official language was an obvious premium.[19]

Thus, the Tamils, who had relied heavily on government jobs and public services, found employment hard to find.[20] It was estimated that from 1956 to 1965, the number of Tamils working in the Ceylon Clerical Service fell from 50 to 30 percent and the number in the Ceylon Administrative Service fell from 30 to 20 percent.[21]

The language policy of 1956 was to have a lasting effect on Sri Lankan politics. It led to "a polarization of sorts between large sections of the Sinhalese, on the one hand, and Sri Lankan Tamils, on the other."[22] In terms of Sinhalese-Tamil relations,

> the 1956 election was a milestone in Sri Lankan politics. In the south, the triumph of ethnic identity amounted to the capture of the state by the majority community for the purpose of political consolidation . . . in the north it represented the beginnings of a serious challenge to the unitary status of that state.[23]

Newspapers and parliamentary debates during the period 1956–77 underscored the communal tension that the "Sinhala-only" policy brought about. TULF's Amirthalingam said, "The 'Sinhala-only' policy . . . means not merely the elimination of the Tamil language from its due place in the public life of this country but the shutting out of the Tamil-speaking people of this country from the political, economic and cultural life of Ceylon."[24] Similar outcries made during parliamentary debates were: "The threat to communal amity, or rather the killing of communal amity, was carried out by the Government by its language policy"[25] and "there can be no communal peace in this country as long as . . . Sinhala Only Act remains on the statute-book."[26] Another Tamil representative noted, "If we submit to the imposition of Sinhala in our areas, we are accepting forever Sinhala domination, Sinhala supremacy, Sinhala rule, which is a substitute for colonial rule. . . . Today the language question has become a question of freedom."[27]

The legislation of successive Sinhalese-dominated governments continued to discriminate against the Tamils by "what has been alternatively called the 'competitive chauvinism' or 'intra-ethnic outbidding' of Sinhalese party politics."[28] In 1958, the government canceled previously made plans for devolution of power to Tamils. The United Front (UF) coalition government, elected in 1970, introduced a new constitution in 1972 making Buddhism the state religion and Ceylon was renamed Sri Lanka. The new constitution "practically amounted to a charter of Sinhalese-Buddhist supremacy."[29]

The UF government introduced unfair policies against Tamils with respect to admission to universities. A system of "standardization" and "district quotas," introduced between 1970 and 1973, resulted in the "weighting of marks in favor of Sinhalese candidates, or 'positive' discrimination."[30] The qualifying number of marks for admission to universities was higher for Tamils than for Sinhalese. In short, students taking the same examination, but belonging to different ethnic groups, had different qualifying marks.[31] Consequently, thousands of qualified Tamil students were denied the right to higher education. It is estimated that between 1970 and 1975, the number of Tamils admitted to medicine and engineering programs fell from 40 percent of the total number of students to 19 percent, whereas the number of Sinhalese students in the same programs rose from 58 to 78 percent.[32] In the words of Walter Schwarz, "nothing arouses deeper despair among the Tamils than the feeling that they are being systematically squeezed out of higher education."[33]

## Mobilization of Tamils

In response to the discrimination, the Tamils began to mobilize. In the 1970s, several secessionist groups came into existence. The first Tamil secessionist group called the Tamil New Tigers (TNT) was formed in 1972. The Tamil Eelam Liberation Organization (TELO), originally created in 1972, was reorganized in 1974.[34] In 1975, Eelam Revolutionary Organization of Students (EROS) was formed. A faction of this group later became the Eelam People's Revolutionary Liberation Front (EPRLF).[35]

In 1976 many Tamil political parties came together to form the TULF and on May 14 of the same year the TULF adopted the "Vadukodai Resolution," which formally demanded a separate Tamil state of "Eelam." Excerpts from the resolution, which openly sanctioned armed struggle, stated:

> This Convention resolves that the restoration and reconstitution of the free, sovereign, secular socialist state of Tamil Eelam based on the right of self-determination inherent

> to every nation, has become inevitable in order to safeguard the very existence of the Tamil nation in this country. . . . This convention directs the Action Committee of the TAMIL UNITED LIBERATION FRONT to formulate a plan of action and launch without undue delay the struggle for winning the sovereignty and the freedom of the Tamil Nation. And this Convention calls upon the Tamil Nation in general and the Tamil youth in particular to come forward to throw themselves fully into the sacred fight for freedom and to flinch not till the goal of a sovereign socialist State of Eelam is reached.[36]

Around the same time, The TNT strengthened and grew in size and became the LTTE on May 5, 1976. The LTTE emerged as the most ruthless and formidable of all the groups. The proliferation of secessionist sentiment among the Tamil minority is attributed to the discrimination they experienced at the hands of the various Sinhalese governments.

As C.R. de Silva has noted:

> By 1977 the issue of university admissions had become a focal point of the conflict between the government and the Tamil leaders. Tamil youth, embittered by what they considered discrimination against them, formed the radical wing of the Tamil United Liberation Front. Many advocated the use of violence to establish a separate Tamil state of Eelam. It was an object lesson in how inept policy measures and insensitivity to minority interests can exacerbate ethnic tensions.[37]

Reporting on the secessionists, the *South* confirmed the above:

> These are not terrorists but youthful politicians of despair. They are among the brightest and the best in Tamil society, who have abandoned careers in such fields as engineering, medicine, and accountancy. They are the flesh and blood of a statistical nightmare in the north and east, where unemployment among the Tamils with "A" level qualifications is as high as 41 per cent, compared with a rate of 29 per cent among their Sinhalese counterparts.[38]

A spokesperson for the LTTE explained, "We took up arms because of the government's failure to approach the ethnic problem with rational methods. . . .The phenomenon of *Eelam* rose out of the failure of the Sinhalese leadership."[39]

## SHIFT IN BALANCE OF POWER

As the Tamil secessionists mobilized and acquired arms and funds, their power rose relative to that of the Sri Lankan government. The power of the Tamils further increased with the 1977 election results. In the 1977 parliamentary elections, the TULF won big in the Tamil areas of the north and east and became the main opposition party in parliament. For the first time since the independence of Sri Lanka, a non-Sinhalese party became the largest opposition party. "[T]he SLFP—which since 1952 had always been the main opposition party whenever it was not in power—was reduced to 8 seats, while the TULF won 17 (almost all of them in predominantly Tamil areas)."[40] The TULF had increased its power and was now able to "bolster the Tamil claim for separation."[41] After all, the TULF election manifesto had clearly stated its commitment to the establishment of a separate state of Tamil Eelam for the Tamil people. The manifesto had stated:

> The Tamil nation must take the decision to establish its sovereignty in its homeland on the basis of its right to self-determination. The only way to announce this decision to the Sinhalese government and to the world is to vote for the Tamil United Liberation Front. The Tamil-speaking representatives who get elected through these votes, while being members of the National State Assembly of Ceylon, will also form themselves into the National Assembly of Tamil Eelam which will draft a constitution for the state of Tamil Eelam and establish the independence of Tamil Eelam by bringing that constitution into operation either by peaceful means or by direct action or struggle.[42]

The TULF election manifesto had asked the Tamil people for a mandate for a separate state of Tamil Eelam. Thus, the 1977 election "at once turned the parliamentary confrontation between government and opposition into one between a Sinhalese government and a Tamil opposition."[43] The powerful position of the leader of the opposition fell into the hands of Mr. Amirthalingam, a staunch advocate of Tamil secession. Mr. Amirthalingam's appointment as leader of the opposition created fear in the minds of the Sinhalese who began to feel that "the TULF had somehow moved closer to its goal of a separate state."[44]

With the TULF as the main opposition party in Parliament and Mr. Amirthalingam as the opposition leader, the Sinhalese government began to perceive a shift in the balance of power in favor of the secessionists. There was a relative decline in the government's power compared with the power of the TULF. Simultaneously, the growth of secessionist groups such as LTTE, TELO, and EROS, among others, and an increased Tamil political mobilization added to the overall power of the secessionists and a further shift in the balance of power between the Tamil secessionists and the Sri Lankan government.

## PREVENTIVE WAR ON TAMIL SECESSIONISTS

Perceiving a shift in the balance of power in favor of the Tamil secessionists, the Sri Lankan government decided to wage a preventive war in order to crush them before they further increased their power. The preventive war on the Tamils took place in July 1983 with preludes in August 1977 and July/August 1981.

Barely a month after coming to power in July 1977, the UNP government, under President Jayewardene, sent in the army with orders to "wipe out" those who were organizing the movement for a separate Tamil state.[45] The idea was to weaken the rising secessionist movement before it became a threat. In August 1977, anti-Tamil violence spread throughout the country. Tamils were attacked and killed by the hundreds, and thousands of Tamils were rendered homeless. According to Satchi Ponnambalam, "It was the government, through the police and the army that had used force against the Tamils and in particular had tyrannized the young Tamils. The government assumed that it had *carte blanche* to use the Sinhalese armed forces against the . . . Tamil youth and the people."[46] He continues, "Without . . . taking any steps to redress Tamil grievances, Jayewardene proceeded to declare war by sending in the army with instructions to wipe out the terrorists."[47]

Following the repression of 1977, the Jayewardene administration introduced draconian legislation to deal with the secessionists. The Prevention of Terrorism Act (PTA) of 1979 allowed detention without trial, confessions extracted under torture, and searches without warrants, among other things. A state of emergency was declared in the Tamil areas soon after the PTA was introduced and once again, the army was instructed by the government to "wipe out" the secessionists.

Evidence gathered by Amnesty International (1980) indicated that soon after the declaration of emergency,

> a pattern of arbitrary arrest and detention existed and torture was used systematically. . . . Six young men, reported arrested in the days after the emergency declaration, died in the custody of the police after having been tortured and the bodies of three of them have still not been found. When the Emergency was declared, the President had instructed the Commander of the Security Forces in the Jaffna District to carry out his mandate before 31 December 1979.[48]

In a subsequent letter to President Jayewardene in 1980, Amnesty International wrote:

> Various methods of torture have been used by both the police and the army in the period immediately after the emergency declaration, including suspending people upside down by the toes while placing their head in a bag with suffocating fumes of burning chillies, prolonged and severe beatings, insertion of pins in the finger tips and the application of broken chillies and biting ants to sensitive parts of the body and threats of execution. After these and other methods of torture had been applied, statements were extracted and recorded.[49]

In the middle of 1981, another anti-Tamil pogrom took place and it is believed that it was government-instigated violence once again. The repression of 1977 had strengthened the resolve of the Tamil secessionists and further radicalized the movement. Perceiving a shift in the balance of power in favor of the secessionists, the central government decided, once again, that it was better to use force to suppress the movement and block its further growth. A British journalist, who was in Sri Lanka at that time, wrote:

> It is clear that . . . violence in July and August, which was directed against Sri Lanka Tamils in the east and south of the country, and Indian Tamil tea estate workers in the central region, was not random. It was stimulated, and in some cases organized, by members of the ruling UNP, among them intimates of the President. In all 25 people died, scores of women were raped, and thousands were made homeless, losing all their

> meager belongings. But the summer madness, which served the dual purpose of quieting Tamil calls for Eelam, that is a separate state, and taking the minds of the Sinhalese electorate off a deepening economic crisis is only one of the blemishes on the face of the island. Since Jayewardene came to power . . . a system of what his critics call "State Terrorism" has brought an Ulster-style situation in the Tamil-majority areas of the north and the east. . . . Hundreds have been detained without charge or trial. This year at least 156 Tamil youths have been detained and tortured, then released. Thirty-five are still held at Colombo's Panagoda Army Camp. Human rights workers, Sinhalese as well as Tamil, told me that the most favored tortures are hanging prisoners upside down on heaps of burning chillies, and inserting needles under their finger nails.[50]

Confirming the torture, Amnesty International (1982) reported:

> In April and May 1981 some 30 members of the Tamil minority were arrested without warrant and held incommunicado following a bank raid in Neerveli in which two policemen were killed. . . . At the end of 1981, 22 were still held without charge or trial in Panagoda Army camp; five in solitary confinement.[51]

The anti-Tamil violence of 1977 and 1981 paled in significance when compared to the preventive war of 1983. The intensity of the "*organized mob violence* at work"[52] in 1983 was incredible. From July 24, 1983, to the beginning of August, over 3,000 Tamils were brutally killed.[53] Around 150,000 Tamils were left homeless and tens of thousands of refugees landed in southern India and the West. Problems of credible commitment created by a shift in the balance of power precluded negotiations between the central government and the secessionists.

There is extensive evidence from media and investigative reports that shows the prior planning of this pogrom by the government. *The Hindu* reported:

> The precision with which the violence was executed is suggestive of a degree of pre-planning and State involvement. Tamil homes would be burnt to the ground while neighboring Sinhalese homes would be left untouched. Tamil businesses in industrial areas were invariably correctly identified and destroyed.[54]

*The Times* (London) stated, "The rioters, seeking out Tamil homes and burning them, had a particularly detailed knowledge of who lived where and who owned what."[55] *India Today* (New Delhi) confirmed, "The mobs were armed with voters' lists, and detailed addresses of every Tamil-owned shop, house, or factory, and their attacks were very precise."[56] In *Unfinished Journey,* Shiva Naipaul wrote about how the Sinhalese planned their attack to single out the Tamils. He said, "Their bloodlust was in effect regulated by the bureaucratic endeavors of the civil service. Before the axes could be wielded, before the petrol bombs could be thrown, before the pillaging could begin, a little paperwork had to be done."[57] The August 5, 1983, issue of *The Times* (London) reported: "Army personnel actively encouraged arson and looting of business establishments and homes in Colombo and absolutely no action was taken to apprehend or prevent the criminal elements involved in these activities."[58]

An editorial in *The Hindu* wrote:

> A look in hindsight at the series of events as they unfolded and evidence collected from witnesses would suggest that the events of July 1983 were far from spontaneous, they were in fact well planned and constitute a well organized massacre, a pogrom. To suggest that the murder of over 3,000 people in the space of a week is a disturbance of public order is at best insulting. . . . [B]efore the violence finally exploded on July 25th the Sri Lankan government promulgated two pieces of legislation, the purposes of which can only be seen with knowledge in hindsight of the terror unleashed on the Tamil people in Sri Lanka. In early July . . . the Jayewardene regime imposed the Public Security Act, which gave the Security forces permission to immediately bury or cremate dead bodies without post mortem examination, inquest or judicial inquiry of any kind. The freedom and impunity that this legislation conferred was taken advantage of by the Sri Lankan security forces with much vigor. . . . The legislation was directed at the security forces who played a full part in the anti-Tamil violence. It gave them the freedom to murder with impunity by allowing them to destroy the evidence.[59]

In his book, *Sri Lanka: The Holocaust and After*, L. Piyadasa described how the Tamils were attacked. According to him, marauding groups ran amok for almost a week killing thousands of innocent Tamils, setting fire to their property, and plundering and looting whatever they could. All of this occurred "while the guardians of the law remained inactive and in some instances even encouraged and assisted the lawlessness."[60] Piyadasa further wrote that a close examination of the preventive war on the Tamils underscored the fact that the actions of the Sinhalese mobs were not spontaneous but part of a carefully planned strategy of the UNP government to drive away the Tamils from their homes, schools, and places of work.[61]

A report on Sri Lanka issued by the U.S. State Department spoke of the physical damage experienced in the country:

> Violence against Tamils in the city of Colombo spread throughout the Sinhalese majority areas in the central and southern parts of the country. . . . As many as 3,100 Tamil shops were damaged or destroyed, and thousands of Tamil-owned or occupied homes were burned or looted.[62]

A survivor who narrowly escaped being killed wrote this account:

> Several government jeeps and buses belonging to the Sri Lanka Central Transport board came speeding and halted suddenly with their brakes screeching. People started alighting from the vehicles with knives and swords in their hands. There were about 200 men. They systematically started to run towards the Tamil houses. About ten people who appeared to be the leaders were holding sheets of paper in their hands. (I later came to know that they were election register lists.) They were directing the mob to the Tamil houses. Two of the men were very familiar. I had seen them speak at an election meeting of the ruling government party (United National Party) recently. There were three Tamil houses opposite mine. The men smashed the windows and threw petrol bombs inside. With a blaze the houses caught on fire and the flames rose

> to the sky. People were screaming. The fire was so intense that it compelled the mob to move further away.[63]

The July violence continued unabated into August when the "Sri Lankan troops set ablaze the Tamil-speaking town of Mannar and opened indiscriminate fire on civilians at two other places in insurgency-hit Northern Province."[64] Reports indicated that "more than 3,000 families had lost their homes in the Army violence in the town, located 80 km South of Jaffna on the gulf of Mannar."[65] By the middle of August, the "army operations . . . covered Jaffna, Velvettiturai, Chunnakam, Mannar and other parts of the Northern Province where the Tamils constituted an overwhelming majority of the population."[66]

In sum, a shift in the balance of power created increased tensions between the Tamils and the central government and the ensuing "problems of credible commitment" between the two parties led to a preventive war on the Tamils by the Sinhalese-dominated central government. Moreover, the central government wanted to prevent the further rise of the secessionists and so, decided to crush them while the military advantage of the government was still high.

## EXPLOSIVE GROWTH OF THE MOVEMENT

Each time the Sri Lanka government tried to suppress the Tamils, the movement only became stronger. There is decisive evidence that the preventive war strengthened the collective identity of the Tamils, who joined the movement in large numbers. Tamils who were not in favor of the movement became radicalized and several new secessionist groups came into existence. Soon after the 1977 attempt to crush the movement, a group of Tamils wrote:

> Since 1977 there has been a reign of terror in the North unleashed by the armed forces. Instead of curbing violence, it has, on the contrary, escalated the incidence of violence, as can be seen from the increasing number of killings of armed personnel. We need hardly state that the terrorism of the armed forces has been counterproductive. . . . The reason is that the grievances of the people are far too deep-seated to be smothered by batons and bullets.[67]

Even the 1979 PTA did not curb the secessionists. Rather, it radicalized the Tamils and increased their acts of sabotage and violence. As Ponnambalam has put it, "No people can be held down by the force of military might, particularly of another oppressive ethnic community. The situation escalated into a 'race' war between the Sinhalese and the Tamils."[68]

The 1983 preventive war on the Tamils by the central government of Sri Lanka led to an explosive growth of the movement. It "left a lasting imprint upon the collective consciousness of Tamils and . . . resulted in the political radicalization of thousands of Tamil youth."[69] These youth began to join Tamil guerrilla groups. As Sumantra Bose has said, "It was only *after* July 1983 that Tamil youth began joining the LTTE and similar radical groups in really significant numbers, and that the armed insurgency spread from the peninsula to other areas of the North and East."[70] High-school dropouts and men in their twenties joined the Tamil movement in droves.

Journalist and author, William McGowan has written:

> After the riots of 1983, the various Tamil rebel groups launched intensive recruitment drives in the refugee camps of southern India and in Tamil areas . . . in the north and east. Issues such as national self-determination, university admissions, and equity in land settlement paled before the basic desire for vengeance and the quest for safety inside an independent Tamil state. Thousands joined the movement.[71]

In a similar vein, J.P. Senaratne has said:

> Within a matter of months after the 1983 riots the Tamil guerrilla offensive escalated to a qualitatively higher level of violence. All five major groups—LTTE, PLOTE, TELO, EROS, EPRLF—became larger and stronger as a consequence of increased Tamil popular support and . . ."[72]

Simultaneously, many new Tamil militant groups came into existence—"a veritable alphabet soup of initials."[73] Some of these post-July 1983 groups were:

| | |
|---|---|
| IFTA | Illkai Free Tamil Army |
| NLFTE | National Liberation Front of Tamil Eelam |
| RELO | Revolutionary Eelam Liberation Organization |
| RFTE | Red Front of Tamil Eelam |
| TEA | Tamil Eelam Army |
| TEC | Tamil Eelam Commandos |
| TEEF | Tamil Eelam Eagles Front |
| TELA | Tamil Eelam Liberation Army |
| TELC | Tamil Eelam Liberation Cobras |
| TENA | Tamil Eelam National Army |
| TERO | Tamil Eelam Revolutionary Organization |
| TERPLA | Tamil Eelam Revolutionary Peoples Liberation Army |

Reporting on the 1983 preventive war on the Tamils, *India Today* stated, "That, indeed, was the turning point, when even those Tamils who had been skeptical of the prospects of secessionism began to take the rebellion more seriously."[74] Commenting on the repeated repression of the Tamils, Tambiah cautioned, "what the Sri Lankan government is achieving by its persistent military action and terrorizing of all Tamils is to drive the latter . . . toward the imagined haven of Eelam and a blanket of ethnic solidarity."[75]

Thus, the preventive wars on the Tamils led to "the consolidation of a composite Tamil national identity"[76] among the various Tamil groups irrespective of religion. This is because in "the riots of 1977 and in the pacification that followed the riots, the Sinhalese-dominated security forces made no distinction between

Tamils on the basis of religion: all Tamils were potential enemies."[77] Thus, Tamil Catholics and Tamil Hindus were members of a "Tamil nation." Their strengthened Tamil identity increased their resolve and led to an explosive growth of the movement.

## ALLIANCE OF SECESSIONISTS AND EXTERNAL POWER

The preventive war on the Tamils of Sri Lanka also led to an alliance between them and India. In order to survive the preventive war of 1983, Tamil refugees from Sri Lanka "estimated to be in the region of 40,000 in the months following July 1983 and about 150,000 by 1985"[78] began to pour into Tamil Nadu, in southern India. Along with the refugees came the secessionists.[79] They needed assistance in the form of arms, funds, and military training to fight the Sri Lankan government.

At the same time, Tamil Nadu politicians lobbied the Indian government to support their ethnic brethren in Sri Lanka. On July 31, 1983, Tamil Nadu chief minister, Mr. M.G. Ramachandran, led a delegation to meet Prime Minister Indira Gandhi in New Delhi and gave her a memorandum that said, "The grim and inhuman killings in Sri Lanka cannot be dismissed as the internal affairs of the country. . . . We definitely feel that the time has come for the Indian government . . . to save the Tamils in Sri Lanka."[80]

Tamil political parties in Tamil Nadu like the Dravida Munnetra Kazhagam (DMK) and the All-India Anna Dravida Munnetra Kazhagam (AIADMK), longtime advocates of Tamil militancy in Sri Lanka, began to lend support to the Tamils of Sri Lanka. Along with the refugees came the militants.[81] The DMK supported the TELO and the AIADMK promoted the LTTE.[82] The leader of the DMK, Mr. Karunanidhi, protested to the UN about what he called the genocide on the Sri Lankan Tamils. It was Karunanidhi who, in 1986, tried to unite the six Sri Lankan Tamil militant groups who were operating from bases in Tamil Nadu.[83]

In an effort to placate Tamil Nadu, Mrs. Gandhi responded that her government would place a high priority on the Tamil situation in Sri Lanka.[84] This is because "with general elections due in 1984 and her electoral base eroding in many parts of India, including some of her strongholds in southern India, Indira Gandhi was anxious to mollify Tamil Nadu and to retain . . . the Congress I party's base there."[85] Moreover, "Gandhi saw in the ethnic crises a golden opportunity to change into a direction she wanted, the Sri Lankan government's pro-Western foreign policy"[86] and "to ascertain her position of regional supremacy in the South Asian region."[87] Thus, the preventive war on the Tamils by the Sri Lankan government opened windows of opportunity for both India and the secessionists to form an alliance.

India's alliance with the Tamil secessionists resulted in overt mediation and humanitarian assistance and the covert arming and training of the Tamils by India.[88] Sri Lankan Tamil guerrilla groups set up bases in Tamil Nadu, where they were arming and training themselves with India's help. India's foreign intelligence agency, the Research and Analysis Wing (RAW)[89] covertly recruited, trained, and armed the Sri Lankan Tamil militants.[90] In his in-depth investigation of RAW involvement in the Sri Lankan secessionist crisis, Gunaratna has reported: "In October 1983 . . . RAW officials . . . planned the Sri Lanka Operation . . . a two-pronged, covertly military and overtly political strategy to 'handle' Sri Lanka."[91] This plan to "recruit, arm, train, and finance Sri Lankan Tamil militancy was secretly prepared and executed under the overall supervision of R.N. Kao, the National Security Advisor to the Prime Minister of India."[92]

There is significant evidence that the Tamil militant group TELO was an Indian creation, a group with no specific ideology, made up of thugs brought in to follow instructions from RAW.[93] In 1982, RAW gave members of TELO and various other Tamil secessionist groups extensive military intelligence and espionage training in Tamil Nadu.[94] These trainees would later return to Sri Lanka and carry out attacks on Sinhalese soldiers, police, and even civilians. The May 1985 bus-stop massacre in Anuradhapura was said to be a collaborative effort between the LTTE and RAW.[95]

According to *Frontline*:

> the "original sin" of permitting the LTTE and other militant groups to operate from Tamil Nadu was committed by the Government of Indira Gandhi and later Rajiv Gandhi, who allowed the Indian external intelligence agency, the Research and Analysis Wing (RAW), to train them in Tamil Nadu and use the State as a base for their operations against the Sri Lankans.[96]

Although the Indian state of Tamil Nadu began to assist the Sri Lankan Tamil separatists in the early 1980s before the 1983 riots, there is evidence that this assistance intensified greatly after the July 1983 riots. The *Frontline* reported:

> Since mid-1983, Tamil Nadu has been a haven for Sri Lankan Tamil militants of various shades—above all the LTTE cadres. With a coastline extending over 1000 km, dotted with nearly 26 big and small urban centers and about 450 fishing hamlets, the State has been regarded as a vital rear base in the armed struggle in the North-East of the island.[97]

In its investigation of India's support to the Sri Lankan Tamil rebels, *India Today* reported:

> The rebels, most of whom escaped by boats from Jaffna in the wake of the July 1983 massacres, are now all over Tamil Nadu. For their leaders, Madras has become a kind of tactical headquarters. They operate out of rooms in the legislators' hostel, allotted in the names of sympathetic MLA's and privately hired houses, while the Government is most accommodating about visa and immigration regulations—some of them even go abroad on Indian passports. . . . Rebels of various groups run regular motorboat ferries between the Indian coast and Jaffna, using the Palk Straits

unmolested. . . . Besides, the width of the Palk Straits is just about 35 km—the maritime boundaries overlap—and the . . . Indian Navy and Coast Guard, it seems, couldn't care less.[98]

On India's role in Sri Lanka, Rajesh Kadian has written:

> the guerrillas were sent to major training institutions in different parts of India. For example, selected militants were sent to Chakrata in the Himalayan foothills of Uttar Pradesh. Here, Establishment 22, a tough, hush-hush organization . . . was used because it is secluded, well-guarded and far from the public eye . . . similarly, the academies of the para-military forces in central India were used to provide basic infantryman's training. . . . In general, the quality of training was high and consisted of fieldcraft, tactics, map—reading, and jungle and guerrilla warfare. They were taught to handle weapons-systems like light and medium machine-guns, automatic rifles, pistols, and rocket-propelled grenade launchers. The AK-47 assault rifle . . . had to be specially procured for this purpose. Regular Indian Army personnel were seconded to provide instruction in the use of bombs, laying of mines, and the establishment of telecommunications.[99]

Reporting on the first training camp for Tamil secessionists, a journalist wrote:

> The place was Chakrata, north of Dehra Dun. Two thousand Tamil terrorists were imparted training there. . . . In November last year (1983), the men were picked up from Dehra Dun by buses . . . and transported in batches of 500 to Madras. Thereupon, the local line to Sri Lanka took over, and the terrorists were crossed over to Jaffna.[100]

Although India repeatedly denied aiding the secessionists and claimed that "in India there were no terrorists but refugees, adding that there were no military training camps but only refugee camps to accommodate those seeking asylum from Sri Lanka following anti-Tamil violence,"[101] official sources in Sri Lanka identified several camps in North and South India where Tamil militants seeking to establish the state of Eelam were being trained to put up a fight against the preventive wars of the Sri Lankan government.[102] Marguerite Johnson wrote in the *Lanka Guardian* that, "Tamil Nadu . . . harbors 39 rebel camps, in which an estimated 3,300 guerrillas are undergoing training."[103] Tables 4.3 and 4.4, published in *South* magazine, show that several groups of militants—TELO, People's Liberation Organization of Tamil Eelam (PELO), EROS, and TELA, among others, received intensive training in India.[104]

Thus, the government of India, as Shelton U. Kodikara has written,

> was certainly infringing the norms if not the rules of international conduct by its tolerance, and even tacit support . . . and its failure to heed repeated Sri Lankan government charges that some of the militant groups operating from Tamil Nadu were not only proclaiming their commitment to a separate state but even attempting the subversion of the democratic process in the island.[105]

**Table 4.3 Military Training in Tamil Nadu**

| Groups | No. Trained | Period of Training | Location of Camp | Subject of Instructions | Name of Instructors |
|---|---|---|---|---|---|
| TELO | | May 5, 1983 | Large house at no. 777 or 977 | Unarmed combat, weapon training .303 rifles, AK-47 Kalashnikov or T 56, piston/revolvers | Subedar Major Narashima Vaman |
| TELO | Not known | October 1982 May 5, 1983 | Parangimali and at a place about 40 km from the Madras airport | Firing practice, leopard crawl, monkey crawl, ghost walk, close quarter unarmed combat, first aid, preparation of Molotov cocktails, fire-fighting, endurance test | Indian instructors |
| TELO | 300 | September 26, 1983 | Salem Kollimalai Kanjipuram | Drill, PT, military subjects | Ex Subedar Major Narashima Vaman of the Indian Army |
| TELO | Not known | October 30, 1983 | Kollimalai, Kanjipuram | Physical training, Military subjects | Ex Subedar Major Narashima Vaman of the Indian Army |

*(continued)*

**Table 4.3 Continued**

| Groups | No. Trained | Period of Training | Location of Camp | Subject of Instructions | Name of Instructors |
|---|---|---|---|---|---|
| TELO | 360 | Later part of 1983 | Kollimalai, Kakavel | AK-47, G3, pistols, SLR, LMG, SMG, No. 36 Browning revolvers, rocket launchers, 2” mortar, explosives | |
| TELO | 24 | November 1982 August 1982 (first visit) | Anna Nagar (2 months), Parangimalai, in close proximity to Meenambakkam Airport (1 month) Salem (2 months) | Physical training, .303 firing | Ex Subedar Major Narashima Varman of the Indian Army |
| | 700 | March 1984 August 1984 (second visit) | Salem (2 months) | G3 rifles, AK-47, military subjects | Ex Subedar Major Narashima Varman of the Indian Army |
| TELO | 350 | October 19, 1983 June 19, 1984 | Kanchipuram | Military Subjects | Ex Subedar Major Narashima Rao of the Indian Army |
| P.L.O.T. | Not known | May 21, 1983 | Sengalpattu Presawakkam | Physical training, weapon handling | Rajah—retired Army soldier |

| | | | | | |
|---|---|---|---|---|---|
| P.L.O.T. | Not known | March 12, 1983 September 12, 1983 | Sengalpattu, Thanathur, Kongurukolam in Erodi | Military tactics, guerrilla warfare, jungle warfare, handling of weapons, .380 and .450 revolvers, .22 air rifle | Sekar |
| T.E.L.A. | 300 | Not known | Valachchari and Thenikramam | Physical training, weapon training | Alagasamy, a retired Indian police officer and an ex-Indian Army officer |

*Source*: *South*, March 1985, 14.

**Table 4.4 Military Training in North India**

| Groups | No. Trained | Period of Training | Location of Camp | Subject of Instructions | Name of Instructors |
|---|---|---|---|---|---|
| TELO | Not known | August 13, 1983<br>February 18, 1984 | A place in close proximity to Greater Kailas 11 in New Delhi | SMG, AK-47, revolver, explosives | "Sir," an Indian who conversed in Hindi Nayar of Kerala |
| TELO | Not known | October 30, 1983<br>July 19, 1984 | Sadtagen development area adjoining Cannal Park in New Delhi (3 months training) | Manufacturing of bombs, handling of SMGG, AK-47, pistols | Narayan and two others of the Indian government |
| TELO | 300 | September 26, 1983<br>September 25, 1983 | At a location about 2 hours journey by bus from New Delhi railway station | PT, SLR, AK-47 weapon handling, guerrilla warfare, firing practice, grenade throwing, rocket launcher | North Indians |
| TELO | 102 60 150 | October 12, 1983 | A camp in Uttar Pradesh close to the Himalayan foothills | PT, weapon training, jungle warfare, map reading, military tactics, communications | One Punjab national, three Malayalees and seven other instructors |
| TELO | 60 | October 20, 1983<br>February 3, 1984 | Green Park, New Delhi, close to the medical college | Trained in using pistols, revolvers, and SMG, firing practice | Narayan and three instructors from Kerala |

| | | | | | |
|---|---|---|---|---|---|
| TELO | Not known | October 19, 1983<br>June 19, 1984 | A camp in Uttar Pradesh not far from the Himalayan foothills | Physical training, weapon training, jungle warfare, map reading, military tactics, communications | Indian instructors |
| PLOT | Not known | May 21, 1983 | The Army camp close to the International Airport, Delhi | Drill, weapon training | Rajah, retired army soldier<br>Shekar, Indian army soldier |
| EROS | 56 | October 5, 1983<br>March 21, 1984 | A camp in Uttar Pradesh close to the foothills of the Himalayas | Drill, weapon training, map reading, communications, field craft, guerrilla warfare, military tactics | Indian instructors |

*Source*: *South*, March 1985, 14.

All of the above available evidence shows that the preventive war on the Tamils by the central government led to an alliance between India and the Tamil secessionists. By mid-1987, it was estimated that around 20,000 secessionists had trained in India.[106]

## NO RIVALRY BETWEEN HOST STATE AND EXTERNAL POWER

India and Sri Lanka have never been rivals. In fact, for strategic reasons, India has always recognized the importance of good relations with Sri Lanka.[107] It has been said:

> As long as Sri Lanka is friendly or neutral, India has nothing to worry about but if there be any danger of the Island falling under the domination of a power hostile to India, India cannot tolerate such a situation endangering her territorial integrity.[108]

In other words, "Sri Lanka is regarded as being integral to India's security"[109] Therefore, India and Sri Lanka have maintained cordial relations with each other.

In this case study, the "rivalry" variable did not play a role in the formation of an alliance between the Tamil secessionists and India. It was ethnic ties between the Tamils of the two countries that was an important factor that brought about the alliance in the wake of the preventive war. However, the absence of rivalry between India and Sri Lanka led to a relatively weak alliance between India and the Tamil secessionists. Ethnic ties alone did not build an alliance strong enough to lead India to militarily intervene in order to break up Sri Lanka.

## ETHNIC/RELIGIOUS KINSHIP BETWEEN SECESSIONISTS AND EXTERNAL POWER

Strong ethnic ties between the Tamils of Sri Lanka and the Tamils of India led to an alliance between India and the Tamil secessionists. The Tamils of both countries "belong not only to the same ethnic stock . . . but also speak the same language and follow the same cultural patterns."[110] For this reason,

> Whenever communal riots between the Sinhalese and the Tamils take place, the fifty million Tamils in the state of Tamil Nadu press the government of India to take up the matter with Sri Lanka and do something or redress the wrong done to their brethren in that country.[111]

After the 1983 riots in Sri Lanka, TULF leaders appealed to Indian Prime Minister Indira Gandhi to "save millions of Tamils on the island from total annihilation."[112] In response to their demand,

> Mrs. Gandhi reiterated that it was not India's intention to interfere in the internal affairs of Sri Lanka, but it could not be a silent and disinterested spectator of this grim

> tragedy, when so many innocent Tamils with strong filial links with their brethren in South India were being killed, rendered homeless and treated in this inhuman fashion.[113]

Thus, the ethnic linkage between the two groups was an important factor in shaping the alliance between India and the Tamil secessionists of Sri Lanka. The alliance must be understood in the context of "the transnational ethno-linguistic affinities"[114] that exist between the Tamils of the two countries. As K.M. de Silva has aptly said,

> [T]he Tamil Nadu factor forms an important facet of India's complex role in the ethnic conflicts of Sri Lanka in the 1980s. . . . Seldom has a constituent unit (a province or state) of one country influenced the relationship between it and a neighboring country with the same intensity and to the same extent that Tamil Nadu did . . . in the case of India's relations with Sri Lanka. Indeed the India-Tamil Nadu-Sri Lanka relationship is unique in international affairs. . . . Tamil Nadu provided Sri Lankan Tamil separatist activists with sanctuaries, training and bases. Not only did the central government connive in this, but it also tolerated the provision of training facilities, and the existence of camps and bases in other parts of the country.[115]

Speaking on India's assistance to the Sri Lankan Tamils, Indian ambassador to Sri Lanka aptly summed up the situation in a speech in March 1989: "we had to respect the sentiments of the 50 million Tamil citizens of India. We felt that if we did not rise in support of the Tamil cause in Sri Lanka, we were not standing by our own Tamils . . . it was a compulsion that could not be avoided by any elected government in this country."[116]

## NO INTERNATIONAL MILITARY INTERVENTION BY EXTERNAL POWER

Besides the preventive war on the Tamils, it was only the "ethnic kinship" variable that led to the alliance. The "rivalry" variable was absent. For this reason, the alliance that was formed was not strong enough to bring about military intervention[117] by India with the goal of breaking up Sri Lanka. Although tensions between India and Sri Lanka did arise, India intervened through humanitarian, peacekeeping, and diplomatic means and not through military invasion.

It is evident from the following sequence of events that the alliance between India and the Tamil secessionists of Sri Lanka was seen as a threat to Sri Lanka, which took steps to diminish the security of the alliance. The creation of the security dilemma and the subsequent spirals of hostility and suspicion between the two parties—Sri Lanka and the Indian alliance—did create tensions.

In the 1980s, especially after 1983, India's massive covert assistance to the secessionists, in the form of sophisticated arms and ammunition, base facilities, training in guerrilla warfare, laying of mines, map reading, and so on, increased the military strength and capability of the various secessionist groups. Not only were the Tamil secessionists able to recover from the preventive war launched on them, but they were also able to fight strongly against the Sri Lankan government. By 1985–86, there was "a virtual setting up of a parallel administration in the Northern Province by the LTTE."[118] The Tigers were literally in control of the Jaffna Peninsula.

In order to get the Tigers to lose control of Jaffna and cause them grave hardship, the Sri Lanka government imposed a food and fuel embargo on Jaffna in January 1987. Soon after that, in May1987, Sri Lanka launched *Operation Liberation,* "a massive land-sea-air offensive"[119] on the Jaffna Peninsula in an attempt to regain control of the area from the LTTE.

Condemning the attack on the LTTE by the Sri Lanka government, India, once again, went to the aid of the secessionists. India's high commissioner in Sri Lanka issued a statement to the Sri Lankan government:

> The population of Jaffna, already suffering extreme hardship under the five month old economic blockade imposed upon them by their own Government are now becoming the victims of an all out military assault as part of what has been described as a "fight to finish." Thousands have already been killed in the ethnic conflict and hundreds more are dying. . . . Although attempts have been made to keep this tragic story from the world by a communication blockade and by sealing off Jaffna from the rest of the world, reports are already filtering out of large scale civilian deaths, property damage leaving thousands homeless and acute shortage of food, medicines and shelter. . . . In response to this tragic situation, and motivated by humanitarian considerations, the Government and people of India propose to send urgently needed relief to Jaffna.[120]

Sri Lanka responded by blaming India for the plight of the people of Jaffna:

> While pointing out that the tragic situation in Sri Lanka would not have become acute as at present but for the patronage of separatist terrorism by the state of Tamil Nadu, a Constituent of the Republic of India, the Government of Sri Lanka wishes to point out that neither has Government of Sri Lanka solicited any humanitarian aid nor does the situation obtaining in the North require any assistance.[121]

Despite the above response from Sri Lanka, India sent a flotilla of 19 boats with food, medicine, and other essentials on a humanitarian mission to Jaffna in June 1987. The Sri Lankan forces turned the flotilla back. This prompted India, in defiance of Sri Lanka's wishes, to air-drop 25 tons of food to the Tamil secessionists in Jaffna. This action on the part of India was seen by Sri Lanka as an outright violation of its airspace and as a result, Indo-Sri Lankan relations reached its nadir. There was fear and distrust of India among the Sinhalese. Sri Lanka was apprehensive about whether India would intervene militarily like it did in Bangladesh. Tensions and security competition between the two countries were high and "Sinhalese perception and fears of a threat from India grew worse."[122]

At the same time, India was not pleased that Sri Lanka was increasing its supply of arms from other countries. Reporting on Sri Lanka's acquisition of new arms, *India Today* stated:

> Indian sources claim that the Sri Lankans have been using far heavier artillery than ever before, including 75 mm rockets fired from pods under the wings of the SIAI Marchettis and 50 lb bombs dropped from helicopters which explode on impact. The army also possesses newly acquired 120 mm mortars. These weapons, sources say, have been arriving in recent months from Indonesia, Singapore and South Korea.[123]

India also claimed that there were around thirty-seven foreign advisors in Sri Lanka, "including some from Pakistan, Israel, and members of the notorious British Keany, Meany Services (KMS)."[124] According to *India Today*, "It was possibly the involvement of Israel and Pakistani advisors that annoyed New Delhi more than anything else and pushed India into making the air-drop."[125]

Uncertainty by one side over the intentions of the other, misperceptions, fear, and distrust of each other led to the creation of the security dilemma, which increased security competition between Sri Lanka and the alliance between India and the Tamil secessionists. Consequently, the risk of an Indian invasion was high.

However, instead of overt Indian military intervention on behalf of the secessionists, India and Sri Lanka signed a peace accord on July 29, 1987. Under the terms of this accord, India was to bring about an end to the hostilities between the Tamil guerrillas and the Sri Lankan military, and to get the secessionists to surrender their arms. An Indian peacekeeping force (IPKF) was sent to Jaffna to disarm the Tamil rebels on July 30, 1987. Thus, India decided to intervene as peacekeepers "to implement the provisions of the Accord and to bring about a resolution of the conflict."[126] However, the IPKF was unsuccessful in its endeavor and ultimately withdrew in 1990.

India intervened first on humanitarian grounds and then by sending peacekeepers but there was no military invasion on the part of India. India did not favor a "Bangladesh-style"[127] intervention in Jaffna. Rather, India wanted a settlement through mediation. "Between 1983 and 1987, Indian diplomats and politicians floated a series of schemes, at the inter-governmental level, all of which postulated a negotiated settlement to the 'ethnic problem' on the basis of varying degrees of limited regional autonomy for the Sri Lankan Tamils."[128] Since India and Sri Lanka are not rivals, it was not in India's interest to break up Sri Lanka. Besides, dividing up Sri Lanka would only give rise to a Sinhalese state in southern Sri Lanka that would be anti-India.

## STALEMATE

Throughout the 1990s, the LTTE continued its struggle for a separate state with intermittent peace negotiations with the government of Sri Lanka. "One of the hallmarks of the civil war in the 1990s was its increasingly brutal nature, involving major human rights abuses perpetrated by both the Sri Lankan army and the Tamil rebels."[129] Currently, the Tamil secessionist movement in Sri Lanka is at a stalemate. Peace talks between the Sri Lankan government and the Tamil Tigers are being brokered by Norway. However, no political settlement between the two sides has been reached and violence between the two sides has erupted again.

## CONCLUSION

As the theory laid out in chapter 2 predicted, a shift in the balance of power between the Sri Lankan government and the Tamil secessionists led to a preventive war on the Tamils by the Sri Lankan government. The preventive war, in turn, led to an explosive growth of the movement and to an alliance between India and the secessionists. Ethnic kinship between the Tamils of India and the Tamils of Sri Lanka encouraged the alliance. However, the absence of rivalry between India and Sri Lanka created an alliance that was not strong enough to cause military intervention by India.

The balance of power shifted in favor of the Tamil secessionists when the Tamil political party TULF, the main proponent of Tamil secession, became the main opposition party in Parliament in 1977, thereby strengthening the Tamil demand for a separate state—Eelam. There was a decline in the power of the Sinhalese government relative to the power of the Tamil secessionists.

When the Jayewardene government of Sri Lanka perceived a shift in the balance of power in favor of the Tamils, it decided to wage a preventive war on the Tamils in 1983 in order to wipe out the movement before it became stronger. Although conditions were still favorable, the Sri Lankan government wanted to crush the Tamil secessionists and not wait till later when conditions might worsen.

The preventive war on the Tamils led to an explosive growth of the movement. Several new secessionist groups sprung up in the months following the preventive war of 1983. The preventive war also led to an alliance between the Tamil secessionists and India. In an attempt to increase their power and military capabilities, the secessionists turned to India for help and the Indian government assisted them with arms, training, finance, and logistical support. The Indian government also stood to gain from the alliance. The Congress (I) party at the Center wanted electoral support from the Tamils of Tamil Nadu.

The "rivalry" variable was not relevant in this case because India and Sri Lanka are not rivals. However, the ethnic kinship between the Tamils of India and the Tamil secessionists did have a strong effect on the formation of the alliance. Lastly, the evidence supported the hypothesis that a weak alliance (in this case, an alliance formed only by ethnic ties) does not lead to external military intervention. Although the security dilemma did build up between India and Sri Lanka, the former did not use military force to break up the latter because the absence of rivalry did not create an alliance that was strong enough to bring about military intervention.

# 5

# Kashmir

AN EXAMINATION OF the events leading to the Pakistan military incursion into the Kargil sector of Kashmir[1] in 1999 reveals the causal sequence that precedes foreign military intervention in a secessionist war. The Kashmir insurgency of 1989 created a shift in the balance of power between the Kashmir secessionists and the Indian government. In order to weaken the growing secessionist movement and retard its further growth, the Indian government resorted to a preventive war on the secessionists starting in 1990. Using its military troops, India tried to crush the secessionists before they accumulated more power. The preventive war on the Kashmiris led to an explosive growth of the secessionist movement and also led to an alliance between Pakistan and the Kashmiri secessionists. The enduring rivalry between India and Pakistan and ethnic/religious ties between the Kashmiri Muslims and Pakistanis formed a very strong alliance that in turn led to Pakistani military intervention in 1999 in an attempt to wrest Kashmir from India. Although Pakistan's military intervention was unsuccessful against India's military prowess, tensions between India and Pakistan over Kashmir have continued.

Kashmir occupies a strategic location in the northernmost part of India, surrounded by Pakistan on one side and China on the other (see figure 5.1). One-third of the state, known as Azad Kashmir, is governed by Pakistan and two-thirds of the state known as Jammu and Kashmir is governed by India. The cease-fire line that divides the state came into being in 1949 after the first Indo-Pak war. With the 1972 Simla Agreement, which was signed by India and Pakistan after the 1971 war, the cease-fire line came to be called the Line of Control (LOC).[2]

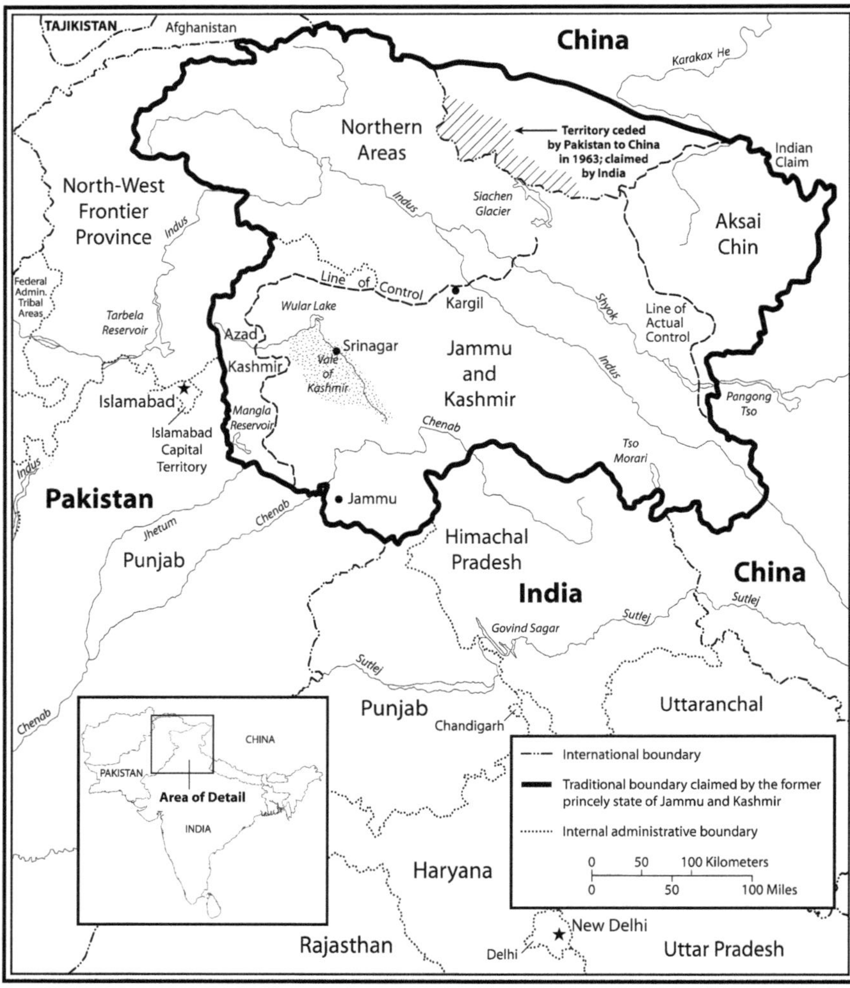


**Figure 5.1 Map of Kashmir Region**

*Source*: Courtesy of the University of Texas Libraries, University of Texas at Austin, September 2006.

## BACKGROUND

In order to understand the Kashmir secessionist movement in its proper perspective, it is necessary to take a look at the history and geopolitics of the region in 1947, the year India gained independence from the British. The controversy in Kashmir originated from unique circumstances that were bound to result in a bitter dispute. Under the British, India was divided into two entities, that is, British India, which was governed directly by the British government, and the quasi-autonomous

Indian states (also called principalities) that were ruled by Indian princes. A little over half of the total area of India was governed directly by the British whereas the rest of the country was divided into more than 550 principalities.[3] The princes were responsible for managing the internal proceedings of the princely states, but it was British doctrine of paramountcy that controlled the military and diplomatic affairs of the princely states.[4]

Within this complex framework, a Hindu prince, Maharaja Hari Singh, was placed in charge of the principality of Kashmir, which was overwhelmingly Muslim. It was agreed that British authority over the princely states including Kashmir would expire on August 15, 1947, when India would gain independence from the British. In keeping with the rules for the partitioning of India, it fell upon Maharaja Hari Singh to decide whether Kashmir would choose to go to Hindu-majority India or Muslim-majority Pakistan. In fact, over 500 princely states decided to accede to either India or Pakistan without a plebiscite. All that was required to complete the legal part of the accession was a prince's signature on the Instrument of Accession.[5] Maharaja Hari Singh of Kashmir failed to make a decision of accession till after the British rule ended. His procrastination meant that Kashmir was "technically independent."[6] As Hayes has said, "The Maharaja, by his delaying tactics, could hardly have had any objective in mind other than independence."[7] However, both India and Pakistan continued to covet Kashmir.

On October 22, 1947, a large number of armed tribesmen from northwest Pakistan invaded Kashmir destroying and looting towns and villages. In an attempt to save Kashmir, Maharaja Hari Singh appealed to India for assistance and in order to receive military help, decided to accede to India.[8] Once the maharaja signed the Instrument of Accession on October 26, 1947, Indian troops were sent to Kashmir. War broke out between India and Pakistan in November 1947 and continued till December 20, 1947, when the case was referred to the UN Security Council.[9] This led to the partitioning of Kashmir along a cease-fire line, which came to be known as the LOC in 1972.[10]

The Maharaja's decision to accede to India was immediately labeled by Pakistan as illegal and nonbinding. It was officially stated as early as October 30, 1947: "The Government of Pakistan cannot accept the version of the circumstances in which Kashmir acceded to the Indian Dominion."[11] Pakistan has never abandoned this position and neither has India been willing to relinquish its own. Therefore, the root cause of the Kashmir problem can be found in the circumstances leading to the partition of the subcontinent in 1947. The dispute over Kashmir has continued for over fifty years and has led to three wars (1947, 1965, and the Kargil War of 1999) between India and Pakistan, the massive military build-up on both sides, and the involvement of both in cold war alliances. Maharaja Hari Singh delayed making a decision about Kashmir's accession and Pakistan has still not accepted his eventual decision of accession to India. Both India and Pakistan have proclaimed their rights over Kashmir. India has tried to retain its hold on Kashmir by maintaining its military superiority over Pakistan; similarly, Pakistan has tried to change the status quo in Kashmir by trying to wrest Kashmir from India.

## Discrimination Against the Kashmiris

Due to the controversy surrounding Kashmir's accession to India, Kashmir was granted a "special status"[12] under Article 370 of the Indian Constitution of 1950. Article 370 was based on clauses 7 and 8 in the Instrument of Accession, which was signed by Hari Singh and designed to safeguard his sovereignty:

> Nothing in this Instrument shall be deemed to commit me in any way to acceptance of any future constitution of India or to fetter my discretion to enter into arrangements with the Government of India under any such future Constitution.[13]
>
> Nothing in this Instrument affects the continuance of my sovereignty in and over this State, or, save as provided by or under this Instrument, the exercise of any powers, authority and rights enjoyed by me as ruler of this State or the validity of any law at present in this State.[14]

According to Article 370, which applied only to Kashmir, the central government of India had jurisdiction over the state's defense, external affairs, and communications, whereas everything else fell under Kashmir's own jurisdiction. However, the Indian government did not honor Article 370, which was "to ensure a fundamental autonomy in the internal administration of Jammu and Kashmir."[15] The central government of India constantly interfered in the internal affairs of Kashmir and tried its best "to integrate Kashmir more tightly with the rest of the nation."[16] Almost every election in Kashmir was rigged by the central government thereby undermining Kashmir's autonomy. Worse still, "starting from the early 1980s, the Congress government at the center indulged in blatant vote fraud and subversion of the electoral process in Kashmir in order to further the interests of the Congress Party in the state."[17]

Listing the serious errors of consecutive Indian governments in Kashmir that resulted in the isolation of the Kashmiris,[18] A.G. Noorani, former advocate of the Bombay High Court and the Indian Supreme Court, has written: "India's record shows lapses on five accounts—rigged elections, failure to respect the State's autonomy, corruption, discriminatory employment practices, and failure to respect human rights."[19]

In 1984, the elected National Conference government in Kashmir was arbitrarily dismissed by the central government in New Delhi. Farooq Abdullah's government in Kashmir had been popularly elected in 1983 with massive support of the people in a fair election. He had run on a pro-Kashmiri autonomy platform and "the reasons that were adduced for his dismissal were, at best, flimsy and, at worst, downright specious."[20] The people of Kashmir saw the dismissal of Abdullah's government by the central government as a gross misuse of power by New Delhi. This interference by New Delhi in Kashmir's affairs was "another nail in the coffin of the Kashmiri's faith in Indian democracy and law."[21] As Victoria Schofield has written, "The fact that the prime minister of India was willing and able to set Abdullah aside for what essentially were personal reasons demonstrated the lack of regard she and the government of Delhi had for Kashmir's so-called special status."[22]

Merely two years after the dismissal, in 1986, Farooq Abdullah's party, the Kashmir National Conference, was urged to form an electoral alliance with Rajiv Gandhi's Congress (I) party in the state. It was a coalition of convenience for the Congress (I) party that was desperate to come to power but could not do so on its own.[23] This alliance that "reduced Farooq Abdullah, the son of the legendary Sheikh Abdullah, to the status of a mere stalking horse for the Congress (I) in Kashmir"[24] was responsible for rigging the Kashmir elections of 1987.

The 1987 Kashmir election was both fraudulent and violent. Not only was the election rigged but also the opposition Muslim United Front party's agents were attacked and evicted from the voting and counting stations.[25] Journalist Tavleen Singh confirms this: "The rigging was blatant. In the constituency of Handwara, for instance, Abdul Ghani Lone's traditional bastion, as soon as counting began on 26 March, Lone's counting agents were thrown out of the counting station by the police."[26]

The flawed 1987 elections in Kashmir "ensured that the last viable avenue for the expression of political discontent was blocked."[27] The Kashmiris were further alienated from the central government of India for its disregard of fair electoral practices and democratic procedures. As Abdul Ghani Lone, a Muslim United Front candidate, told *India Today*: "If people are not allowed to cast their votes where will their venom go except into expressions of anti-national feelings?"[28] Journalist Inderjit Badhwar wrote: "These events, some of them witnessed by *India Today*, have only served to produce a deeper feeling of alienation among the youth who have flocked to the opposition—even the MUF—in search of an alternative power structure in Kashmir."[29]

A.G. Noorani has cogently summed up the political discrimination the Kashmiris felt at the hands of the central government: "the political coup ousting Chief Minister Farooq Abdullah in July 1984, the forced marriage of his National Conference with the Congress party in November 1986, and the rigging of the 1987 state election was enough to drive the Kashmiris to desperation."[30]

The economic plight of the Kashmiris, overlooked by the central government, has also been a factor that has contributed to their alienation. In 1990, *The Times of India* stated:

> The national investment in public sector enterprises during the past 40 years has been of the order of Rs. 86,000 crores and Jammu and Kashmir's share has remained as low as 0.03 per cent. The ratio of grant and loan from the Central Government to Jammu and Kashmir has all along been unfavorable even though the state has sought justice. Whereas Himachal Pradesh with its much better agricultural infrastructure and industrial base when compared to Jammu and Kashmir, has been receiving Central funding at the ratio of 90 per cent as grant and 10 per cent as loan, Jammu and Kashmir has been getting 70 per cent as loan and 30 per cent as grant. The ratio never left more than a wage-bill in the hands of the state government. Owing to this discrimination, no real

> development has taken place. . . . The absence of any industry on the one hand and availability of free education in school and college on the other hand naturally raised the level of unemployment. Needless to add, unemployment has been the most important factor responsible for the alienation of the Kashmiris.[31]

## Mobilization of Kashmiris

Unable to find a viable democratic outlet for protest, the dissidents in Kashmir looked for other means to express their grievances against the corrupt central government. They turned to militancy. The alienation of the Kashmiris led to the growth of secessionist sentiment among the Muslims especially after the elections of 1987. The *Time* magazine reported the following:

> The last straw for Kashmiri political activists who would eventually become guerrillas was [Rajiv] Gandhi's tolerance of, if not connivance in, overt election fraud in 1987 to help a local ally win control of the state. As a consequence, the political moderates, who looked to New Delhi for leadership, have all but vanished, at least in Jammu and Kashmir.[32]

Another account stated:

> The rigged election was the beginning of the end. When I next went to Kashmir . . . nearly everyone I met said that most of the youths who had acted as election agents and workers for the MUF candidates were now determined to fight for their rights differently. They had no choice but to pick up the gun, was the message I was given.[33]

*India Today* reported:

> A look at the intelligence agencies' lists of the A and B category extremists shows how much the rigging of the 1987 poll has cost the nation and [then Chief Minister] Farooq [Abdullah] himself. Nearly all the young men on the wanted list today were guarding ballot-boxes for the Muslim United Front (MUF) candidates in the last election.[34]

Educational opportunities and a rise in literacy fueled the mobilization of young Kashmiris. As one journalist wrote:

> A new generation of Kashmiris, who knew little or nothing of the freedom movement against the Maharaja's rule or the tribal invasion, had gone to the polls, and were disappointed. They had benefited from the free education—from primary to university levels—available since the early fifties, but were frustrated because there were few jobs available for them. Educated unemployed are the most eruptive element in any society; here, they blamed lack of opportunities in the rest of India for their plight.[35]

An increase in unemployment exacerbated the situation. Rajesh Kadian has said, "in the fifteen years after the 1971 war the unemployed in Kashmir had increased from 10,000 to 150,000. Therefore, jobless or under-employed young men became increasingly available to the militants."[36] Unemployed Kashmiris joined secessionist groups in large numbers.

By 1989 a rapid spread of militant sentiment contributed to the proliferation of several insurgent groups. On one side, groups were formed of Muslim fundamentalists who are pro-Pakistan and want Kashmir to be part of Pakistan. These fundamentalist groups are the Hezb-i-Islami (founded in 1982), the Muslim Students' Federation, and the Islami-Jammiat Tulba.[37] On the other side exists a group of secessionists linked with the Jammu and Kashmir Liberation Front (JKLF), which was founded in 1965. The secessionist groups tied to the JKLF are the Mahaz-i-Azadi, the Kashmir Students' Liberation Front, and the Kashmir Mujahideen Liberation Front.[38] These secessionists do not want to join Pakistan, but wish to have a separate and independent state of Kashmir. Former governor of Kashmir, Jagmohan listed 44 secessionist groups operating in Kashmir before he took over as governor on January 19, 1990.[39]

## SHIFT IN BALANCE OF POWER

There is substantial evidence to indicate that a shift in the balance of power took place in favor of the Kashmir secessionists. First of all, a rapid proliferation of secessionist groups in Kashmir was accompanied by a decline in the power of the central government of India. The nationally dominant Congress (I) party underwent a steady organizational decline in the 1980s, first under Indira Gandhi and later under her son Rajiv Gandhi. In 1983, strong opposition parties to Congress (I) appeared in the states of Tamil Nadu, Karnataka, Andhra Pradesh and West Bengal. These regional parties together with Farooq Abdullah's Kashmir National Conference became part of an unofficial alliance against the central government.[40]

In order to compensate for this decline, the Congress (I) party tried to gain power in states where the party did not have a substantial constituency.[41] To achieve this, the Congress (I) forged alliances of convenience with the leaders of some states. Within Kashmir there was widespread opposition to the Kashmir National Conference—Congress (I) coalition state government formed in 1986. The Congress (I) government at the center was distracted on several fronts, which led to a further decline in its power. Commenting on the declining power of the Indian government, Sumit Ganguly has written:

> The Congress (I) government in New Delhi was preoccupied with its own problems and paid little attention to Jammu and Kashmir. At a domestic level, the regime faced an increasingly hostile opposition, which accused the ruling party of having received substantial kickbacks for the purchase of the Bofors field gun for the Indian Army. The party's electoral base had also shrunk considerably, with the Congress (I) in power in only twelve states. At the foreign policy level, in January 1987 India and Pakistan had teetered on the brink of war. "Brasstacks,"[42] India's largest military exercise in its postindependence history and a brainchild of General Krishnaswami Sundarji had precipitated this crisis. Furthermore, several divisions of the Indian

> Army that had been deployed in Sri Lanka as the Indian Peace Keeping Force (IPKF) became steadily embroiled in the civil war there.[43]

A decline in the power of the central government of India in the 1980s was accompanied by a rapid spread of fundamentalist Islam in Kashmir, which followed from a big change in Pakistani political culture. Pakistani President Zia-ul-Haq's politics of Islamization had a substantial effect on nurturing fundamentalist groups inside Kashmir "either as subsidiaries of the parent groups in Pakistan or as pirated versions of the original."[44] Muslim fundamentalist groups in Kashmir, which were financed with money from Pakistan, tried to convert Kashmiri Muslims to fanaticism and fundamentalism by encouraging them to consider non-Muslims as "kafirs" or infidels.[45] This gradual "Islamization" of Kashmir played a big role in undermining the common Kashmiri identity called "Kashmiriyat" that had developed among the Kashmiris over the centuries. The people of Kashmir began to think of themselves in terms of Hindus and Muslims rather than just "Kashmiris." In this way, "the precious secular harmony of the once-placid Valley"[46] of Kashmir was eroded.

Throughout 1988 and 1989, the power of the secessionist groups was on the increase. Bomb blasts, violent clashes, protests, and terrorist activities by the secessionists continued unabated. In his memoirs, *My Frozen Turbulence*, former governor of Kashmir, Mr. Jagmohan has written extensively about the increasing power of the secessionists in Kashmir in February 1989 and the inefficiency of the Indian government in dealing with it:

> The subversionists are proving successful in their designs to inject heat in the political environment. . . . New terrorist outfits like "Al Jung" and "Zia Tigers" are emerging. Militancy is mounting. Hit-and-run tactics are being increasingly employed. . . . The continued failure of the State Government to redress the grievances of the people and to show results in the realm of development add to the tension and enable the fundamentalists and secessionists to exploit religious frenzies. . . . In fact, to a considerable extent, the present troubled state of affairs is the result of the accumulated anger of the people against the malfunctioning of the Government.[47]

In a letter to Prime Minster Rajiv Gandhi on April 8, 1989, Jagmohan lamented on the relative increase in the power of the secessionists:

> The situation is fast deteriorating. It has almost reached a point of no return. For the last five days, there have been large-scale violence, arson, firing, hartals, casualties and what not. Things have truly fallen apart. . . . The Chief Minister stands isolated. He has already fallen—politically as well as administratively; perhaps only constitutional rites remain to be performed. His clutches are too soiled and rickety to support him. Personal aberrations have also eroded his public standing. The situation calls for effective intervention. Today may be timely; tomorrow may be too late.[48]

A decline in the power of the central government of India and the Kashmir state government and the spread of Islamic militant sentiment led to a shift in the balance of power in favor of the secessionist groups in 1989. Evidence of this shift is reported in several newspapers in 1989. On October 24, 1989, a commentary in the *Patriot* read:

> Kashmir is heading toward a crisis. Srinagar is daily rocked by bursts of explosives aimed mainly at Central Government offices, installations and officials. There is a leadership vacuum in the Valley. The main crisis, which manifests is the disquieting hold the Pakistan-based Kashmir Liberation Alliance has gained on the Valley.[49]

On November 6, 1989, *The Statesman* reported:

> The Kashmir Valley has been effectively left at the mercy of the militants. . . . The administration ceased to exist several months ago. . . .To the people, the absent administration and a totally deaf Center are the last straws.[50]

*The Times of India* on November 23, 1989, lamented:

> There seems to be a strange conspiracy of silence about the reign of terror, subversion and lawlessness in the once happy and now apparently helpless valley of Kashmir. For the daily outrages by Pakistani-trained militants . . . have gone on without evoking even a semblance of concern from New Delhi and nothing more than a few thundering speeches by the State Chief Minister, Dr. Farooq Abdullah. The paramount cause of the apparent paralysis of the law enforcement agencies is the lack of political will and direction in Srinagar and New Delhi's unwillingness or the inability to do anything that might invigorate the political set-up at the state level.[51]

The *Hindustan Times* commented on December 17, 1989:

> Today in Kashmir the cult of violence is spreading very fast. Since there is not even a semblance of the Government in the Valley . . . the Valley has been left free to the militants. "There is no rule of law but the rule of the bullet," a tourist who returned from the Valley remarked.[52]

The Pakistan press also wrote about the decline in the power of the Indian government. The *Nation* commented in two editorials in December 1989: "The message from Srinagar is loud and clear. New Delhi's writ is no longer operative in the Valley and Dr. Farooq Abdullah has more glamorous pursuits to chase than putting the act of his crumbling administration together,"[53] and "[t]here is a virtual uprising against the Indian rule. . . . The Kashmiri Muslims' struggle for freedom is at crossroads and a historic opportunity awaits them to transform it into the decisive assault for breaking the shackles of Indian bondage."[54]

Summing up the dire conditions in Kashmir in the late 1980s, Jagmohan wrote:

> To sum up, the trends and undercurrents reveal that the polity and the administration of the state are not in good health. The Congress (I) is in disarray. The National Conference shows no spark, no vigour. The drumbeaters of parochialism and fundamentalism

> are working overtime, and the secularists have surrendered initiative. Subversion is on the increase. The shadows of events from across the border are lengthening. Lethal weapons have come in. More may be on the way. The intelligence agencies have not proved equal to the task. The chinks in their armour stand exposed by the undetected movement across the border. As if these problems were not sufficient to fill the cup of trouble, regional agitations have cropped up. The face of democracy is being increasingly pimpled by exploitation. The overall fabric of the State shows too many loose threads, too many weak stitches.[55]

The violent incidents in Kashmir during most of 1988 and 1989 crested with the kidnapping of the daughter of the union home minister in Srinagar on December 8, 1989. The kidnappers who were members of the Jammu and Kashmir Liberation Front (JKLF) demanded the release of five incarcerated political activists. "The government's willingness to concede emboldened the insurgents and very soon the Valley was aflame."[56]

## PREVENTIVE WAR ON KASHMIRI SECESSIONISTS

The events of the 1980s in Kashmir clearly showed how a shift in the balance of power in favor of the Kashmir secessionists took place. A shift in the balance of power led New Delhi to use force to crush the uprising. New Delhi deployed nearly 400,000 Indian security personnel to Kashmir. These included members of the Indian Army, the Border Security Force, and the Central Reserve Police Force, among others. Mr. Jagmohan, well known for his ruthlessness in dealing with crises, was sent to Kashmir where he took over as governor on January 19, 1990. From January 1990, the "crackdown was marked by brutality against civilians, including the shooting of unarmed demonstrators, civilian massacres and summary executions of detainees."[57] The July 1990 *Armed Forces Special Ordinance* gave the security forces power to search and arrest people without a warrant, shoot and kill under immunity from prosecution. According to one estimate, Kashmir has "the highest ever per capita ratio of troops per population in contemporary human history, with a ratio of one Indian armed military man for roughly every 3–4 Kashmiri youth."[58]

The following extensive evidence from journalists and human rights groups clearly indicates that the preventive war occurred soon after the shift in the balance of power in 1989. A report by *Asia Watch,*[59] a division of Human Rights Watch, contrasts the pre-insurgency killings in Kashmir with those that took place in 1990:

> According to one account, in the 17 months . . . before January 19, 1990, 96 people were killed in Kashmir by militants or police forces. Another report noted that the number of persons killed in demonstrations and police firings between mid-1988 and mid-1989, approximately 50, was more than in any period in the previous two decades. By contrast, most estimates indicate that in 1990 alone more than 2,000 persons were

> killed in war-related violence in Kashmir. According to press reports, there have been a comparable number of disappearances and hundreds of cases of rape, sexual abuse and torture.[60]

The report continued:

> In the first few weeks of 1990, government forces arrested hundreds of young men and opened fire on unarmed demonstrators, killing scores of civilians. Since then, the central government has pursued a policy of repression in Kashmir that has resulted in massive human rights violations by the army and the security forces, including extra judicial executions, disappearances, arbitrary arrest, prolonged detention without trial, and widespread and widespread torture.[61]

According to journalist Tavleen Singh:

> Having been to the Valley barely a week before [Jagmohan] took over as governor, I can say, with certainty, that although the situation was bad it was nowhere near as bad as it became within weeks of Jagmohan taking over. Before he arrived, despite the militancy, the civil curfews and the general sense of non-government, Kashmir was not the killing field it became with his advent. In fact, before he went there the number of deaths caused by the violence could be counted in double figures. Within two months of his arrival more than 200 people had been killed. Before he took over there was a semblance of normalcy in the Valley, which allowed tourists to continue to visit and people to go about their daily activities despite the militancy. After he took over almost the first thing that happened was that the Valley was put under a state of almost perpetual curfew. . . . Jagmohan clearly had a brief to unleash as much repression as possible.[62]

Describing the actions of the Indian security forces, *Asia Watch* has reported:

> In a pattern that is repeated everyday in Kashmir, the security forces detain young men during "crackdowns"—cordon and search operations during which all the men of a neighborhood or village are called to assemble for an identification parade in front of hooded informers. According to journalists and human rights activists in Kashmir, the informers are often detainees themselves who have been threatened with death unless they identify a quota of militants. Those whom the informers point out are taken away for torture and interrogation. A number of detainees are simply taken out and shot.[63]

The report also stated:

> In August 1992, Indian government forces launched a new offensive against the militants, called Operation Tiger, a campaign of surprise raids designed to capture and kill suspected militants and terrorize civilian sympathizers. Summary executions of detainees and indiscriminate attacks on civilians escalated during the operation, and during another which followed, called Operation Shiva. Over the next several months, the security forces also engaged in frequent arson attacks, burning houses, shops

> and entire neighborhoods. . . . By mid-1993, human rights groups and journalists in Kashmir reported figures of several hundred executions of detainees since Operation Tiger began.[64]

The use of repressive force by the Indian security personnel against the insurgents has killed thousands. The human toll has extended to the security forces and innocent civilians. The *Washington Times* reported in 1992:

> In this active rebellion, up to 30,000 people have been killed by a regional military and paramilitary force fluctuating between 350,000 to 430,000 in just the last two years. Torture, gang rape and various other heinous acts are commonplace by uniformed members of the security forces.[65]

There have been repeated human rights violations against peaceful demonstrators:

> On January 6, 1993, in the single largest civilian massacre of the conflict, at least 43 people were shot dead or burned to death when Indian paramilitary forces rampaged through a neighborhood in the city of Sopore. . . . A local police official at the scene stated that the security forces "ran amok" and prevented police and fire fighters from intervening.[66]

*Asia Watch* further reports:

> In the first four months of 1993, more than 130 persons are reported to have died in custody in Kashmir. Asia Watch and PHR[67] directly investigated 19 custodial executions and 47 other extrajudicial killings by government forces that occurred between July 1992 and April 1993.[68]

Table 5.1 lists the deaths in custody during the years 1985–91 in Jammu and Kashmir.[69] There is clear evidence from the table that the deaths in custody took place in 1990 and 1991 after the shift in the balance of power took place.

## EXPLOSIVE GROWTH OF THE MOVEMENT

The massive preventive war by the central government resulted in the strengthening of the Kashmir secessionist movement. It was said that the 1990 *Armed Forces Special Ordinance,* described earlier, turned "innocents into militants."[70] New Delhi's repressive tactics created a situation where those who were initially against the militants began to feel that secession from India is the best way to escape the brutal Indian crackdown. One Kashmiri official aptly summed up the situation: "Till January 19 (the day Jagmohan returned as Governor of Kashmir) I was against militants. Today I am for them."[71]

There is evidence that the preventive war on the Kashmiris resulted in an explosive growth of the movement. It was estimated by the press that in the beginning of 1990 there were around 400 militants in the Kashmir valley but by

**Table 5.1 Deaths in Custody During the Years 1985–91**

| Name (age) | Date of Death | Circumstances of Arrest | Circumstances of Death | Official Action Known |
|---|---|---|---|---|
| Mumtaz | September 13, 1991 | Between September 12 and 19, the army conducted cordon and search operations, during which Mumtaz's brother was shot dead | Beaten to death by the army when performing the last rites for his brother | |
| Khazir Mohammed Abdul Aziz | August 24 or 25, 1991 | The two men were arrested by the security forces during a crackdown on their village on August 24 | They died in an interrogation center, according to official sources | |
| Mohammed Ashraf | July 1991 | Arrested by security forces during counter insurgency operations and taken to an interrogation center | On July 18, his body was taken home, reportedly showing signs of torture | |
| Ghulam Mohammad | July 1991 | Detained by the security forces and taken to an interrogation center | Body was handed over to the relatives on July 18 | |
| Abdul Gani Khan | December 3, 1990 | Detained on December 3 by the security forces | Body was found in Habak village. Locals said he had died in custody | Official announced an investigation |

(*continued*)

**Table 5.1 Continued**

| Name (age) | Date of Death | Circumstances of Arrest | Circumstances of Death | Official Action Known |
|---|---|---|---|---|
| Imtiaz Ahmed Mir (30) | October 1990 | Arrested in October in Anantnag by the Central Reserve Police Force (CRPF), 53rd battalion | The next day his body was found by a roadside, marked by torture and a bullet wound | Relatives filed a complaint with the police. The CRPF denied his arrest |
| Bashir Ahmad | July 11, 1990 | Arrested with two others on July 10 by the security forces | Died in custody, reportedly of torture. Police refused to take his body, which was thrown into a river by the security forces | |
| Ghulam Hassan Sheikh | July 11, 1990 | Arrested by the security forces on July 10 | Died the following day reportedly of torture during interrogation | |
| Fayaz Ahmed Mattoo | June 21, 1990 | Shot dead while bathing in a pond, then detained by CRPF; taken to an interrogation center | Two days later his body was returned to relatives without explanation | |
| Mangta Khan | June 3 or 4, 1990 | Arrested by the army with other villagers on June 3 and taken to an army camp | The following day his dead body was taken to a hospital, reportedly with a fractured skull | |

| | | | |
|---|---|---|---|
| Ghulam Qadir War | June 1990 | Arrested by the security forces and taken to Akhnoor interrogation center, Jammu | Died in custody and despite a court order his body was not returned to his home for burial |
| Mohammad Sultan Malik | June 1990 | Arrested by the security forces and taken to an interrogation center | Died reportedly of torture |
| Mohammad Ayub Khan (35) | May 14, 1990 | Arrested May 14 by the 68 Mountain Brigade from his home | Reportedly tortured during interrogation, then killed by five bullets fired at close range |
| Abdul Majid Khan (22) | May 1990 | Arrested by the 68 Mountain Brigade on May 22 with his father, shot and injured. Taken for interrogation | Several days later, body was found with an eye missing and numerous bruises and burns |
| Shabir Ahmad Sulati (about 19) | May 1990 | Arrested by the security forces and taken to an interrogation center | Died as a result of torture. His body was returned on May 15 by the police |
| Altaf Aly | May 1990 | Detained mid-May with 14 others from Haihama- Payerpora, Kupwara district by the security forces. Subjected to electric shocks | The 14 other men were later released, but he was reportedly beaten to death in custody |

(*continued*)

**Table 5.1 Continued**

| Name (age) | Date of Death | Circumstances of Arrest | Circumstances of Death | Official Action Known |
|---|---|---|---|---|
| A. Razak | April 7, 1990 | Arrested by the armed forces in March | Died due to torture during interrogation | |
| Hilal Ahmad (early 20s) | Probably 1990 | Arrested by the security forces in Kupwara district and taken to an interrogation center | Died in custody. His body had one ear missing and burn marks | |
| Ghulam Mohammad Shah (70) | April 5, 1989 | Police claim he was taken into custody after he refused to hand over some people who had taken refuge in his house | Died in hospital. Police say he had a cerebrovascular attack and was taken to hospital immediately. One of his sons alleged that he had been "hit and severely beaten up by police" | |
| Ghulam Mohiuddin Ganai | October 1991 | | Died reportedly in interrogation center after torture. Body handed over to police by security forces | |

*Source*: *India: Torture, Rape and Deaths in Custody* (New York: Amnesty International, 1992), 124.

August 1990 this figure had risen to 1,500 militants.[72] Two months later in October 1990 the *Indian Express* reported that there were 4,000 militants operating in the valley with 4,000 more waiting to cross the border from Pakistan.[73] In 1990, the Hibz-ul-Mujahideen emerged as the biggest and best-armed group in Kashmir. Since 1994, the Lashkar-e-Tolba has been the most active. By the mid-1990s, there were around 130 insurgent groups in Kashmir.

*The Independent* reported:

> in Kashmir, waves of brutal state repression have sparked off a powerful mass response. A great majority of Kashmiris who were uncommitted before Jagmohan's rule are today in favor of independence. It will be such a mass movement that will pose a much graver challenge and a much less manageable situation in Kashmir for the Indian government.[74]

On January 15, 1990, the *New York Times* reported: "Visitors to. . . Kashmir find a common theme in most conversations: admiration for the militants, anger towards the government and a wish for separation from India."[75]

The *Committee for Initiative on Kashmir* reported in March 1990:

> ironically, the government's plan to suppress "terrorism" is ending up in a situation where the hitherto non-committed masses are being pushed to a position where they feel that "independence" from New Delhi—as demanded by the assortment of secessionist militant groups—is the only way of escape from state repression.[76]

*India Today* described the situation in April 1990:

> In a cartographic and military sense, Kashmir remains with India. There's Ladakh in the north, Jammu in the south. And the Indian Army all along the actual line of control. . . . In Kashmir, nobody . . . now talks for India or even of a settlement with the Center. That part is over. Done with. The movement has now arrived at different crossroads. The debate is now whether they choose independence or Pakistan.[77]

By August 1990, Kashmiris openly showed disgust and hatred for Indian rule and support for the secessionists. It was reported:

> A walk through the narrow alleys of Srinagar shows how uniformly committed Kashmiris seem to be. Toddlers flash victory signs and chant, "Indian dogs go home!" and "We want freedom!" An elderly woman confronts an Indian soldier beneath her window with cries of "Murderer! You rape our girls, you shoot our boys. God will punish you." For the average Kashmiri, the violence is becoming a way of life.[78]

In May 1992, a human rights group reported:

> Although the militancy in the valley has been curbed to a noticeable extent, the brutal methods by which this result was brought about have increased the bitterness of the

people against the Indian Government as well as the Indian State . . . the people on the whole have become even more sullen and more hostile to the Indian State than what they used to be. The frequent military crackdowns, the inhuman torture of innocent persons, the indiscriminate shooting at people, the frequent thefts, and the occasional rapes committed by the security forces have increased the disgust and resentment of the people in the valley.[79]

## ALLIANCE OF SECESSIONISTS AND EXTERNAL POWER

Although Pakistan has denied giving material support to the secessionists, there is abundant evidence, both from Indian and western sources, that Pakistan was "waging its own 'proxy war' in Kashmir, not only by supporting the militants by giving them arms but also by allowing them to train in their territory."[80] In January 1990, it was reported that residents of Pakistan Occupied Kashmir or Azad Kashmir were openly helping their Muslim brethren across the LOC. "Students boast of helping guerrillas from Indian Kashmir to buy weapons or to train for combat, activities that officials deny are taking place with Government sanction, but do not deny are taking place."[81]

In February 1990, Indian intelligence sources revealed over 46 camps in the Azad Kashmir area where secessionists were being trained and armed.[82] A journalist who visited these camps in Azad Kashmir in June 1990 described them as follows:

> In the Jamaat camps, there are no women, children, or older men. They are all young men coming from different towns and villages in the Valley . . . their morale is high. They say they are well looked after . . . they describe themselves as refugees. But stickers on the wall proclaim they are members of the Hibz-ul-Mujaheddin.[83]

In 1991, a correspondent for *The Economist* reported:

> Refugees from Indian Kashmir pour over, to be housed in camps run by Pakistan's military intelligence outfit, the Interservices Intelligence Directorate (ISI). Pakistan denies that it trains or arms insurgents—rather unconvincingly, since guerrillas have been photographed in spanking new uniforms and are known to have modern weapons.[84]

Figure 5.2 shows the location of camps in Pakistan, which are used to train the JKLF secessionists.

Describing Pakistan's "frenzied" assistance to the Kashmir secessionists after 1989, former governor of Kashmir, Jagmohan has written:

> Pakistan provided not only moral, political and propaganda support to the subversionists in the Valley, as it itself admitted, but also actively helped them in training in guerrilla warfare and techniques of contemporary terrorism. Batches after batches of the Kashmiri youth were trained in POK and Pakistan. Sophisticated weapons and

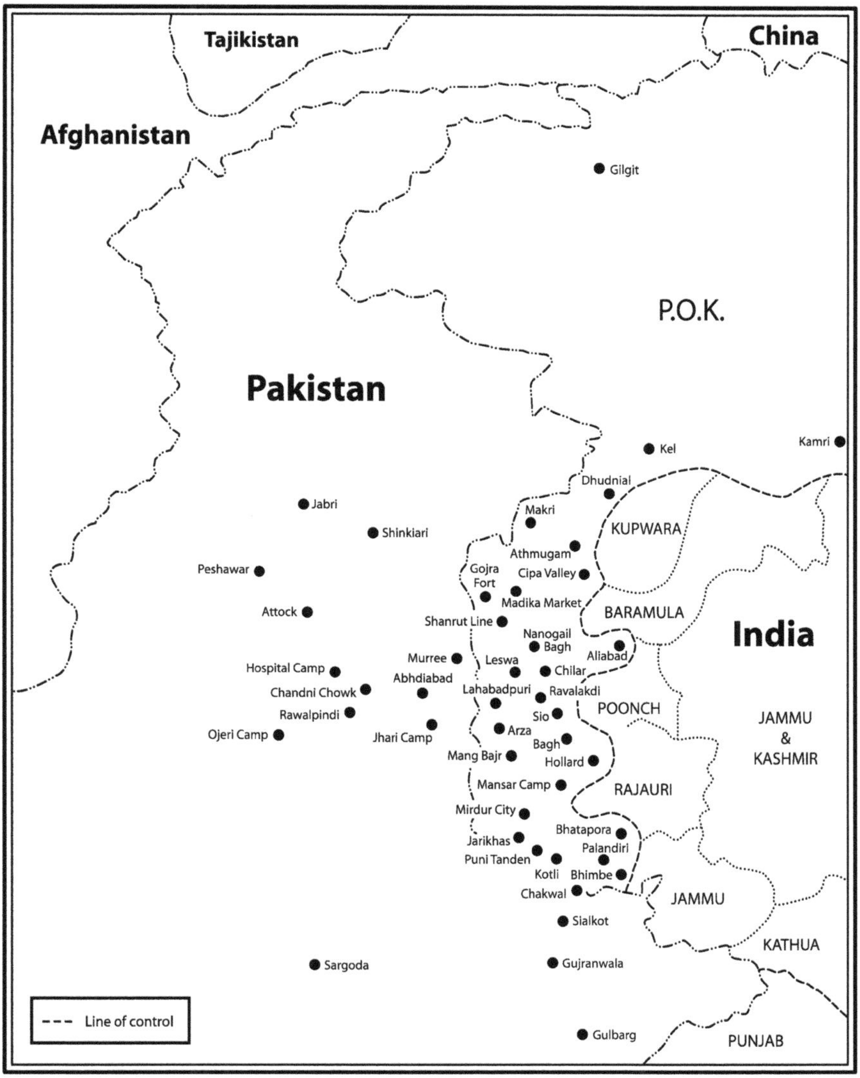


**Figure 5.2 Training Camps in Pakistan**

*Source*: V.D. Chopra, *Genesis of Indo-Pakistan Conflict on Kashmir* (New Delhi: Patriot, 1990), 237.

finances were made available. A strong underground network for motivation, recruitment and guidance was set up. Besides the houses of Ghulam Mohammad Wani at Athmuqam and Raja Mazaffar at Muzaffarabad, the barracks of the Field Intelligence Unit of Pakistan at Kalamulla Chakothi, Tilwari, Nausheri, Dudbnial, Kel, Kamri and Minimarg were used as launching pads for the purpose. An overall strategy was also worked out to ensure that in the long run Kashmir fell like a ripe apple in the lap of Pakistan. The operation was largely conceived, controlled, and directed by the Inter Services Intelligence of Pakistan, which virtually functioned as a "state within a state."[85]

In 1993, a U.S. House of Representatives "Task Force on Terrorism and Unconventional Warfare" confirmed reports of the Interservices Intelligence (ISI) involvement in the Kashmir insurgency: "The ISI . . . was completing a vast training infrastructure for the Afghan resistance movement that could just as well be used for the training and support of other regional groups."[86] The report continued that Pakistan "began expanding its operation to sponsor and support separatism and terrorism primarily in Kashmir as a strategic long-term program."[87] In September 1994, the Human Rights Watch Arms Project reported that "the diffusion of vast quantities of weapons to militants in Punjab and Kashmir is linked to the so-called Afghan pipeline: massive, covert transfers of arms by the US CIA through Pakistan's ISI to the Afghan mujahidin after the Soviet invasion of Afghanistan. . . . [These] weapons have made their way into the hands of Sikh and Kashmiri militants."[88] An *India Today* story entitled "Exporting Terror" reported that the ISI brought Libyan instructors to train the Kashmir secessionists in terrorism.[89]

Indian officials have continued to point a finger at Pakistan for its material and financial support of the secessionists. Former governor Saxena said in 1994:

> Pakistan took a firm and bold decision to meddle. . . . This time they pulled out all the stops and went about creating trouble in a big way, training thousands of youths, giving huge quantities of arms to them, and not bothering so much as they earlier did about the threshold of India's tolerance, with the result that the environment acquired the proportions of a widespread terrorist movement and armed insurgency, which was conducted at the initiative of Pakistan by youth trained in Pakistan.[90]

Although Pakistan repeatedly denies arming and training the Kashmir militants, several newspaper reports provide evidence of Pakistan's continued alliance with the secessionists. An article in the May 16, 1994, issue of *The Washington Post* stated:

> Pakistan has resumed arming, training and providing logistical support to militants fighting security forces in the troubled Indian state of Kashmir less than a year after convincing the U.S. government that it had adopted a hands-off policy there, according to Pakistani military sources. The Pakistani army's Inter Services Intelligence (ISI) directorate—akin to the CIA—and its Field Intelligence Unit are coordinating the shipment of arms from the Pakistani side of Kashmir to the Indian side, where Muslim insurgents are waging a protracted war, the sources said.[91]

*India Today* reported that the "U.S. State Department's 1995, 1996, and 1997 annual reports *Patterns of Global Terrorism* spoke of Pakistan's alliance with the Kashmir secessionists. The 1997 report stated that the Harkat-ul-Ansar (HUA), an Islamic secessionist group formed in 1993, was based and trained in Pakistan and operated mainly in Kashmir."[92] *Jane's Intelligence Review* declared that the "HUA owes its considerable arsenal in large measure to the generosity of the Pakistani Government, more specifically, its intelligence service."[93]

Training camps have continued to flourish inside Pakistan. A BBC documentary in 1995 "showed evidence of camps supported by the Jamaat, where fighters trained and openly professed their intention of going to fight a holy war in Kashmir."[94] In 1999, a report on the training camps described what the secessionists underwent: "They crawl on their bellies, plant land mines and practice marksmanship. Their enemies are the Indian soldiers trying to crush a decade-old insurgency in the Indian-controlled portion of Kashmir."[95]

Robert Wirsing has written:

> Pakistan's support . . . has unquestionably been a key organizational variable in Kashmir; and its patronage has no doubt exerted a powerful influence on the rise and fall in fortunes of practically every militant group active there. Some of the militant organizations may be largely or even entirely the creatures of the ISI, and all of the principal groups, according to most informants, are dependent to some extent for their financing and supplies on the resources of that intelligence unit.[96]

## RIVALRY BETWEEN HOST STATE AND EXTERNAL POWER

"A legacy of misperception"[97] and "a culture of distrust"[98] between India and Pakistan followed the partition of India in 1947. The Hindu-Muslim antagonism, which was the cause of partition, has remained as interstate rivalry between the two countries. Leaders of India and Pakistan have always misunderstood each other's intentions and motives and an atmosphere of mutual suspicion has governed their relations. As early as 1950, Liaquat Ali Khan, the first prime minister of Pakistan, stated:

> I charge the Government of India: first, it has never wholeheartedly accepted the Partition scheme, but her leaders paid lip service to it merely to get British troops out of the country. Secondly, India is out to destroy the State of Pakistan which Indian Leaders persistently continue to regard as part of India itself.[99]

India and Pakistan have gone to war four times since they became independent states in 1947 and three of these wars have been over Kashmir. In 1947–48 and in 1965 Pakistan tried to wrest Kashmir from India through military force. In 1971 India waged war against Pakistan in order to liberate Bangladesh, and in 1999,[100] the two countries fought over Kashmir once again. As recently as 2001, India and Pakistan came to the brink of war[101] with military build up on both sides of the LOC in Kashmir.

The relationship between the two countries has been marked by arms races, and the explosion of nuclear devices by both countries in the late 1990s has meant that the discord over Kashmir continues into the twenty-first century. As Robert Wirsing has said:

> Having far more in common with one another than either would ever admit, they enter upon the turbulent political terrain of the twenty-first century bent with a burden of fear and distrust that neither, whether acting alone or even in company with its hostile neighbor, is fully empowered to remove.[102]

Partha Ghose has aptly described Indo-Pak relations:

> Like Bismarck's proverbial gout the conflict between India and Pakistan finds expression in several forms—sometimes it is over Kashmir, sometimes it is over terrorism in Punjab, sometimes it is over the question of the US arms aid to Pakistan, sometimes it is over India's alleged support for the democratic and autonomist demands in Pakistan, sometimes it is over Pakistan's alleged strivings to acquire nuclear weapons, or at still other times, it is over the question of the "plight" of the Indian Muslims. In short, the two countries are always at war—at times with weapons, at times with words.[103]

According to a former chief of the Indian Army:

> As part of its prolonged jihad against India, peace is perceived as a temporary phase, to last only until preparations for the next round can be made. We must heed this strategic lesson of the last fifty years, and plan our long-term national security—Pakistan's hostility will stay with us for a long time and the nation must be prepared to sleep next to its weapons for the foreseeable future.[104]

This intense rivalry between India and Pakistan led Pakistan to form an alliance with the Kashmir secessionists in 1990 and help them with arms and ammunition, training camps, and sanctuaries. Having failed to seize Kashmir by military force in 1947–48 and 1965, it was in Pakistan's interest to keep the insurgency in Kashmir alive through the 1990s in an effort to dismember India from within.[105] Pakistan figured that "providing military and financial support to the Kashmiri secessionists is a less costly and less risky course of action"[106] than "initiating a war against India."[107]

## ETHNIC/RELIGIOUS KINSHIP BETWEEN SECESSIONISTS AND EXTERNAL POWER

The Muslims of Kashmir share strong religious and ethnic ties with the Muslims of Pakistan and for this reason Pakistan was keen on allying with the Kashmiri secessionists. Religion has certainly played a very important role in the Kashmir secessionist movement. On July 5, 1990, the leader of the Jama'at-I-Islami party in Pakistan emphasized the salience of religion in the movement when he said, "We are a small power but a Muslim country. We live in an ocean of Muslim brotherhood. The Hindus are not like us. . . . The people in Kashmir have carried the Pakistani flag. It is our religious duty to support the Muslims of Kashmir."[108]

As Sumantra Bose has said, "the central importance of a deeply-felt collective Muslim identity in the Kashmiri struggle for 'self-determination' cannot and need not be denied."[109] On February 10, 1990, the prime minister of Pakistan, Benazir Bhutto spoke about Pakistan's concern for the Kashmiris: "Pakistanis have blood relations with the Kashmiris, besides having with them historical, geographical and cultural affinity. That is why the people of Pakistan have demonstrated total solidarity with the Kashmiris."[110] Earlier, on January 26, 1990, several thousand protesters in Muzaffarabad in POK (or Azad Kashmir) assembled in support of the Kashmiris on the Indian side. "We will go and fight if necessary. . . . No sacrifice is too great for our brothers on the other side."[111]

Soon after the preventive war on the Kashmiris began in January 1990, Pakistani Foreign Minister Sahabzada Yakub Khan told his fellow Pakistanis in a broadcast to the nation on January 30, 1990, that it was not possible for Pakistanis "not to raise their voice in support of the Kashmiris."[112] He further stated, "Pakistan cannot be cowed down by any pressure or threats and it will continue to support the right of self-determination of the Kashmiri people."[113]

## INTERNATIONAL MILITARY INTERVENTION BY EXTERNAL POWER

The alliance between Pakistan and the Kashmiri secessionists in 1990 increased the distrust between India and Pakistan. Each side viewed the other's intentions as hostile. India perceived Pakistan as interfering in its internal affairs by supporting the Kashmiri secessionists with arms. Pakistan perceived India as being determined to wipe out the Kashmiri secessionists and their movement through a gross violation of human rights. "Even though war did not ensue in 1990, Indo-Pakistani relations remained strained throughout the decade. The situation in Kashmir continued to deteriorate throughout the early 1990s."[114]

The alliance between Pakistan and the Kashmir secessionists was seen as potentially threatening by India. The ensuing security dilemma, uncertainties, and fear of the future led to a nuclear arms race between the two countries. According to one report:

> Even before conducting its May 1998 nuclear tests and declaring itself a nuclear-weapon power, India had been pressing ahead with sensitive nuclear activities in enrichment, plutonium reprocessing, and breeder reactor installation, as well as with ballistic missile development. India apparently was barely restrained by diplomatic intervention from new nuclear testing in 1995 and again . . . in early 1996. . . . Pakistan was responding in 1996–97, trying to match each nuclear and missile development in India. Most hesitated then to label the South Asia action-reaction cycle as a full-fledged nuclear arms race, but that conclusion was unavoidable after May 1998.[115]

Thus, arms races between the two countries, which began in the 1950s, eventually led to the nuclearization of the subcontinent. In May 1998, "India and Pakistan jettisoned the officially preferred status of 'nuclear ambiguity' and 'recessed' (or 'nonweaponized') deterrence and became overt nuclear weapon states."[116] On May 11, India successfully carried out three tests, followed by an additional two on May 13. In order "to restore the strategic balance"[117] with India, Pakistan followed suit with five nuclear tests on May 28, followed by a sixth test on May 30.[118]

"Mutual antagonisms and fear continue to mark Indo-Pak relations."[119] Describing the ongoing tensions between India and Pakistan, Navy Vice Admiral Thomas Wilson, the director of the Defense Intelligence Agency has said: "Both sides operate from 'zero-sum perspectives,' retain large forces, in close proximity, across a tense line of control. . . . The potential for mistake and miscalculation remains relatively high."[120]

These words rang true in 1999. Miscalculating Indian military strength, Pakistan undertook a military incursion across the LOC into Kashmir along three points: Kargil, Dras, and Batalik. In May 1999, over 800 hostile intruders—Pakistani forces and Kashmir secessionists—crossed over the LOC in the Kargil sector and "were now in a position to cut off the northern portions of Kashmir from the rest of the state."[121] The diary of a captured Pakistani army officer Captain Hussain Ahmad referred to this incursion as a plan to set up a "new LOC" in Kashmir.[122] The Kargil Review Committee reported: "It was an extraordinary war, this Fourth War of Kashmir, fought at impossible heights in what will go down as the most inhospitable and unlikely battleground in the history of warfare."[123]

Misperception, misinformation, and the misreading of "relative military strength"[124] led Pakistan to intervene militarily on behalf of the secessionists. As Sumit Ganguly has said, "Pakistani decision-makers grossly underestimated Indian military prowess and likely Indian responses to military challenges. . . . The anti-Indian and chauvinistic ideology of the authoritarian Pakistani state repeatedly contributed to a flawed assessment of India's military capabilities and will."[125] Ganguly has further stated: "it is not unreasonable to infer that Pakistan's acquisition of an incipient nuclear capability and the communication of that information to India further emboldened Pakistani military decision-makers."[126]

Thus, miscalculation and information failures were responsible for Pakistan wrongly assuming that

> the Indian leadership, cognizant of Pakistan's nuclear capabilities, would decline to use overwhelming force and would also avoid a dramatic escalation or expansion of the conflict. . . . Pakistan's overt nuclearization had . . . bolstered this sense of false optimism. Pakistan decision-makers had convinced themselves that their achievement of rough nuclear parity with India now enabled them to probe along the LoC with impunity.[127]

Pakistan's military incursion into Kargil did catch India by surprise. However, after the initial shock and setback, the Indian Army and Air Force battled Pakistan in a 73-day conflict. With a series of air strikes, India dislodged the intruders and managed to recapture key positions occupied by Pakistan. It was only by the end of July that the infiltrators withdrew and gave up their positions to the

Indian forces. Thus, Pakistan's military intervention in Kashmir proved to be a failure.

An arms race continues between India and Pakistan. This has led to warnings being issued about the danger of nuclear war in South Asia. One such warning wrote:

> In South Asia, India and Pakistan are in a period of accelerated nuclear weapons and missile development. Political tensions and domestic politics have driven the two countries to test nuclear weapons in 1998, and to develop and test longer-range missiles in 1998 and 1999. Tensions in the region will likely remain high. . . . Given the long-standing hostility between the two countries, even a minor conflict runs the risk of escalating into an exchange of missiles with nuclear warheads, which would have disastrous consequences for the region and beyond. . . . Additional nuclear tests are possible. . . . [M]ore missile tests are likely. . . . [T]he potential for the proliferation of technologies and expertise will increase in the future, as both countries become more self-sufficient in the production of nuclear weapons and missiles and subsequently become potential suppliers.[128]

## STALEMATE

Currently, the Kashmir secessionist movement is at an impasse. Peace talks between the leaders of India and Pakistan have begun in 2004 but given the long history of mutual distrust and rivalry between the two countries, a solution is a long way off. Both sides will have to make difficult concessions in order to have peace. As Sumit Ganguly has written:

> Will Pakistan finally abandon its quest to wrest Kashmir from India through the use of force? Will India be willing to settle the dispute by legally ceding the portions of Kashmir under Pakistan and Chinese control? Will Pakistan accept such a dispensation? Finally, will the vast majority of the Kashmiris in Indian-controlled Kashmir settle for a substantial degree of autonomy under the aegis of the Indian constitutional framework?[129]

## CONCLUSION

There is more than sufficient evidence to conclude that a shift in the balance of power between the government of India and the Kashmir secessionists in the late 1980s led to a preventive war on the secessionists by the Indian government. As the power of the Congress (I) party at the center fell in relation to the secessionists, the government of India feared that if the Kashmir insurgency were not suppressed with force, it would increase in strength and power and could succeed in reaching its goal of secession from India. Therefore, it was imperative for the Indian government to weaken the secessionist movement while the latter was still on the rise. The evidence in this case thus supported the preventive war hypothesis.

The preventive war launched on the Kashmiri secessionists led to an explosive growth and strengthening of the movement. By the mid-1990s, there were around 130 insurgent groups in Kashmir fighting either for an independent Kashmir or for union with Pakistan. The preventive war also led to the formation of an alliance between Pakistan and the Kashmiri secessionists. Being an enduring rival of India, it was in Pakistan's interest to go to the aid of the secessionists. Moreover, ethnic/religious ties between the Kashmiris and Pakistan made the alliance stronger.

The formation of a strong alliance and the ensuing security dilemma, arms race, and increased suspicion between India and Pakistan heightened tensions and security competition between India and Pakistan and eventually led to Pakistan's military intervention in 1999 in an effort to wrest Kashmir from India.

Thus, the historical evidence put forth in this chapter supports all the hypotheses in chapter 2. As the theory predicted, a shift in the balance of power in favor of the Kashmiri secessionists resulted in a preventive war on the secessionists, which in turn caused an explosive growth of the movement and led to an alliance between the secessionists and the Pakistani government. Rivalry between India and Pakistan and ethnic/religious ties between the Kashmiri secessionists and the Muslims of Pakistan were also responsible for the formation of the alliance. Finally, the alliance led to spirals of suspicion, hostility, and arms racing between India and Pakistan. In addition, uncertainty, misinformation, and misperception exacerbated the tensions between the two countries resulting in Pakistan's military intervention.

# 6

# Punjab

THE SIKH SECESSIONIST movement in Punjab and its demand for a separate state of Khalistan, which raged in the 1980s and early 1990s, ended in 1993. However, just like the East Pakistan, Sri Lanka, and Kashmir cases, a shift in the balance of power between the Sikh secessionists and the Indian government led to a preventive war on the Sikhs. In other words, fearing a further increase in the power of the secessionists, the Indian government sent in the army in 1984 to wipe out the Sikh secessionists who had taken refuge in the Golden Temple, the holiest Sikh shrine in Amritsar. The preventive war on the Sikhs resulted in a strengthening of the Sikh secessionist movement. It also led to an alliance between the Sikh secessionists and Pakistan. Rivalry between India and Pakistan fueled this alliance. Yet, owing to the lack of religious ties between the Sikhs of Punjab and the Pakistanis, the alliance that was formed was not strong enough to bring about military intervention from Pakistan. After a human toll of 21,469[1] by 1993(secessionists, civilians, and security personnel), the movement eventually subsided, and except for a few hardcore secessionists who may still be at large, it can safely be said that the movement is dead.[2] In order to understand the tragic events of the 1980s and early 1990s in Punjab, it is important to take a look at the historical background of the Sikhs.

## BACKGROUND

The Sikhs of Punjab have always been very mindful of their distinct identity and have resented any suggestion that Sikhism is a part of Hinduism. The Sikhs who originate from Punjab[3] are disciples of Guru Nanak, born in AD 1469.

They speak Punjabi with its own script—Gurmukhi—distinct from the Devnagari script of the Punjabi Hindus. "Their scriptures, ceremonies, code, customs, appearance and modes of dress"[4] differ from the rest of India, and for this reason the Sikhs have considered themselves a separate nation. Sikh men are clearly distinguished from Hindus by their turbans and beards and Sikh women usually wear "salwar-khameez"—a loose-fitting trouser and tunic. Yet, despite these differences, it is important to note that before the 1980s, Sikhs and Hindus lived in harmony in Punjab.

When India was partitioned in 1947, Punjab was divided between India and the newly created Pakistan, and Sikhs and Hindus from the western part of Punjab (now in Pakistan) moved into eastern Punjab, which remained a part of India. Muslims from the eastern part of Punjab moved into the western part. As a result of the transfers of population between India and Pakistan, the percentage of Hindus rose to 64 percent of the population in postindependence Indian Punjab, the Sikhs 33 percent, and the Muslims 2 percent.[5] Being a minority in Punjab, the Sikhs were afraid that they might not be able to retain their separate identity and that their language, culture, and religion might be absorbed within Hinduism. It must be remembered, "Sikhism was born out of Hinduism. All the ten Sikh gurus were Hindus till they became Sikhs. . . . Sikhism broke away from its parent Hindu body and evolved its own distinct rites of worship and ritual, its own code of ethics, its separate traditions which cumulatively gave it a distinct religious personality."[6] For this reason, the Sikhs who constitute only 2 percent of the entire population of India were fearful that in the future, "the Sikhs would lapse back into the Hindu fold and become Hindus believing in Sikhism."[7] As journalist Khushwant Singh has written:

> The chief cause of Sikh uneasiness in free India was the resurgence of Hinduism, which threatened to engulf the minorities. Renascent Hinduism manifested itself in phenomenal increase in Hindu religious organizations, the revival of Sanskrit, and the ardent championing of Hindi.[8]

Therefore, when India became independent, the Sikhs asked the government of India for safeguards so that the majority Hindus would not exploit them. As early as 1949, the Sikhs felt that justice was being denied to them and these feelings were made known by Sardar Hukum Singh in the Constituent Assembly of India on November 21, 1949:

> The Congress was announcing again and again that all minorities shall have proper safeguards. The Muslims refused to be contented with any safeguards, but insisted on having a home for themselves. They got Pakistan, and can have no further grievance. The Anglo-Indian community has been sufficiently protected. They can have no grouse. The Parsees and Christians are far more advanced educationally and economically and have declared that they do not want any safeguards. It is only the Sikh community that earnestly desired, repeatedly requested and constantly cried for safeguards but have been denied any consideration.[9]

Without any safeguards, the Sikhs continued to harbor a deep resentment that they lost very heavily as a result of the partition of India. Not only did the Sikh farmers from western Punjab suffer the psychological trauma of uprooting themselves and their families from their homes, but they also lost their farmlands, which were their sole means of livelihood. They had to "start from scratch," so to speak, in the "underdeveloped" east Punjab. Similarly, Sikh traders who had to abandon their businesses in western Punjab did not get money from the government to restart their businesses in eastern Punjab. "The Partition is now so routinely reduced to statistics about death and migration that it is difficult to imagine the sheer enormity of what each individual and family—even people who did not suffer a loss of life among those they loved—had endured."[10]

It has been repeatedly written that the Sikhs were

> the worst losers in the partition. Hindus were largely an urban people and were able to salvage some of their properties and cash, which enabled them to rehabilitate themselves in cities and large towns. The majority of Sikhs were farmers. They lost not only their homes but also their lands and cattle which were their only means of livelihood. They had been the richest landowners in undivided Punjab (13 percent of the population paying over 40 percent of the land revenue and water rates). They had to change places with the landless Muslim peasantry of East Punjab. With rustic logic they maintained that while Hindus got Hindustan and the Muslims got Pakistan, all they got was poverty.[11]

Being extremely insecure, the Sikhs began demanding a Punjabi-speaking state or *Punjabi Suba* in 1953. The Akali Dal,[12] the main political party of the Sikhs, wanted a state where Punjabi (with the Gurmukhi script of the Sikh scriptures) was spoken. This meant that the Sikhs wanted a homeland just for themselves—a region where the Sikhs would predominate. The Hindus considered this demand by the Sikhs as a communal demand—a demand based on religion—the obvious reason being to form a state in which the Sikhs would be a majority.[13] In view of the fact that India is a secular state, the then Prime Minister Jawaharlal Nehru refused to concede to the Sikh demands of a *Punjabi Suba*. Finally, after continued and increased protests and agitation by the Sikhs, the boundaries of Punjab were redrawn in 1966 and the Sikh demand for a Punjabi-speaking state was met. The Punjab Reorganization Act of 1966 went into effect on November 1, 1966.[14] The linguistic reorganization of Punjab resulted in the Sikhs comprising 60 percent of the population and the chances of electoral success by the Akali Dal were boosted considerably.[15] However, even the formation of a *Punjabi Suba* did not seem to satisfy the Sikhs.

Khushwant Singh comments:

> Much as the Indian Government tried to appease the Sikhs it was never enough. The Bhakra Dam with its irrigation canals, the electrification of villages and the agricultural university in Ludhiana where Norman Bourlaug developed new strains of Mexican wheat produced the Green Revolution. The wheat yield per acre was trebled and

> the Sikh farmer once again became prosperous. But the clamour against discrimination and injustice continued to grow.[16]

Singh, a Sikh himself, lists the honors and privileges the Sikhs enjoyed after 1966:

> [A]ll chief ministers of the state (of Punjab) were Sikhs and Sikhs were fully represented in the central cabinet; many were appointed governors of states. Two Air Chief Marshals of the Indian Air Force have been Sikhs. In 1982, Giani Zail Singh was elected President of the Republic, the first Sikh to become Head of State. Even this did not appease the Akalis.[17]

The Akalis, involved in a power struggle with the Congress party in Punjab, constantly looked for "issues that could improve their standing in Sikh society and in election results."[18] For this reason, the Akali Dal came forward in 1973 with the historic Anandpur Sahib Resolution in which a number of political, economic, and religious issues were demanded from the government.[19] Among other things, the resolution sought changes in the relationship between the central government and Punjab limiting the role of the former to defense, foreign policy, communications, and currency and leaving the rest under the control of the local Punjab authorities. In other words, the resolution was a demand for greater autonomy for Punjab. True to the expectations of the Akalis, the resolution "improved Akali Dal's standing among Sikhs and the Akali Dal cashed in on its new-found popularity in the Punjab elections of 1977."[20] It was at this time in 1977 that the Akalis formed a coalition government with the Janata Party in Punjab.

## SHIFT IN BALANCE OF POWER

The late 1970s saw the rise of the fundamentalist Sikh preacher, Jarnail Singh Bhindranwale, initially encouraged by Prime Minister Indira Gandhi to weaken the Akali Dal, the Sikh political party that posed a threat to her Congress (I) party. Indira Gandhi wanted to weaken the Akali Dal because she felt that the Sikh party, if too powerful, would defeat the Congress (I) party in the 1980 elections. Having lost the 1977 elections to the Akalis, the Congress (I) party looked for a Sikh religious leader who could divide the Punjab electorate by getting the Sikhs to vote for the Congress party. In other words, the strategy of the Congress (I) party's "factional penetration of Akali Dal"[21] was to ensure the Congress (I) party's rule in Punjab. In Bhindranwale, Mrs. Gandhi found a charismatic preacher who, with her encouragement, could break the Akali Dal's hold on the Sikhs.[22] During a 1980 election campaign, Bhindranwale shared the stage with Mrs. Gandhi as he campaigned for her in Gurdaspur.[23] The Congress (I) party succeeded in winning the 1980 Center and Punjab state elections but not before Bhindranwale got thrown into the spotlight "as a fundamentalist alternative to the Akalis."[24]

Gradually, the Akalis found their influence over the Sikh masses declining and Bhindranwale's credibility increasing.[25] It seemed that the Congress party's plan of dividing the Sikhs was working. Bhindranwale's support and popularity increased rapidly attracting a huge following of Sikhs who eventually became extremists demanding a separate homeland called Khalistan. It was apparent that the masses of rural Sikhs whose voices were not being heard by the government "were ripe for new political mobilizations and they came under the spell and umbrella of Sant Jarnail Singh."[26] Bhindranwale firmly inculcated his ideas of Punjab's secession from India in the minds of his followers. Ironically, he had turned against the government that had supported his rise to power.

Bhindranwale's influence on the uneducated Sikh masses was enormous. Besides being a Sikh fundamentalist preacher, he became an arbitrator of disputes among the people.[27] The masses looked upon him to solve their problems and settle their conflicts. They trusted his judgment and in return for his services followed his fundamentalist teachings. Not only did he preach his warped version of Sikhism but he also advocated violence and hatred for the Hindus and the central government. Those who did not follow his fundamentalist teachings were killed and, therefore, he instilled a sense of deep fear into those around him. The police were forced to turn a blind eye because they feared retaliation.

The storm of secession, which began to brew in the years 1980 and 1981, "could easily have been nipped in the bud by timely administrative and political measures."[28] However, the central government was more bothered about sustaining Congress rule in the country rather than maintaining law and order in Punjab.[29] Violence, murders, hijackings, kidnappings, and a host of other terrorist activities became the order of the day.

In June 1982, "Bhindranwale and several hundred of his heavily armed followers . . . entered the Golden Temple in search of sanctuary."[30] The Golden Temple was misused "to accumulate large quantities of arms and ammunition, to shelter murderers and criminals, and to make detailed preparations for subversion and insurgency."[31] Many of these men had been accused of murders and they found a safe haven in the Golden Temple. As the *Indian Express* reported:

> Though the CBI has solved the murder case of the Nirankari guru, Baba Gurcharan Singh, and his aide last year, it is almost certain that the killers will never be arrested because they are alleged to be in the protection of Sant Jarnail Singh Bhindranwale. . . . Besides, the State police is not prepared to involve itself in the case by arresting the culprits.[32]

For the next couple of years, Bhindranwale's campaign intensified against the government of India. The Akali Dal leaders, afraid of Bhindranwale and his armed men, did not condemn the misuse of the temple nor did they denounce the hatred that was being preached from the temple.[33] "The Akalis had begun to feel that things had gone beyond their control—and that even they were now controlled by the extremists."[34] The secessionists were emboldened by the lack of opposition to their spurious activities. It seemed like the secessionists were taking shelter under the cover of the Akali Dal's agitations and demands "to pursue a systematic plan of stockpiling of arms and ammunitions in places of worship and of misusing the sacred precincts of the Golden Temple and other gurudwaras to direct and commit acts of murder, sabotage, arson and loot."[35] Two disgruntled former major-generals of the Indian Army joined Bhindranwale and trained the secessionists in military operations, the extensive use of weapons and explosives. One of these advisers, Shabeg Singh, had played a major role in the 1971 Indian war against Pakistan where he trained the Bengali insurgents in guerrilla warfare. This military expertise led Shabeg Singh to form an excellent plan of defense around the Golden Temple.[36]

Throughout 1983, Bhindranwale and his followers, who were demanding secession from India, were responsible for hundreds of killings in Punjab. The victims included anybody who opposed the secessionists. Supporters of the government were attacked and it seemed that "Bhindranwale and his men were above the law."[37] Bhindranwale's influence appeared to be growing "and the situation in Punjab continued to deteriorate, largely due to the passivity of the central government which shied away from . . . taking bold decisions on the issues involved."[38] The failure of the Indian government in dealing with the situation pointed to the poor "political management of the State by Indira Gandhi since the early 1970s characterized by attempts to outflank the religious platform of the Akali Dal, and manipulation of the rules governing center-state relations."[39]

On October 6, 1983, due to widespread lawlessness, Prime Minister Indira Gandhi brought Punjab under president's rule[40] or central government rule. Tully and Jacob have written:

> It was a difficult decision to take because it meant admitting that her own party had failed to rule Punjab. In 1980 Mrs. Gandhi had fought her way back to power with the slogan, "Elect a government that works." In Punjab it was now clear that her government had not worked.[41]

However, the power of Bhindranwale and the secessionists continued to grow. On December 15, 1983, Bhindranwale moved into the Akal Takht,[42] inside the Golden Temple complex, making it harder for him to be captured. The high priests of the temple were unable to prevent him from taking this step. "The Akal Takht was thus transformed into his personal 'Court.'"[43] Once inside the Akal Takht, Bhindranwale accelerated his campaign. His preaching of hatred for the Hindus became more inflammatory alienating them even more. His plan was to create unprecedented tension and fear among the Hindus forcing them to flee Punjab. Simultaneously, "he hoped for a backlash against the Sikhs in other parts of the country as a result of which those living outside the state would be forced to return to Punjab."[44] This would pave the way for the creation of a Sikh-only Khalistan.

Things were getting so out of control that on India's Republic Day—January 26, 1984—Bhindranwale and his men flew a Khalistani flag from the Golden Temple.[45] The government, once again, seemed powerless and refused to move against the secessionists. Bhindranwale began to wield enormous power over government officials. The police dared not arrest him and his men because they feared retaliation. "Past experience had shown that those policemen who had arrested Bhindranwale's followers and close associates, had sooner or later been eliminated."[46]

By early 1984, the Golden Temple

> bore the semblance of a fortress with an elaborate network of warlike defenses manned by highly motivated fanatics, armed to the teeth. This group of misguided militants committed to the goal of carving out a separate Sikh State, Khalistan, had already spread fear and panic through numerous acts of violence. They had taken a sacred vow before the *Guru Granth Sahib* (the holy book of the Sikh scriptures) to undertake any sacrifice that was necessary to achieve their ends.[47]

In fact,

> the Akal Takht had been restructured, with steel and cement bunkers, into a last-ditch battle fort. Every floor was fortified; every door and window was fashioned into a gun port. The high water tank was a machine-gun nest. A maze of tunnels and manholes were used for a ground level attack by machineguns and grenades.[48]

It was evident that there was a shift in the balance of power in favor of the secessionists, numbering in the thousands. The *White Paperon the Punjab Agitation* (1984) describes the situation:

> The essence of the problem in Punjab was not the demands put forward by the Akali Dal in 1981 but the maturing of a secessionist and anti-national movement. . . . The terrorists escalated their violence. With each passing day the situation worsened. The subversive activities of groups inside the Golden Temple had assumed menacing proportions in the context of India's security.[49]

The inability of the central government to control the situation and stem the violence was proof of its weakness. A decline in the power of the central government relative to the secessionists had taken place. This was evident from the fact that president's rule in Punjab had done nothing to improve the situation; the government appeared paralyzed and the police seemed totally ineffective.[50] The explosive situation had definitely threatened the security of the country.

Around April, the Khalistan secessionists began to fortify the neighborhood around the Golden Temple complex. Bhindranwale's men forcibly occupied several buildings adjacent to the complex and converted them "into well defended 'Observation and Early Warning Posts,' manned with light machine guns and other automatic firing weapons with their sights directed towards the open spaces along the approaches to the Temple and the narrow, labyrinthine maze of lanes running below."[51] Inside the complex, fortifications were completed much earlier. Every vantage point was covered: rooftops, balconies, and other high points from where the view was clear and a good defense possible.[52]

By May 1984, "information was received by Government that . . . Bhindranwale had advocated the killing of Hindus in Punjab so as to set in motion a general exodus . . . it was obvious that a situation of insurgency in open defiance of constituted authority was building up."[53] Then, on May 29, 1984, India received intelligence reports that the "establishment of Khalistan would be proclaimed from the Golden Temple" on June 4, 1984, and "immediately thereafter, an army of some forty thousand Sikhs including Muslims would invade India from the side of Wagah border between India and Pakistan."[54]

## PREVENTIVE WAR ON SIKH SECESSIONISTS

Perceiving a shift in the balance of power in favor of the Sikh secessionists, the government of India ordered the army to storm the Golden Temple to wipe out the secessionists. And, "to save the situation from irretrievable deterioration, there was utmost necessity for speed in completion of Army operations."[55] So, in June 1984, the Indian army launched *Operation Bluestar*—an attack on the Golden Temple in Amritsar, the holiest shrine of the Sikhs, to flush out the Sikh militants who had taken refuge there. From June 5 to 7, a full-scale military operation on the Sikh Temple killed hundreds of Sikhs, both secessionists and innocent civilians visiting the temple.[56] The Indian government launched this preventive war on the Sikhs in order to suppress the Sikh secessionist movement before it became even more powerful. The power of the movement was threatening the unity and security of India. "The forces of secession, operating from inside the Temple, had to be removed or eliminated, in order to prevent the break up of the country. It had become an escapable necessity to cry halt before it was too late."[57]

On June 5, "tanks of the 16th Calvary Regiment of the Indian army started moving up to the Golden Temple complex."[58] Facing stiff resistance[59] from the secessionists inside the temple, the Indian Army was compelled to use much greater force than it had originally intended to.[60] Intelligence reports had failed to assess the extent of the fortifications and the resistance the Indian army was likely to face.[61] "As far as the fortification was concerned, the roof tops, the first floor, the second floor and all parts and buildings of the Temple Complex were heavily fortified. They had bunkers, they had fire trenches and they had converted all the doors and windows into fixed defenses. . . . In fact, the Temple was fortified into an impregnable bastion."[62]

So, after suffering casualties from heavy machine gun fire and grenades from the secessionists inside the well-fortified temple, the Indian Army was forced to escalate their attack:

> (Bhindranwale) was blasted out of the Akal Takht by the 105-mm. main armaments of Indian Vijayanta (Victory) tanks. In the process much of the Akal Takht, the shrine, which according to original orders was to suffer "as little as possible damage," was reduced to rubble. At the start of the operation, troops had even been forbidden to use

automatic weapons against the Akal Takht. The evacuation of the hostel complex was completed but not without heavy casualties.[63]

A soldier who took part in *Operation Bluestar* described the scene on June 6, 1984:

> On the morning of June 6, the Golden Temple complex was like a graveyard. Bodies lay all around in the buildings. . . . Bodies of *jawans* (soldiers) were identified and handed over to their respective regiments. . . . The civilians, who had died, about 1500 of them, were piled in trollies and carried away.[64]

Although the exact number of people killed is not certain,

> the clear conclusion emerges that hundreds and hundreds of people were killed, during the Army Action on Golden Temple in June 1984, most brutally. It was indeed a mass massacre mostly of innocents. Most of the dead bodies had their hands tied behind their backs implying that they had not died during the action, but . . . lined up before the firing squad, all of them must have been shot after being captured alive. . . . At the time of the post-mortem, the bodies were in a putrid and highly decomposed state—they had been brought for post-mortem after 72 hours implying a totally callous attitude towards the injured and the dead.[65]

Journalist Tavleen Singh, who visited Punjab soon after *Operation Bluestar,* had this to say:

> the state was still virtually under martial law. No civilian vehicles were allowed on the roads and there were tanks stationed on all main roads leading into Amritsar city. There was curfew even in the countryside because the army was afraid of villagers marching to the Golden Temple.[66]

The government was following a ruthless preventive war in order to crush the secessionist movement before it became stronger. A shift in the balance of power between the central government and the Sikh secessionists created problems of credible commitment, which precluded negotiations between the two parties. "Last minute efforts made by the Center to defuse the situation, and to arrive at a peaceful settlement . . . had yielded no fruit."[67] Before undertaking *Operation Bluestar*, Prime Minister Indira Gandhi had appealed for peace. She had explained that she had consented to most of the demands of the Akali leaders but had not succeeded in satisfying them because they always wanted more. It was apparent to the prime minister that the Akalis had no intention or desire to solve their problems through negotiations with the government but on the contrary, they were permitting Bhindranwale to represent them by force.[68] She had come to this conclusion that the Akalis did not want to negotiate because talks with them in October 1981, November 1981, April 1982, and several times after that had reached no settlement.[69] Negotiations, as late as May 1984, had yielded no positive results. It was evident that "coercive measures were to take a priority over political bargaining in resolving the Punjab problem."[70]

So, repression by the government continued. Soon after *Operation Bluestar,* the army launched *Operation Woodrose* to arrest secessionists who roamed the Punjab countryside. Describing *Operation Woodrose,* General Narinder Singh, a retired general and vice-chairman of the Punjab Human Rights Organization, told author Joyce Pettigrew:

> The real scar was operation Woodrose. . . . The men were taken out of the houses. . . . They then searched and removed many precious things from the homes. Systematically, everyone wearing the saffron *patka*[71] or having a flowing beard was branded a terrorist and eliminated. This went on for three months. It occurred primarily in the Majha region but throughout other districts they searched pockets of marked influence, which were given the same treatment. . . . The army took the help of the Hindu population. So a certain amount of polarization between the two communities, Sikh and Hindu, did occur at that time.[72]

These repressive measures of the government were facilitated by the introduction of draconian legislation like the Terrorist and Disruptive Activities (Prevention) Act or TADA[73] as it came to be known in 1985, and the National Security Act or NSA,[74] introduced in 1987. A number of innocent people were detained under these laws that were described as follows:

> There is no constitutional protection of one's rights. Suspects are tried in designated courts. Each district has a designated court and there is no provision for bail unless the court is satisfied the man will not commit the crime again. In cases where bail is denied, the right to approach the High Court is also denied. The case then goes to the Supreme Court, which is expensive and time-consuming and there is difficulty getting advocates to take on the cases. The innocent are detained under TADA for there is a vast difference in the mode of trial under TADA and the mode of trial under normal law. He has to prove his innocence.[75]

The governor of Punjab S.S. Ray and director-general of police Julio Ribeiro were entrusted with the suppression of the secessionist movement in Punjab in the late 1980s. Their rigorous implementation of the draconian antiterrorist laws resulted in them being "commonly accused of operating a non-accountable police state."[76] Commenting on TADA, the *Economic and Political Weekly*, April 23, 1988, stated:

> While newspaper headlines keep assuring us that "terrorists" of all grades and categories are being arrested everyday in Punjab, one wonders how many among them are really terrorists. The difference between suspicion and sure knowledge has been blurred by the catch-all provisions of the Terrorists and Disruptive Activities (Prevention) Act which whet the subjective inclinations of any policeman who wants to settle old scores or impress his bosses with the greatest number of catches.[77]

It was said, "In the ten years following 1984, some seventy thousand people were detained under TADA though only 1 percent of them were eventually convicted of a crime."[78] Human rights violations have run rampant in Punjab. Detainees have been tortured to such an extent that many of them have died in custody.

Investigating human rights violations in Punjab, *Asia Watch* has concluded:

> Government forces operating in Punjab have systematically violated international human rights law as well as the laws of war governing internal armed conflict. Members of the Punjab police, the federal paramilitary troops of the Central Reserve Police Force and the Border Security Force and, to a lesser extent, the Indian army have engaged in widespread summary executions of civilians and suspected militants. Many of these executions involve persons who were first detained in police custody and then subsequently reported by the authorities as having been killed in an encounter with the security forces.[79]

Table 6.1 from an Amnesty International report lists the deaths in custody that took place in Punjab from 1985 to 1991.[80]

## EXPLOSIVE GROWTH OF THE MOVEMENT

The preventive war on the secessionists strengthened the resolve of the Sikhs for a separate homeland. Evidence from several sources supports this argument. In the words of a leader of the Khalistan Commando Force (KCF):

> Prior to June 1984 we used to talk about . . . the right to self-determination within India. After 1984 we needed our own independent home. The government that could kill hundreds, send thousands to prison, rape our women and generally humiliate our people, there could never be a compromise with them! We now needed an independent home for the Sikhs.[81]

After *Operation Bluestar,* Khushwant Singh wrote:

> Things have never been the same again. Sikhs who had nothing to do with Bhindranwale or politics felt deeply humiliated. Bhindranwale was killed which gave a halo of martyrdom he did not deserve. It gave a fillip to the terrorist groups.[82]

Indeed, "Operation Bluestar left a deep scar on the Sikhs."[83] In a show of outrage, Sikh troops mutinied in several places. The wife of a former Sikh soldier aptly summarized the general feeling among the Sikhs:

> The Indian government is our enemy, and it is clear that we cannot live with them. If they are calling us terrorists or something like that, it doesn't make much difference as they are our enemy and they can be expected to say anything. That only makes us more firm in our resolve that we can't live with these people and the only solution for us is an independent sovereign nation.[84]

**Table 6.1 Deaths in Custody in Punjab, 1985–91**

| Name (age) | Date of Death | Circumstances of Arrest | Circumstances of Death | Official Action Known |
|---|---|---|---|---|
| Gurinder Singh | May 10, 1985 | Arrested on May 4 after an encounter with police in which he was alleged to have killed two police personnel | Admitted to hospital with multiple injuries allegedly from torture. He told doctors he was tortured after arrest | An executive magistrate conducted an inquest and reportedly found that the injuries were "justified" as he resisted arrest |
| Pramod Kumar | Between March 2 and 14, 1986 | Detained by two subinspectors and taken to Araghar police outpost for questioning on March 2 | Died reportedly from injuries sustained during interrogation | |
| Mukhtiar Singh | September 1986 | He was wanted in connection with a shooting incident and was handed over to the police on August 19 | Allegedly tortured by Chheharta police. Police stated that he had a fever and that he died on his way home | |
| Sarbjit Singh Johal (21) | September 12, 1987 | Arrested on September 10 in Amritsar | Reportedly died due to police torture | |
| Suresh Pal Singh, student | Between February 10 and 17, 1988 | Arrested February 10. Taken to Bijoi Police Station | Allegedly beaten to death by police. Police claimed he died from drinking | An inquiry was ordered and a police official stated that the police responsible were being charged with manslaughter |

| | | | | |
|---|---|---|---|---|
| Balraj Singh Raji | Between March 29 1989 and April 15, 1989 | Reportedly taken to Nurmahil police station on March 29. Police allege he was arrested after an encounter with police on April 15 | Died in custody allegedly as a result of torture. Police initially denied arrest, then claimed that he committed suicide by taking poison | The body was cremated before the relatives could see it |
| Surinder Singh (22) | April 30, 1989 | Arrested for questioning about Sikh groups on April 24. Phillaur police denied he was in their custody | His parents located him and secured his release but he had been badly tortured and died later. | |
| Gurmit Singh Machaki | July 11, 1989 | Arrested at the Bombay airport in connection with terrorist crimes | Died in police custody at Muktsar. An official said he was bitten by a snake | |
| Raghbir Singh | July 19, 1989 | Arrested July 19 and held in police post, Khassa | Died allegedly from beatings by police | Subdivision magistrate undertook an inquiry. Local police reportedly refused to give evidence |
| Bahadur Singh (28) | February 28, 1990 | He attended a protest and was allegedly hit by police on February 26. He stated he had been tortured in police custody | Found later semiconscious. Police stated he died from alcohol | A doctor found his legs paralyzed and considerable injuries |

*Continued*

**TABLE 6.1 Continued**

| Name (age) | Date of death | Circumstances of arrest | Circumstances of death | Official action known |
|---|---|---|---|---|
| Karamjit Singh (24) | May 30 or 31, 1990 | Reportedly abducted on May 30 | The police registered a case of suicide. His father alleged he died from torture by the police or CRPF | Postmortem indicated he had a variety of external injuries |
| Sukhdev Singh (also known as Kaka) (22) | October 2, 1990 | Jalandhar police raided Nandpur village on October 1 looking for him | Police reportedly beat him to death. Police denied his arrest and claimed that he poisoned himself | Postmortem recorded at least 10 injuries. Despite three summonses the police did not appear before the magistrate |
| Partwinder Singh Ropar | January 1, 1991 | Arrested on December 31, 1990 by the BSF and taken to Beco interrogation center | Reportedly received fatal injuries as a result of torture and died the next day | |
| Gurpreet Singh and Sohan Singh | February 5, 1991 | Detained by police outside Dakha village on January 31 | Reportedly killed on the outskirts of Dakha village while in police custody | |
| Tarsem Singh, member of Punjab home guards | May 15, 1991 | Arrested on May 9, held at Civil Lines Police Station, Amritsar | Police claim he fell ill and was taken to hospital. Others state he died as a result of torture | Announced that action would be taken against five policemen and that a murder case would be registered |

| | | | | |
|---|---|---|---|---|
| Avtar Singh | Probably July 1991 | Reportedly detained on July 26 by the Patiala police. Illegally detained in an interrogation center at Patiala | Reportedly died as a result of torture in Patiala police custody. Police allege he died in an encounter | |
| Manjit Singh (24), police constable | August 17, 1991 | Arrested under TADA on August 8. Charged with involvement in violent attacks, including the murder of a policeman | Died in hospital after telling doctors that he had been tortured. Police claimed he suffered from dysentery. Medical report allegedly noted a number of external injuries | Inquest conducted. Several people told a magistrate that he died as a result of torture. Magistrate stayed cremation while allegation of torture was investigated |

*Source*: Amnesty International USA, *India: Torture, Rape and Custody*, 1992.

The preventive war on the Sikh secessionists contributed to an explosion of the secessionist movement. There is overwhelming evidence to corroborate this statement. It was noted:

> [F]ar from containing militancy the Ray-Ribeiro[85] strategy provided it with a rich breeding ground. The killing rate rose dramatically from 1246 (1987) to 3074 (1988). . . . Instead of marginalizing the militants, they were transformed into martyrs; and the regular deaths of innocent individuals touched a raw nerve in the violent culture of rural Punjab.[86]

*Operation Woodrose*, which followed *Operation Bluestar* "only whetted extremism. Harassment of innocent people further alienated the Sikhs. Those in their teens and early twenties suffered the most which made their impressionable minds more susceptible to the separatist viewpoint."[87] Gurdarshan Singh Grewal, former Punjab advocate-general believed that imprisoning innocent people resulted in an increase in militancy.[88] From June to September 1984, large numbers of Sikh youth between the ages of 15 and 25 were whisked away from their homes.[89] Although some remained in police custody for a long time, others "disappeared" while in police custody. Those who survived (most of them innocent) were ready to join secessionist groups.

The media described the increasingly horrible situation in Punjab in 1991. *India Today* reported:

> the fear of the unknown is the engine that powers the juggernaut of terror. Inexorably, quietly and in a most un-Punjabi-like resignation the people have surrendered to the law of the gun. There is no such thing as a government. There is no such thing as a society with its own corrective mechanisms. There are the police and there are terrorists . . . Today's Punjab, held to terror's ransom, is a state of every man for himself. Of Punjab's three socio-geographical regions, Majha, west of the Beas is increasingly like the Wild West. Doaba, the fertile delta between the Beas and the Sutlej is rocked by new militant inroads. And Malwa, including Patiala is fast succumbing to the rule of the gun. . . . In parts of rural Punjab, particularly along the border, the militants no longer run a parallel government. They run *the* government.[90]

*The Sunday Times of India* reported:

> In today's Punjab the militant's word is law. In the rural areas of the worst-affected districts, his rule is absolute. The substantial, brave section of the Punjab police, which has decided to fight the battle, is doing so unaided. Crucial government wings like the judiciary, public works and local administration have long collapsed. The Punjab politician has become a marginal figure, only aggravating the problem by trying to exploit it. And Delhi remains the most irresponsible culprit, with no cohesive policy and conflicting hot-and-cold signals, which only serve to demoralize the administrators and encourage the militants.[91]

U.S. State Department document of January 19, 1993, stated:

> In Punjab there were credible reports that police in particular continued to engage in faked encounter killings. In the typical scenario, police take into custody suspected

> militants or militant supporters without filing an arrest report. If the detainee dies during interrogation or is executed, officials deny that he was ever in custody and claim he died during an armed encounter with police or security forces. Afterwards the bodies reportedly are sometimes moved to distant police districts for disposal, making identification and investigation more difficult. Indian human rights groups estimated that 1,350 people were killed in fake encounters during the first nine months of 1992. . . . There was no indication that any police officers were held responsible and punished.

The preventive war also resulted in a proliferation of secessionist groups demanding a separate state. The *Frontline* reported in December 1990:

> These major groups include the Babbar Khalsa, the Khalistan Commando Force (KCF—Paramjit Singh Panjwar group), the Khalistani Liberation Force (Gurjant Singh Buddhsinghwala group), the KCF (Pipal Singh group), the Bhindranwale Tiger Force of Khalistan (BTFK—Gurbachan Singh Manochahal group), the BTFK (Sangha group), the KCF (Wassan Singh Zaffarwal group), the Sikh Students' Federation (Daljit Bittoo group) and others of the All-India Sikh Students Federation (AISSF), the Damdami Taksal and the Gurjant Singh Rajasthani group. The Satta Chinna gang is another feared group while a dominant organization, the Khalistan National Army (KNA), is active once more.[92]

As figure 6.1 shows, three key Panthic committees controlled and coordinated the activities of the various militant groups and organizations.[93]

## ALLIANCE OF SECESSIONISTS AND EXTERNAL POWER

Following *Operation Bluestar*, "many supporters of the militant Sikh leader Bhindranwale fled across the border and with the encouragement from Pakistani officials organized themselves to mount a bigger challenge to the Indian control of the State."[94] Pakistan was very willing to ally with the Sikh secessionists because this was an opportunity to destabilize India and avenge India's assistance to the East Pakistan secessionists in 1970. India and Pakistan are archrivals and, therefore, it was in Pakistan's interest to encourage the Sikh secessionists.

There is compelling evidence that from 1985 Pakistan provided the secessionists with training camps, logistical support, weapons, and financial assistance. Avtar Singh Khalsa, a captured secessionist revealed on interrogation that he had escaped to Pakistan after *Operation Bluestar* in 1984. He disclosed that he and other Sikhs were trained in terrorist activities in Sialkot and Lahore in Pakistan. Detailed plans of terrorism against India were found on him.[95]

By mid-1987, it was learnt that 144 AK-47 rifles had made their way into the hands of the Sikhs.[96] Evidence suggested "a lot of weaponry made available by the United States to the Pak ISI to equip the mujahideens against the Soviet Army was siphoned off to arm the Sikh rebels."[97] Journalist Shekhar Gupta of *India Today* reported on the wide availability of arms and ammunition in Pakistan: "Just fifty

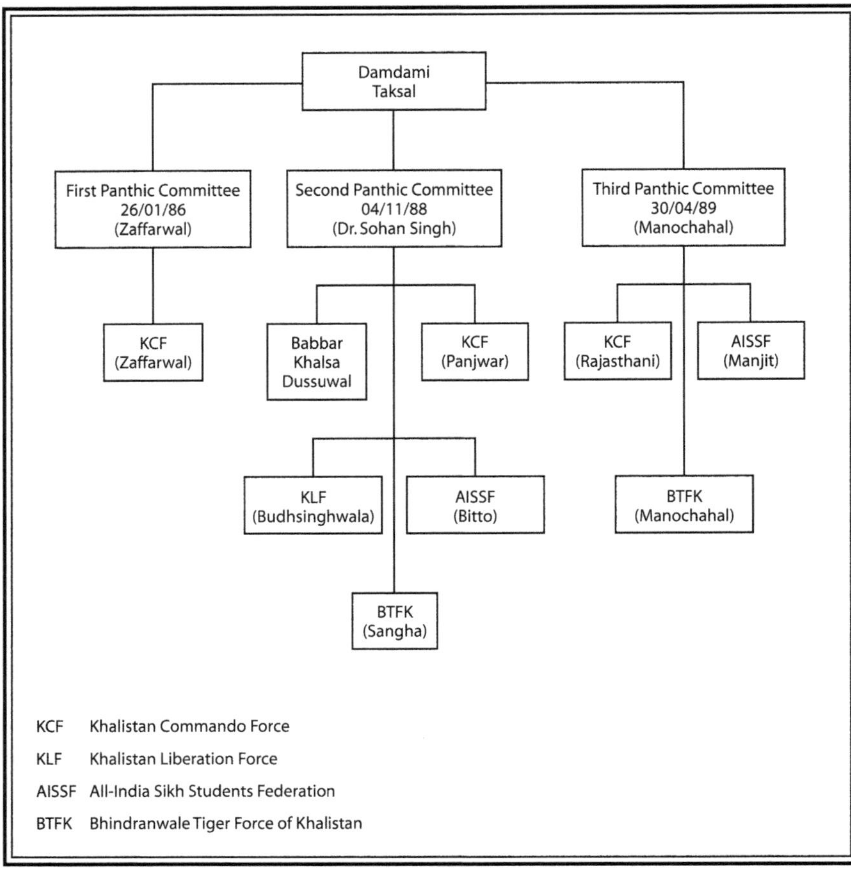


**Figure 6.1 Sikh militant groups and organizations**

*Source*: Gurharpal Singh, *Ethnic Conflict in India* (New York: St. Martin's Press, 2000), 151.

kilometers south of the Pakistani frontier city of Peshawar, lies the world's most unusual arms bazaar frequented by the sub-continent's extremists. Here, lethal weapons sell openly alongside narcotics."[98] According to his report, the weapons included Kalishnikovs, antiaircraft guns, rocket-propelled grenade launchers, sniper rifles, all kinds of rocket launchers, and gas masks.[99]

There is substantial evidence that the ISI Directorate of Pakistan was responsible for carrying out President Zia's policy of "destabilizing India by supporting militancy in Punjab and Kashmir."[100] It was learnt that a plan was made by the ISI to get the Punjab and the Kashmir secessionists to work together against India.[101] It was the ISI that helped reconcile the various Punjab militant groups in 1987 and boost their morale when they began to fight among themselves.[102]

The Indian government suspected Pakistan assistance when the secessionists

> brought in some 150 Chinese-made AK-MS (popularly listed as AK-47s) assault rifles . . . apparently bought in the arms bazaar in Pakistan's North-West Frontier

> Province. . . . The Indian Government's case was simple. Smuggling in .455 pistols and using weapons snatched from licensees were one thing, but bringing in AK-47 rifles and the large amount of ammunition that the fast-firing weapons require smacked of Pakistan's complicity. . . . The suspicion was strengthened by the sudden arrival of rocket-propelled grenades (RPGs) in Punjab. Once again it was clear that the consignments could not have come to India without "facilitative assistance" from the Pakistani authorities.[103]

*Frontline* reported:

> The accusation of Pakistani involvement began to gain ground in 1986–87. The Government did not produce any explicit evidence, but there were "leaks" of the interrogation records of some of the terrorists who had been apprehended.[104]

Table 6.2 has been compiled from interrogation reports of several key secessionists. "The interrogation reports are quite damning. The statements are not of some misguided youth caught on the border, but of high, and sometimes the topmost functionaries of the terrorist groups."[105] The disclosures confirm the accusations that Pakistan facilitated a widespread supply of arms to the Sikh secessionists. In fact, there is overwhelming evidence that the Sikh insurgents had easy access to Pakistan's stockpiles of weapons and explosives. The statements show it was after the preventive war on the Sikhs that they sought Pakistan's assistance.

There is evidence that training camps were set up in Pakistan to train the Sikh secessionists in the use of weapons and explosives. Figure 6.2 shows the location of these training camps in 1988.

## RIVALRY BETWEEN HOST STATE AND EXTERNAL POWER

The following evidence shows that it was rivalry between India and Pakistan that led Pakistan to ally with the Sikh secessionists. Explaining the reasons why Pakistan went to the aid of the Sikh secessionists, the Amritsar Senior Superintendent of Police Hardeep Singh Dhillon said:

> India had won freedom for Bangladesh and Pakistan was thenceforth a divided nation. Especially under Zia-ul-Haq, the aim became to repay India in the same coin. . . . So Zia's intention was to utilize the Punjabis. They . . . managed indeed to achieve considerable internal turmoil and the Punjab police have not been able to curb terrorism but only to manage it. . . . During Operation Woodrose, many rural youth crossed the border. They were hence available to Pakistan and were launched back into India by the Inter Services Intelligence (ISI). The ISI pumped a huge number of AK-47s into the Punjab.[106]

*Frontline* commented:

> Pakistan has no love lost for India. It considers India as the principal villain of the piece with regard to everything, especially because of Bangladesh. Would Pakistan

**Table 6.2 Evidence of Pakistani Aid to the Sikh Secessionists**

| Name of Secessionist and Group Affiliation | Disclosures Revealing Pakistan Assistance to Sikh Secessionists |
|---|---|
| Amrik Singh of Gurdaspur district in Punjab, president of the Akal Federation, a terrorist group with headquarters in Pakistan | He told interrogators that at the request of Pakistani intelligence official named "Malik," he and Panthic Committee member, Wassan Singh Zafarwal, sent 100 "boys" into Pakistan for weapons training, soon after *Operation Bluestar* in 1984. Then, on April 1 and 2, 1985, he and other Sikh secessionists from various militant groups met with three Pakistani intelligence officials to learn how to improve the effectiveness of the groups. After being trained in Pakistan, more than 100 secessionists were sent across the border into Punjab in 12 teams between February and July 1986 |
| Mohan Inder Singh Sachdev, member of the International Sikh Youth Federation in Canada (arrested in January 1987) | He gave details of the money trail from Canada to Pakistan to buy weapons for transfer to Punjab |
| Anokh Singh Babbar, head of the Babbar Khalsa group based in Punjab (arrested in January 1987) | He confessed that he went to Pakistan in July 1984, after *Operation Bluestar.* He was accompanied by Sukhdev Singh Dassuwal (head of the group based in Pakistan). They received extensive explosives training. Anokh Singh was later responsible for the transistor bomb blasts in New Delhi |
| Dalip Singh Rode, former chauffeur of Bhindranwale (arrested in November 1987) | He confirmed that several top secessionists were trained in Pakistan. Some of them were Gurjit Singh (convener of the AISSF), Nirvair Singh (spokesman of the Panthic Committee in the Golden Temple), Malkiat Singh Ajnala ("Lieutenant General" of the KCF—Khalistan Commando Force who surrendered in 1988), and Ajaib Singh (Damdami Taksal). He also stated that Gurjit Singh and Ajaib Singh were threatened by Pakistani intelligence official, Iqbal Chowdhury to declare the creation of Khalistan on April 29, 1986, otherwise the flow of weapons into Punjab would be stopped |

| Name of Secessionist and Group Affiliation | Disclosures Revealing Pakistan Assistance to Sikh Secessionists |
|---|---|
| Buta Singh of Kalanaur village, Punjab (arrested on April 13, 1988) | He disclosed that in a consignment of AK-47s that he brought from Pakistan were 16 antitank RPG-7s. He stated that he had visited Lahore, Pakistan, twice with Jasbir Singh and picked up this huge consignment from a house that was guarded by Pakistan intelligence officials. Stored in this house were massive quantities of missiles, explosives, and rifles for use by the secessionists |
| Nirvair Singh, member of KCF/Panthic Committee, surrendered during *Operation Black Thunder* in the Golden Temple on May 15, 1988 | He confessed that he had gone to Pakistan after *Operation Bluestar* and stayed there till April 1986. He was kept in a camp at Faislabad Jail with around 275 Sikh youth. He came in touch with several pro-Khalistani leaders. He was well looked after by the Pakistani authorities and was paid cash by them when he returned to Punjab |
| Baldev Singh Dorangla . . . self-styled area commander of Babbar Khalsa (arrested on November 29, 1988) | Dorangla made 7 trips to Pakistan between September 1984 and November 1988, during which he came in contact with important Babbar Khalsa leaders in Pakistan. He had extensive arms training and learned how to make and use explosive devices. He confessed to smuggling a large number of AK-47 rifles, rockets, and rocket launchers besides explosive material and detonators. One portable Pak-made rocket launcher, 40 rockets, 48 gun cotton slabs, and 2 HE-36 grenades were recovered from him |
| Davinder Singh, an activist of BTFK (arrested on April 21, 1989) | He accompanied a group of 10 extremists to Pakistan in the last week of June 1988. They were received at Pak Rangers picket Gillanwali by Gurbachan Singh Manochahal, Wassan Singh Zaffarwal, Mohinder Singh Manochahal (since killed in an encounter), and a Pak official named Choudhary. This party smuggled 8 AK-47 assault rifles with 8,000 cartridges, eight 9 mm stun guns with 7,000 cartridges, 4 pistols of .45 bore and 12 hand grenades into India |

*Source:* V.D. Chopra, *Genesis of Indo-Pakistan Conflict on Kashmir* (New Delhi: Patriot, 1990), 243–248 and Manoj Joshi, "The Pakistan Connection," *Frontline*, May 28–June 10, 1988, 13–15.

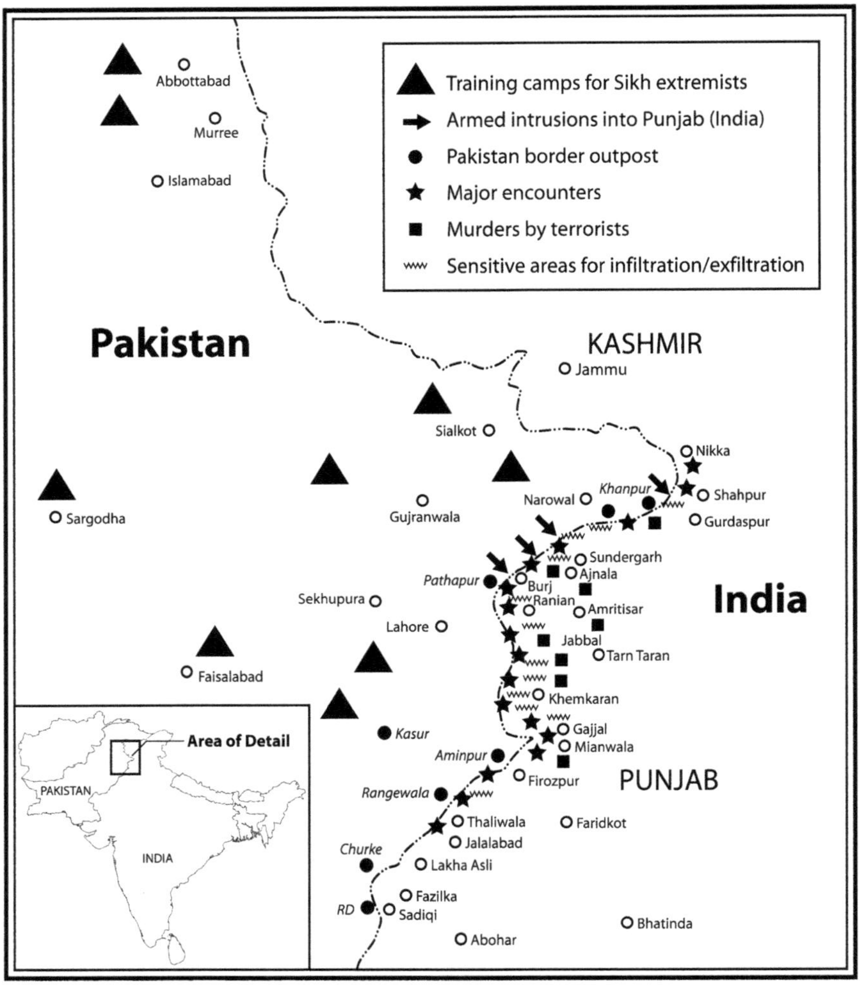


**Figure 6.2 Training Camps in Pakistan**

*Source*: *Frontline*, May 28-June 10, 1988, 14.

> hesitate to support a group of Sikhs who had gained considerable sympathy among the local populace in its struggle to destabilize a key Indian state? [107]

Other reasons made Punjab "the target of destabilization."[108] Punjab borders Pakistan and therefore, it "occupies a key position in India's defense."[109] Punjab "makes a significant contribution to the country's armed forces. Punjab is also the granary of India. The state accounts for valuable share of India's export trade."[110] Being an enduring rival of India, it was in Pakistan's interest to ally with the Sikh secessionists and try to break up India.

## NO RELIGIOUS TIES BETWEEN SECESSIONISTS AND EXTERNAL POWER

The Sikhs of Indian Punjab (East Punjab) and the Muslims of Pakistani Punjab (West Punjab) do have a common cultural heritage in the sense that they are all Punjabis. Before the partition of India in 1947, all of them occupied what was known as British Punjab.[111] However, the religions of the Sikhs and the Muslims—Sikhism and Islam—differ in a manner that far outweighs the bond that the Punjabi culture provides. Their religious customs and traditions are very different. Their religious beliefs and outward appearance are different—the Sikhs wear their distinctive turban. In the absence of strong religious ties with the Sikhs, Pakistan does not have much interest in Punjab like it does in Kashmir.[112] That is why the alliance between Pakistan and the Sikh secessionists was not very strong. It was rivalry between India and Pakistan that led to the alliance and not ethnic/religious ties.

The Sikhs have always been conscious of their separate religious identity—separate from the Hindus and the Muslims. As early as the sixteenth century, the fifth guru of the Sikhs, Arjan (1563–1606) wrote:

> I do not keep the Hindu fast, nor the Muslim Ramadan . . .
> I will not pray to idols nor say the Muslim prayer.
>
> I shall put my heart at the feet of the One Supreme Being.
> For we are neither Hindus nor Mussulmans.[113]

Later, historians and authors voiced similar thoughts. Khushwant Singh has written that by the time of Arjan's death, "the Sikhs had become conscious of the fact that they were . . . neither Hindus nor Muslims but formed a third community of their own."[114] W.H. McLeod has written, "For Nanak, conventional Hindu belief and Islam were not regarded as fundamentally right but as fundamentally wrong. . . . The two were to be rejected, not harmonized."[115]

## NO INTERNATIONAL MILITARY INTERVENTION BY EXTERNAL POWER

After *Operation Bluestar* in 1984 and with Pakistan's covert assistance to the Sikh secessionists thereafter, the military capabilities of the Sikhs increased immensely. Every year after 1984,

> the quality of weaponry and training of the terrorists seemed to improve. Between 1985 and 1986 murders and even massacres were carried out with .455 pistols with Indian-origin rifles and sten-guns, and from 1987 onwards AK-47s started appearing. 1988 began with attacks on the security forces with RPG-7 rockets besides well-coordinated and highly damaging bomb-blasts. Later, terrorist equipment was standardized to versions of the AK rifles, General Purpose Machine Guns (GPMGs) and explosives, with some sophisticated "add-ons" and accessories such as night-vision equipment, Dragunov sniper rifles, Kenpro transceiver sets and so on.[116]

It is evident that the alliance with Pakistan provided the Sikh secessionists with superior weapons, which helped them offer a strong resistance against the Indian government. However, in the absence of strong religious ties between the Sikhs and the Pakistanis, the alliance that was formed was not strong enough to increase security competition between India and the alliance. India was not threatened by the weak alliance. When India confronted Pakistan with evidence of its assistance to the secessionists, Pakistan brushed aside India's accusations and continued to deny any involvement. However, Pakistan agreed to a joint patrolling of the border between Indian Punjab and Pakistani Punjab. India, of course, went a step further by deciding to build a fence along the border to stop infiltrators from Pakistan.

So, from February 1993, Pakistani aid to India was reduced because "553 km of land and riverine tract between Indian and Pakistani Punjab . . . has been fenced and provided with floodlights, with observation posts every 500 yards."[117] Such action had become necessary in view of the evidence that Pakistan was responsible for the flow of arms into Punjab. It was "decided that if terror has to be checked, then the flow of arms has to be stopped and, since Pakistan was at the back of this flow of arms, there had to be border fencing."[118] Moreover, the army was called in to "guard the border in places where infiltration was still easy. They formed a second line of defense to check the smuggling of arms and that paid dividends."[119]

Thus, the events described above show that a weak alliance between Pakistan and the Sikh secessionists did not lead to military intervention by Pakistan. The alliance did increase the military capabilities of the Sikhs but not to the extent of leading to a security dilemma between the two countries. This is because the alliance was not seen as potentially threatening by India. Unlike the Kashmir case where both "rivalry" and "ethnic ties" led to a strong alliance and increased the security competition between India and Pakistan, the alliance in this case was the result of only "rivalry." Consequently, there was no military intervention by Pakistan.

## CONCLUSION

As the theory in chapter 2 predicted, a shift in the balance of power in favor of the Sikh secessionists led to a preventive war on the Sikhs by the Indian government in 1984. India's preventive war led to an explosive growth of the Sikh secessionist movement. There is evidence to show that the preventive war also resulted in an alliance between the Sikh secessionists and Pakistan. Rivalry between India and Pakistan promoted the formation of the alliance. However, the absence of religious ties between the Sikhs and the Pakistanis created an alliance that was not strong enough to cause military intervention by Pakistan.

The events in the Punjab case unfolded in the following way. As the power of the Sikh secessionists increased inside the Golden Temple, there was a decline in the power of the Indian government relative to the secessionists. Perceiving a shift in the balance of power, the Indian government decided to crush the secessionists before the movement grew stronger. Although conditions were still favorable for the Indian government, it waged a preventive war on the Sikhs rather than risk war later when conditions might have worsened. Negotiations between the Indian government and the Sikh secessionists failed because of problems of credible commitment.

The preventive war only resulted in strengthening the resolve of the Sikh secessionists. Sikhs who had never been in favor of a separate state of Khalistan began to support the secessionist movement after the preventive war. The preventive war also led to an alliance between the Sikh secessionists and Pakistan. The Sikhs turned to Pakistan for arms, training, and logistical support, and being a rival of India, Pakistan was very interested in aiding and abetting the Sikhs. The "rivalry" variable was strong in this case. However, the "ethnic/religious kinship" variable did not have an effect on the alliance. Last, there was a positive correlation between the strength of the alliance and the risk of military intervention by the external power. Devoid of religious ties, the alliance was not strong enough to bring about military intervention by Pakistan. The weak alliance between the Sikhs and Pakistan did not give rise to a security dilemma and the ensuing spirals of suspicion and hostility between India and the alliance. In the absence of increased security competition between India and Pakistan, military intervention did not take place.

# 7

# Conclusion

THIS STUDY HAS addressed the ways in which secessionist movements affect international security. The theoretical model developed here clearly predicts a causal sequence that precedes international military intervention in a secessionist war. I argued that a shift in the balance of power between a secessionist group and the host state leads to a preventive war on the former by the latter. The preventive war, in turn, results in an explosive growth of the movement and also increases the chances of an alliance being formed between the secessionists and an external power. The risk of alliance formation is strengthened by the presence of rivalry between the host state and an external power and ethnic/religious affinities between the secessionist group and the external power. Finally, I argued that a strong alliance increases the chances of external military intervention.

I tested these arguments by an in-depth historical analysis of four case studies: East Pakistan (Bangladesh), Sri Lanka, Kashmir, and Punjab. I focused on the causal mechanisms in each case rather than just a broad narration of events. By comparing the pattern of events among the cases, I uncovered similarities as well as differences. The cases confirmed the main arguments put forth in chapter 2. Although military intervention did not take place in all the four cases examined here, this study identified the conditions that made international military intervention in a secessionist war more or less likely.

This chapter is divided into three sections. First, the results of the four case studies are summarized and compared in order to underscore the main theoretical conclusions we may draw from the sequence of events. Second, the policy implications of the results are emphasized: how should a government respond to an increase in the power of a secessionist group? Finally, the long-term relevance of the study is highlighted: the significance of secessionist movements in the present post-9/11 world.

In the East Pakistan case, India's military intervention on behalf of the East Pakistan (Bengali) secessionists was successful, resulting in the state of Bangladesh. The evidence put forth in chapter 3 has clearly shown that a shift in the balance of power in favor of the Bengalis led to a preventive war on them by the Pakistan government. In December 1970, when the Awami League of East Pakistan won an absolute majority in Parliament in the Pakistan general elections, it gave Sheikh Mujib (the leader of the Awami League) the mandate to become prime minister of Pakistan. Perceiving a shift in the balance of power and before Mujib could assume this position and draft a new constitution based on his program of autonomy, the Pakistan government, in March 1971, decided to launch a preventive war on the Bengali secessionists to wipe them out. Historical evidence has shown that the West Pakistan army was out to destroy the Awami League before it could form a new government and accumulate even greater power.

After the preventive war on the Bengalis of East Pakistan, the movement, which had started out as a movement for autonomy, was strengthened and transformed overnight into a secessionist movement for an independent state of Bangladesh. The preventive war on the Bengalis led to an alliance between them and India. The Bengali secessionists turned to India for military training, arms, financial, and logistical assistance. India was keen on helping the Bengalis of East Pakistan because India and Pakistan are enduring rivals, and breaking up Pakistan would be advantageous to India. Moreover, the ethnic ties that linked the Bengalis of India and the Bengalis of East Pakistan also contributed to the formation of the alliance. The presence of both variables in this case—rivalry and ethnic kinship—led to a strong alliance between India and the Bengali secessionists. The strong alliance culminated in military intervention by India. Thus, the evidence in this case supported all the six hypotheses mentioned in chapter 2.

In Sri Lanka, external military intervention (as in the case of Bangladesh) did not take place on behalf of the Tamil secessionists. This is because the alliance that was formed between the Tamil secessionists and India was not strong enough to bring about military intervention. Besides the "preventive war" variable, it was only ethnic kinship between the Tamils of India and the Tamils of Sri Lanka that led to the alliance. The "rivalry" variable was absent because India and Sri Lanka are not rivals and for this reason, the alliance formed was not very strong.

The historical evidence laid out in chapter 4 on Sri Lanka supported five of the six hypotheses. The rivalry hypothesis (H4) was not an issue in this case. For example, a shift in the balance of power in favor of the Tamil secessionists led to a preventive war on them by the Sri Lankan central government. In the 1977 parliamentary elections in Sri Lanka, the Tamil party TULF became the main opposition party in parliament. The TULF had certainly increased its power and was able to reinforce its claim for a separate state of Tamil Eelam. When the Sinhalese government perceived a relative decline in its power and a shift in the balance of power in favor of the secessionists, it resorted to a series of preventive wars on the Tamils (1977, 1981, and 1983) to squash the movement before it became stronger. Each time a preventive war took place, the collective identity of the Tamils was strengthened and the movement became more radicalized. Each time, new secessionist groups came into existence and the movement grew. The growth of the movement had a further effect on the shift in the balance of power, and the cycle continued. The preventive war on the Tamils in 1983 led to an alliance between India and the Tamil secessionists.

In the Kashmir case study, Pakistan intervened militarily in 1999 on behalf of the Kashmir secessionists when it carried out a military invasion across the LOC at three points: Kargil, Dras, and Batalik. The alliance between the Kashmir secessionists and Pakistan was a strong one—the result of bitter rivalry between India and Pakistan and ethnic/religious kinship between the Muslims of Kashmir and the Muslims of Pakistan. A strong alliance led to military intervention.

A relative decline in the power of the Indian government and an increase in the power of the Kashmir secessionists led the Indian government to fight a preventive war on the secessionists in Kashmir. In January 1990, New Delhi sent around 400,000 Indian security personnel that included members of the Indian Army, the Border Security Force, and the Central Reserve Police. The preventive war radicalized the militants and led to a strengthening of the movement, which in turn led to a further shift in the balance of power. The preventive war also led the secessionists to ally with Pakistan for military training, arms, and monetary aid. Finally, the presence of both variables—rivalry and ethnic ties—strengthened the alliance leading to Pakistan's military intervention.

In the Punjab case, external military intervention did not take place because the alliance between Pakistan and the Sikh secessionists was not very strong. The preventive war on the Sikhs by the Indian government and rivalry between India and Pakistan led to the alliance, but in the absence of religious ties between the Sikhs of India and the Muslims of Pakistan, the alliance that was formed was not strong enough to result in military intervention.

A shift in the balance of power did take place in Punjab when Sikh secessionists under the leadership of Bhindranwale assembled with arms inside the Golden Temple and were believed to be ready to proclaim the establishment of Khalistan (a separate state for the Sikhs). When the Indian government perceived a shift in the balance of power in favor of the Sikhs, it waged a preventive war on the latter in June 1984. The preventive war on the Sikhs strengthened the resolve of the secessionists and brought about a huge increase in the number of groups. With the growth of the movement, there was a further shift in the balance of power.

Thus, the main theoretical arguments in chapter 2 were confirmed by the case studies examined. Did the evidence support all the six hypotheses? The study reveals that H1: *The more the balance of power between a secessionist group and the host state shifts in favor of the former, the greater the risk of a preventive war on the secessionists by the central government* is supported by the evidence in all four cases. In the East Pakistan, Sri Lanka, Kashmir, and Punjab movements, a shift in the balance of power in favor of the secessionists did result in a preventive war by the central government of each host state. The central government was unable to negotiate with the secessionists in each of the four movements because a shift in the balance of power created problems of credible commitments. Therefore, as the power of the central government declined relative to the secessionists, it feared that bargains that were previously enforceable would become unenforceable. In each case, the government felt that today's agreements or contracts with the secessionists would not be honored in the future. Therefore, the government chose to fight a preventive war on the secessionists rather than be exploited by them in the future.

All the four case studies support H2: *A preventive war on the secessionists by the central government will result in an explosive growth of the secessionist movement.* A preventive war by the central government strengthened the collective identity of the secessionists in each case. The actions and goals of the secessionists became radicalized, and movements that had started out as autonomous movements were transformed into secessionist movements. Also, several new secessionist groups came into existence after the preventive war in each case. The growth of each movement resulted in a feedback effect on the shift in the balance of power.

The third hypothesis H3: *A preventive war on the secessionists by the central government increases the chances that the secessionists will ally with an external power for its support and assistance* is also supported by the evidence in all the four cases. In order to withstand the preventive war, the secessionists in each case tried to increase their power by forming an alliance with an external power for military training, arms, and monetary assistance. In the East Pakistan and Sri Lanka movements, India became an ally of the secessionists, and in the Kashmir and Punjab movements, the secessionists allied with Pakistan. Also, with the security of the secessionists threatened in each case, they decided to form an alliance with an external power to balance against the threats from the host states.

H4: *Rivalry between the host state and an external power increases the likelihood of an alliance being formed between the secessionists and an external power* is supported by the East Pakistan, Kashmir, and Punjab cases because of the intense rivalry between India and Pakistan. Since India and Pakistan are enduring rivals, India was very willing to ally with the Bengali secessionists of East Pakistan. It was in India's interest to break up Pakistan. Pakistan, in turn, was very willing to ally with the Sikh and Kashmir secessionists. Rivals are always keen on ironing out past differences, so it was payback time for Pakistan who is always willing to stir up trouble in India. However, in the Sri Lanka case, there was no support for the hypothesis because India and Sri Lanka are not rivals.

H5: A *strong ethnic or religious kinship between the external power and the secessionists will increase the chances of an alliance being formed between them* is supported by the East Pakistan, Sri Lanka, and Kashmir cases. In each of these cases, the secessionist group looked to an external state for ethnic brethren who could help them with military, financial, and logistical support. In the Punjab case, however, the hypothesis is not supported. As explained in chapter 6, the Sikhs of Indian Punjab and the Muslims of Pakistani Punjab do share a common cultural heritage because they are all Punjabis. They were all part of the same state of

Punjab before it was divided during the partition of India in 1947. But, their religions are distinct. The differences between Sikhism and Islam weaken the bond that the Punjabi culture provides. For this reason, it was not ethnic/religious kinship that led to the alliance between the Sikh secessionists and Pakistan.

The last hypothesis, H6: *The stronger the alliance between the secessionists and an external power, the greater the risk of military intervention in the secessionist war by the external power* is supported by the evidence in all the four cases. In the East Pakistan and Kashmir cases, military intervention took place due to the strong alliance formed. In the Sri Lanka and Punjab cases, a weak alliance did not lead to military intervention. In East Pakistan, India's alliance with the Bengali secessionists was seen as a threat to Pakistan who took steps to diminish the security of the alliance. Pakistan moved its troops and tanks to its borders with India and tensions increased between the two countries. Because India and Pakistan are rivals, the ensuing uncertainty, misinformation, and misperceptions of each other led to the creation of the security dilemma and ultimately, to India's intervention on behalf of the Bengali secessionists. India's alliance with the Bengali secessionists was strong enough to bring about intervention because besides rivalry, ethnic ties also contributed to the alliance. Similarly, in the Kashmir case, the alliance between the Kashmir secessionists and Pakistan was strong because both rivalry and ethnic/religious ties led to the alliance. A strong alliance increased the security competition between India and Pakistan and eventually brought about military intervention by Pakistan. However, military intervention did not take place in Sri Lanka and Punjab. In the Sri Lanka case, the absence of the rivalry variable and in the Punjab case, the absence of religious bonds between the Sikhs and the Pakistanis resulted in weak alliances and no military intervention by the external power.

## IMPLICATIONS FOR POLICY

The historical evidence collected not only proves that leaders of states look upon secessionist movements as threatening, but also confirms that the usual way of dealing with such movements is not very useful. We have seen that a preventive war to crush a movement is counterproductive and results in strengthening the movement. What follows is even more violence and bloodshed. The case for support of a secessionist group through an alliance with an external power is also weak. It only complicates matters and increases security competition between the host state and the external power bringing about military intervention if the alliance is strong. Preventing military intervention is important because it is a threat to international security and "the instigator of all modern international war and a determinant of its geographic scope."[1]

Given the ethnic and religious differences that exist within states, what can be done to mitigate the problems created by these structural factors that could eventually lead to secessionist movements? In all the cases studied here, we saw that political, economic, and/or cultural discrimination by the central government against a minority group produced secessionist impulses. Therefore, addressing these grievances, by protecting minorities' economic and political interests, and cultural rights could go a long way in preventing secessionist tendencies.

If, however, secessionist movements do start, what measures can be taken to prevent violence? In all the case studies discussed here, we have seen that external support to the secessionists increased violence due to an increase in the supply of arms. Therefore, the international community can help by preventing external powers from aiding and abetting secessionists.

What political solutions can be found for secessionist movements? A policy of devolution as a political process is probably the best solution. Devolution of power is a federalist arrangement in which a central government grants self-governing powers to an ethnic group within the political framework of a state. In other words, ethnic autonomy or self-rule by an ethnic group is a great way to dampen secessionist inclinations. For example, in Sri Lanka, if the government had granted the Tamils autonomy within a united Sri Lanka, all the bloodshed and violence would have been prevented. Similarly, in Kashmir, if the Indian government had allowed Kashmir to have the "special status"[2] it was granted under Article 370 of the Indian Constitution, it would not have demanded secession from India. If the Kashmiris had been allowed to manage matters such as law and order, education, and taxation, among others at the local level and leave defense, communications, and foreign affairs to the central government, the protracted secessionist movement would have been avoided.

## LONG-TERM RELEVANCE OF THE STUDY

This study has been done at a time when the United States is fighting a war on terror in the post-9/11 era. Will the U.S. war on terrorism have an impact on the terror that secessionist groups often unleash in their host states? Will the secessionists who are branded as terrorists be forced to give up or suspend their activities in view of the current war on terror? What does the future hold as far as external powers becoming involved in secessionist movements?

The long-term repercussions from the war on terror are likely to be substantial. With the United States clamping down on countries that assist terrorists, there has been a reduction in the external support afforded to secessionists worldwide. It is heartening that Indian Prime Minister Manmohan Singh and Pakistan President Pervez Musharraf have started peace talks in an attempt to resolve the Kashmir conflict and combat terrorism along their common border. Both sides have honored the cease-fire that began in 2004 along the LOC that divides Kashmir between Pakistan and India, and hopes for a peaceful settlement are more encouraging than previous attempts at peace. The events of 9/11 may have opened new doors in the transformation of regional security in South Asia. Because Pakistan has assumed a new role as an ally of the United States in its war on terror, it has intensified its search for the remnants of the Taliban and al-Qaeda militants hiding along the Pakistan-Afghanistan border. Pakistan has also promised to close down several terrorist training camps located within its borders.

However, the threat of violence in South Asia is far from over. The recent disclosure of a Pakistan scientist's illegal sales of nuclear know-how to Iran, Libya, and North Korea has raised concerns of nuclear proliferation among rogue states. Also, unlike India, Pakistan has refused to introduce a no-first use policy with regard to its nuclear weapons. Given the historical animosity and enduring rivalry between India and Pakistan, it will be years before both sides make important concessions to achieve peace.

# Appendix 1

## Statement Issued by Mr. Tajuddin Ahmed, Prime Minister of Bangladesh, on April 17, 1971, After the Inauguration of the Government of the People's Republic of Bangladesh

BANGLA DESH IS at war. It has been given no choice but to secure its right of self-determination through a national liberation struggle against the colonial oppression of West Pakistan.

In the face of positive attempts by the Government to distort the facts in a desperate attempt to cover up their war of genocide in Bangla Desh, the world must be told the circumstances under which the peace-loving people of Bangla Desh were driven to substitute armed struggle for parliamentary politics to realize the just aspirations of the people of Bangla Desh.

The Six Point Programme for autonomy for Bangla Desh within Pakistan had been put forward in all sincerity by the Awami League as the last possible solution to preserve the integrity of Pakistan. Fighting the elections to the National Assembly on the issue of Six Points, the Awami League won 167 out of 169 seats from Bangla Desh out of a house of 313. Its electoral victory was so decisive that it won 80% of the popular votes cast. The decisive nature of its victory placed it in a clear majority within the National Assembly.

The post election period was a time of hope, for never had a people spoken so decisively in the history of parliamentary democracy. It was widely believed in both wings that a viable constitution based on six points could be worked out. The Pakistan Peoples party which emerged as the leading party in Sind and Punjab had avoided raising the issue of Six Points in their election campaign and had no obligation whatsoever to its electorate to resist it. In Baluchistan the dominant party, National Awami Party, was fully committed to Six Points. In NWFP, the NAP

---

Reproduced from *Bangla Desh Documents*, vol. I (New Delhi: Ministry of External Affairs, Government of India, 1971), 291–298.

dominant in the Provincial Assembly, was also a believer in maximum autonomy. The course of the elections, which marked the defeat of the reactionary parties, therefore, gave every reason to be optimistic about the future of democracy in Pakistan.

Preparatory to the convening of the National Assembly talks were expected between the main parties in the political areas. However, whilst the Awami League was always willing, preparatory to going to the Assembly, to explain its constitutional position and to discuss alternative proposals from other parties, it is believed that the spirit of true democracy demanded that the constitution be debated and finalized in the National Assembly rather tan in secret sessions. To this end, it insisted on an early summoning of the National Assembly. In anticipation of this session, the Awami League worked day and night to prepare a draft constitution based on Six Points and fully examined all the implications of formulating and implementing such a constitution.

The first major talks over Pakistan's political future took place between General and Sheikh Mujibur Rahman in Mid-January. In this session General proved the extent of the Awami Leagues commitment to its programme and was assured that they were fully aware of its implications. But contrary to expectation did not fully spell out his own ideas about the constitution. General gave the impression of not finding anything seriously objectionable in Six Points but emphasized the need for coming to an understanding with the PPP in Western Pakistan.

The next round of talks took place between the PPP and the Awami League from 27th January, 1971 in Dacca where Mr. Bhutto and his team held a number of sessions with the Awami League to discuss the constitution.

As in the case with, Mr. Bhutto did not bring any concrete proposals of his own about the nature of the constitution. He and is advisors were mainly interested in discussing the implications of Six Points. Since their responses were essentially negative and they had no prepared brief of their own, it was not possible for the talks to develop into serious negotiations where attempts could be made to bridge the gap between the two parties. It was evident that as yet Mr. Bhutto had no formal position of his own from which to negotiate.

It must be made clear that when the PPP left Dacca there was no indication from their part that a deadlock had been reached with the Awami League. Rather they confirmed that all doors were open and that following a round of talks with the West Pakistani leaders the PPP would either have a second and more substantive round of talks with the Awami League or would meet in the National Assembly whose committees provided ample opportunity for detailed discussion on the constitution.

Mr. Bhutto's announcement to boycott the National Assembly, therefore, came as a complete surprise. The boycott decision was surprising because Mr. Bhutto had already been accommodated once by the President when he refused Sheikh Mujib's plea for an early session of the Assembly on the 15th of February and fixed it, in line with Mr. Bhutto's preference, for 3rd March.

Following his decision to boycott the Assembly, Mr. Bhutto launched a campaign of intimidation against all other parties in West Pakistan to prevent them from attending the session. In this task there is evidence that Lt. Gen. Umer, Chairman of the National Security Council and close associate of, with a view to strengthening Mr. Bhutto's hand, personally pressured various West Wing leaders not to attend the Assembly. In spite of this display of pressure tactics by Mr. Bhutto and Lt. Gen. Umer, all members of the National Assembly from West Pakistan, except the PPP and the Qayyum Muslim League, had booked their seats to East Pakistan, for the session on 3rd March.

Within the QML itself, half their members had booked their seats and there were signs of revolt within the PPP where many members were wanting to come to Dacca. Faced with the breakdown of this joint front against Bangla Desh, General obliged Mr. Bhutto on 1st March by postponing the Assembly, not for any definite period, but sine die. Moreover he dismissed the Governor of East Pakistan, Admiral S. M. Ahsan, who was believed to be one of the moderates in his administration. The Cabinet with its component of Bengalis was also dismissed so that all power was concentrated in the hands of the West Wing military junta.

In these circumstances Yahya's gesture could not be seen as anything but an attempt to frustrate the popular will by colluding with Mr. Bhutto. The National Assembly was the only forum where Bangla Desh could assert its voice and political strength, and to frustrate this was a clear indication that Parliament was not to be the real source of power in Pakistan.

The reaction to the postponement in Bangla Desh was inevitable and spontaneous and throughout the land people took to the streets to record their protest at this arbitrary act. People now felt sure that never really intended to transfer power, and was making a mockery of parliamentary politics. The popular mood felt that the rights of Bangla Desh could never be realized within the framework of Pakistan, where could so blatantly frustrate the summoning of an assembly proclaimed by his own writ and urged that Sheikh Mujibur Rahman must go for full independence.

Sheikh Mujib however continued to seek a political settlement. In calling for a programme of non-cooperation on 3rd March he chose the weapon of peaceful confrontation against the army of occupation as an attempt to bring them to their senses. This was in itself a major gesture in the face of the cold blooded firing on unarmed demonstrators on the 2nd and 3rd March which had already led to over a thousand casualties.

The course of the non-cooperation movement is now a part of history. Never in the course of any liberation struggle has non-cooperation been carried to the limits attained within Bangladesh between first and 25th March. Non-cooperation was total. No judge of the High Court could be found to administer the oath of office to the new Governor Lt. General Tikka Khan. The entire civilian administration including he police and the Civil Service of Pakistan, refused to attend office. The people stopped supply of food to the army. Even the civilian employees of the Defence establishment joined the boycott.

Non-cooperation did not stop at abstention from work. The civilian administration and the police positively pledged their support to Sheikh Mujibur Rahman and put themselves under his orders.

In this situation the Awami League without being a formally constituted Government, was forced to take on the responsibility of keeping the economy and administration running whilst non-cooperation lasted. In this task they had the unqualified support not only of the people but the administration and the business community. The latter two subordinated themselves to the directives of the Awami League and accepted them as the sole authority to solve their various problems.

In these unique circumstances the economy and administration were kept going in spite of the formidable problems arising out of the power vacuum which has suddenly emerged in Bangla Desh. In spite of the lack of any formal authority, Awami League volunteers, in cooperation with the police, maintained a level of law and order which was a considerable improvement on normal times.

Faced with this demonstration of total support to the Awami League and this historic non-cooperation movement, General appears to have modified his tactics. On the 6th March, he still seemed determined to provoke a confrontation when he made his highly provocative speech putting the full blame on the crisis, on the Awami League and not even referring to the architect of the crisis, Mr. Bhutto. It seems that he expected a declaration of independence on 7th March. The Army in Dacca was put on full alert to crush the move and Lt. Gen. Tikka Khan was flown in to replace Lt. Gen. Yakub to signify the hardening of attitudes within the Junta.

Sheikh Mujib, however, once again opted for the path of political settlement in spite of massive public sentiment for independence. In presenting his 4-point proposal for attending the National Assembly he not only had to contain the public mood but to leave a way open for to explore this last chance of a peaceful settlement.

It is now clear that Yahya and his Generals never had the slightest intention of solving Pakistan's political crisis peacefully but were only interested in buying time to permit the reinforcement of their military machine within Bangla Desh. Yahiya's visit to Dacca was a mere cover for his plan of genocide. It now becomes clear that contingency plans for such a crisis had already begun well in advance of the crisis.

Shortly before 1st March tanks which had been sent north to Rangpur to defend the borders were brought back to Dacca. From the 1st March the families of Army personnel were being sent off to West Pakistan on a priority basis as were the families of West Pakistani businessmen.

The military build-up was accelerated after 1st March and continued throughout the talks up to 25th March. Members of the armed forces dressed in civilian clothes were flown in PIA commercial flights via Ceylon. C 130s carrying arms and provisions for the garrisons flew in to Dacca. It is estimated that up to one division, with complementary support, was brought into Bangla Desh between 1st and 25th March. To ensure security, the airport was put under strict airforce control and heavily guarded with artillery and machine gun nets whilst movement of passengers was strictly supervised. As SSG commando group especially trained in operations in sabotage and assassinations was distributed in key centers of Bangla Desh and were probably responsible for the attacks on Bengalis in Dacca and Saidpur in the two days before 25th march to provoke clashes between locals and non-locals so as to provide a cover for military intervention.

As part of this strategy of deception adopted the most conciliatory posture in his talks with Mujib. In the talks beginning on the 16th of March, he expressed regrets for what had happened and his sincere desire for a political settlement. In a crucial meeting with Sheikh Mujib he was asked to positively state the Juntas position on the Awami Leagues 4-point proposal. He indicated that there was no serious objection and that an interim constitution could be worked out by the respective advisors embodying the four points.

The basic points on which agreement was reached were:

1. Lifting of Martial Law and transfer of power to a Civilian Government by a Presidential Proclamation.
2. Transfer of power in the provinces to the majority parties
3. To remain as President and in control of the Central Government
4. Separate sittings of the National Assembly members from East and West Pakistan preparatory to a joint session of the house to finalize the constitution.

Contrary to the distortions now put out by both and Bhutto the proposal for separate sittings of the Assembly was suggested by to accommodate Mr. Bhutto. Hi cite the practical advantage that whilst 6-points provided a viable blueprint to regulate relations between Bangla Desh and the Center its application would raise serious difficulties in the West Wing. Fro this reason West Wing MNAs must be permitted to get together to work out a new pattern of relationships in the context of the Six-point constitution and the dissolution of One Unit.

Once this agreement in principle had been reached between Sheikh Mujib and there was only the question of defining the powers of Bangla Desh vis-à-vis the Centre during the interim phase. Here it was again jointly agreed that the distribution of power should as far as possible approximate to the final constitution approved by the National Assembly which, it was expected, would be based on Six Points.

For working out this part of the interim settlement Mr. M. M. Ahmed, the Economic Advisor to the President was specially flown in. In his talks with the Awami League advisors he made it clear that provided the political agreement had been reached there were no insuperable problem to working out some version of Six Points even in the interim period. The final list of three amendments to the Awami League draft which he presented as suggestions, indicated that the gap between the Government and Awami League position was no longer one of principle but remained merely over the precise phrasing of the proposals. The Awami league in its sitting of 24th March had accepted the amendments with certain minor changes of language and there was nothing to prevent the holding of a final drafting session between the advisors of and Mujib when the interim constitution would be finalized.

It must be made clear that at no stage was there any breakdown of talks or any indication by General or his team that they had a final position which could not be abandoned.

The question of legal cover for the transfer of power is merely another belated fabrication by to cover his genocide. He and his team had agreed that, in line with the precedence of the Indian Independence Act of 1947, power could be transferred by Presidential Proclamation. The notion that there would be no legal cover to the agreement raised subsequently by Mr. Bhutto and endorsed by General was never a bone of contention between Sheikh Mujib and. There is not the slightest doubt that had indicated that a meeting of the National Assembly was essential to transfer power, the Awami League would not have broken the talks on such a minor legal technicality. After all as the majority party it had nothing to fear from such a meeting and its acceptance of the decision for a separate sitting was designed to accommodate Mr. Bhutto rather than a fundamental stand fro the party.

Evidence that agreement in principle between contending parties had been reached is provided by Mr. Bhutto's own Press Conference on 25th March. It is not certain what passed in the separate session between General and Mr. Bhuttto but there is evidence that deliberate falsehoods about the course of the talk with the Awami League were fed to the PPP who were told that Sheikh Mujib was determined to have a showdown and was daily escalating his demands. Needless to say not the slightest indication of these misgivings has been raised in the meetings between the Awami League team and General Yahiya's advisors where amicability and optimism prevailed to the end.

Whilst hope for a settlement was being raised more ominous signs of the intentions of the army were provided by their sudden decision to unload the munition ship M.V. Swat berthed at Chittagong Port. Preparatory to this decision, Brigadier Mazumdar, a Bengali officer commanding the garrison in Chittagong had been suddenly removed from his command and replaced by a West Pakistani. On 24th night he was flown to Dacca under armed escort and has probably been executed. Under the new command notice was given to local authorities of the decision to unload the ship in spite of the fact that the army had abstained from doing so for the last 17 days in the face of non-cooperation from the port workers. The decision to unload was a calculated provocation which immediately brought 100,000 people on the streets of Chittagong and led to massive firing by the Army to break their way out. The issue was raised by the Awami League with General Peerzada as to why this escalation was being permitted whilst talks were still going on. He gave no answer beyond a promise to pass it on to General.

Following the final meeting between General Yahiya's and Awami Leagues advisors on 24th March where Mr. M.M. Ahmed passed on his amendments, a call was awaited from General Peerzada for a final session where the draft could be finalized. No such call materialized and instead it was learnt that Mr. M. M. Ahmed, who was central to the negotiations, had suddenly left for Karachi on the 25th morning without and warning to the Awami League team.

By 11P.M. of the 25th all preparations were ready and the troops began to take up their positions in the city. In an act of treachery unparalleled in contemporary history a programme of calculated genocide was unleashed on the peaceful and unsuspecting population of Dacca by midnight of 25th March. No ultimatum was given tot he Awami League by, no curfew order as even issued when the machine guns, artillery and canon on the tanks unleashed their reign of death and destruction. By the time the first Martial Law proclamations issued by Lt. General Tikka Kahn were broadcast the next morning some 50,000 people, most of them without offering any resistance, and many women and children, had been butchered. Dacca had been turned into an inferno with fires raging in most corners of the city. Sleeping inhabitants who have been drawn from their homes by the fires started by the military, were machine gunned as they ran to escape the flames.

Whilst the police, EPR, and armed volunteers put up a heroic resistance, the main victims remained the weak, the innocent and the unsuspecting who were killed at random in their thousands. We are compiling a first hand account of the details of genocide committed by the Pakistani Army on the orders of the President of Pakistan which we will publish shortly. The scale and brutality of the action exceeds anything perpetrated in the civilized world.

Yahya himself left Dacca on the night of 25th March after having unleashed the Pakistan Army, with an open license to commit genocide on all Bengalis. His own justification for this act of barbarism was not forthcoming till 8 P.M. the next day when the world was given its first explanation for the unleashing of this holocaust. This statement was self-contradictory and laced with positive lies. His branding of a party as traitors and outlaws, with whom he had only 48 hours ago been negotiating for a peaceful transfer of power, bore no relationship to the situation in Bangla Desh or the course of the negotiations. His promise to hand over power to the elected representatives of the people after banning the Awami League which was the sole representative of Bangla Desh and held a majority of seats in the National Assembly was a mockery of the freely recorded voice of 75 million Bengalis. The crudity of the statement was clear evidence that was no longer interested in taking shelter behind either logic or morality and had reverted to the law of the jungle in his bid to crush the people of Bangla Desh.

Pakistan is now dead and buried under a mountain of corpses. The hundreds and thousands of people murdered by the army in Bangla Desh will act as an impenetrable barrier between West Pakistan and the people of Bangla Desh. By resorting to pre-planned genocide must have known that he was himself digging Pakistan's grave. The subsequent massacres perpetrated on his orders by his licensed killers on the people were not designed to preserve the unity of a nation. They were acts of racial hatred and sadism devoid of even the elements of humanity. Professional Soldiers, on orders, violated their code of military honour and were seen as beasts of prey who indulged in an orgy of murder, rape, loot, arson and destruction unequaled in the annals of civilization. These acts indicate that the concept of two countries is already deeply rooted in the minds of and his associates who would not dare commit such atrocities on their own countrymen.

Yahya's genocide is thus without political purpose. It serves only as the last act in the tragic history of Pakistan which has chosen to write with the blood of the people of Bangla Desh. The objective is genocide and scorched-earth before his troops are either driven out or perish. In this time he hopes to liquidate our political leadership, intelligence and administration, to destroy our industries and public amenities and as a final act he intends to raze our cities to the ground. Already his occupation army has made substantial progress towards this objective. Bangla Desh will be set back 50 years as West Pakistan's parting gift to a people they have exploited for 23 years for their own benefit.

This is a point of major significance to those great powers that choose to ignore this largest single act of genocide since the days of Belsen and Auschwitz. If they think they are preserving the unity of Pakistan they can forget it because himself has no illusions about the future of Pakistan.

They must realize that Pakistan is dead and murdered by - and that independent Bangla Desh is a reality sustained by the indestructible will and courage of 75 million Bengalis who are daily nurturing the roots of this new nationhood with their blood. No power on earth can unmake this new nation and sooner or later both big and small powers will have to accept it into the world fraternity.

It is therefore, in the interest of politics as much as humanity for the big powers to put their full pressure on to cage his killers and bring them back to West Pakistan. We will be eternally grateful to the people of USSR and India and the freedom loving people of all countries for their full support they have already given us in this struggle. We would welcome similar support from the Peoples Republic of China, USA, France, Great Britain and all Afro Asian countries who have freed themselves from colonial rule and from all freedom loving countries. Each in their own way should exercise considerable leverage on West Pakistan; and were they to exercise this influence, could not sustain his war of aggression against Bangla Desh for a single day longer.

Bangla Desh will be the eighth most populous country in the world. Its only goal will be to rebuild the nation from the ashes and carnage left behind by Yahya's occupation army. It will be a stupendous task because of destruction of economy by Yahya's army in our already underdeveloped and overpopulated region. But we now have a cause and a people who have been hardened in the resistance, who have shed their blood for their nation and won their freedom in an epic struggle which pitted unarmed people against a modern army. Such a nation cannot fail in its task of securing the foundations of its nationhood.

In our struggle for survival we seek the friendship of all people, the big powers and the small. We do not aspire to join any bloc or pact but will seek assistance from those who give it in a spirit of goodwill free from any desire to control our destinies. We have struggled far too long for our self determination to permit ourselves to become anyone's satellite.

We now appeal to the nations of the world for recognition and assistance both material and moral in our struggle for nationhood. Every day this is delayed a thousand lives are lost and more of Bangla Desh's vital assets are destroyed. In the name of Humanity act now and earn our undying friendship.

This we now present to the world as the CASE of the people of Bangla Desh. Bangla Desh has earned her right to recognition at great cost, as the people of Bangla Desh made sacrifices of unequal magnitude and fought hard in order to establish the rightful place for Bangla Desh in the community of Nations.

# Appendix 2

## Vaddukoddai Resolution

THE RESOLUTION WAS adopted at the first National Convention of the Tamil United Liberation Front (TULF) on 14 May 1976. TULF's participation in the 1977 general elections was anchored in this Resolution. In this Resolution, the TULF declared its intent of forming a sovereign State of Tamil Eelam. S. J. V. Chelavanayakam presided over the Convention. The following is a translation of the Resolution, which was originally adopted in Tamil.

Whereas, throughout the centuries from the dawn of history, the Sinhalese and Tamil nations have divided between themselves the possession of Ceylon, the Sinhalese inhabiting the interior of the country in its Southern and Western parts from the river Walawe to that of Chilaw and the Tamils possessing the Northern and Eastern districts; And,

Whereas, the Tamil kingdom was overthrown in war and conquered by the Portuguese in 1619, and from them by the Dutch and the British in turn, independent of the Sinhalese Kingdoms; And,

Whereas, the British colonists, who ruled the territories of the Sinhalese and Tamil kingdoms separately, joined under compulsion the territories of the Sinhalese and the Tamil Kingdoms for purposes of administrative convenience on the recommendation of the Colebrooke Commission in 1833; And,

Whereas, the Tamil leaders were in the forefront of the freedom movement to rid Ceylon of colonial bondage which ultimately led to the grant of independence to Ceylon in 1948; And,

---

Reproduced with permission from *South Asia Terrorism Portal* http://www.satp.org/satporgtp/countries/shrilanka/document/papers/vaddukoddai_resolution.htm

Whereas, the foregoing facts of history were completely overlooked, and power over the entire country was transferred to the Sinhalese nation on the basis of a numerical majority, thereby reducing the Tamil nation to the position of subject people; And,

Whereas, successive Sinhalese governments since independence have always encouraged and fostered the aggressive nationalism of the Sinhalese people and have used their political power to the detriment of the Tamils by:

(a) Depriving one half of the Tamil people of their citizenship and franchise rights thereby reducing Tamil representation in Parliament,
(b) Making serious inroads into the territories of the former Tamil Kingdom by a system of planned and state-aided Sinhalese colonization and large scale regularization of recently encouraged Sinhalese encroachments, calculated to make the Tamils a minority in their own homeland,
(c) Making Sinhala the only official language throughout Ceylon thereby placing the stamp of inferiority on the Tamils and the Tamil language,
(d) Giving the foremost place to Buddhism under the Republican Constitution thereby reducing the Hindus, Christians, and Muslims to second class status in this country,
(e) Denying to the Tamils equality of opportunity in the spheres of employment, education, land alienation and economic life in general and starving Tamil areas of large scale industries and development schemes thereby seriously endangering their very existence in Ceylon,
(f) Systematically cutting them off from the main-stream of Tamil cultures in South India while denying them opportunities of developing their language and culture in Ceylon, thereby working inexorably towards the cultural genocide of the Tamils,
(g) Permitting and unleashing communal violence and intimidation against the Tamil speaking people as happened in Amparai and Colombo in 1956; all over the country in 1958; army reign of terror in the Northern and Eastern Provinces in 1961; police violence at the International Tamil Research Conference in 1974 resulting in the death of nine persons in Jaffna; police and communal violence against Tamil speaking Muslims at Puttalam and various other parts of Ceylon in 1976—all these calculated to instill terror in the minds of the Tamil speaking people, thereby breaking their spirit and the will to resist injustices heaped on them,
(h) By terrorizing, torturing, and imprisoning Tamil youths without trial for long periods on the flimsiest grounds,
(i) Capping it all by imposing on the Tamil nation a Constitution drafted, under conditions of emergency without opportunities for free discussion, by a Constituent Assembly elected on the basis of the Soulbury Constitution distorted by the citizenship laws resulting in weightage in representation to the Sinhalese majority, thereby depriving the Tamils of even the remnants of safeguards they had under the earlier constitution; And,

Whereas, all attempts by the various Tamil political parties to win their rights, by co-operating with the governments, by parliamentary and extra-parliamentary agitations, by entering into pacts and understandings with successive Prime Ministers, in order to achieve the bare minimum of political rights consistent with the self-respect of the Tamil people have proved to be futile; And,

Whereas, the efforts of the All Ceylon Tamil Congress to ensure non-domination of the minorities by the majority by the adoption of a scheme of balanced representation in a Unitary Constitution have failed and even the meager safeguards provided in article 29 of the Soulbury Constitution against discriminatory legislation have been removed by the Republican Constitution; And,

Whereas, the proposals submitted to the Constituent Assembly by the Ilankai Thamil Arasu Kadchi for maintaining the unity of the country while preserving the integrity of the Tamil people by the establishment of an autonomous Tamil State within the framework of a Federal Republic of Ceylon were summarily and totally rejected without even the courtesy of a consideration of its merits; And,

Whereas, the amendments to the basic resolutions, intended to ensure the minimum of safeguards to the Tamil people moved on the basis of the nine point demands formulated at the conference of all Tamil Political parties at Valvettithurai on 7th February 1971 and by individual parties and Tamil members of Parliament including those now in the government party, were rejected in toto by the government and Constituent Assembly; And,

Whereas, even amendments to the draft proposals relating to language, religion, and fundamental-rights including one calculated to ensure that at least the provisions of the Tamil Language (Special Provisions) Regulations of 1956 be included in the Constitution, were defeated, resulting in the boycott of the Constituent Assembly by a large majority of the Tamil members of Parliament; And,

Whereas, the Tamil United Liberation Front, after rejecting the Republican Constitution adopted on the 22nd of May, 1972, presented a six point demand to the Prime Minister and the Government on 25th June, 1972, and gave three months time within which the Government was called upon to take meaningful steps to amend the Constitution so as to meet the aspirations of the Tamil Nation on the basis of the six points, and informed the Government that if it failed to do so the Tamil United Liberation Front would launch a non-violent direct action against the Government in order to win the freedom and the rights of the Tamil Nation on the basis of the right of self-determination; And,

Whereas, this last attempt by the Tamil United Liberation Front to win Constitutional recognition of the rights of the Tamil Nation without jeopardizing the unity of the country was callously ignored by the Prime Minister and the Government; And,

Whereas, the opportunity provided by the Tamil United Liberation Front leader to vindicate the Government's contention that their constitution had the backing of the Tamil people, by resigning from his membership of the National State Assembly and creating a by-election was deliberately put off for over two years in utter disregard of the democratic right of the Tamil voters of Kankesanthurai, And,

Whereas, in the by-election held on the 6th February 1975, the voters of Kankesanthurai by a preponderant majority not only rejected the Republican Constitution imposed on them by the Sinhalese Government, but also gave a mandate to Mr. S.J.V. Chelvanayakam, Q.C. and through him to the Tamil United Liberation Front for the restoration and reconstitution of the Free Sovereign, Secular, Socialist State of Tamil Eelam.

The first National Convention of the Tamil United Liberation Front meeting at Pannakam (Vaddukoddai Constituency) on the 14th day of May, 1976, hereby declares that the Tamils of Ceylon by virtue of their great language, their religions, their separate culture and heritage, their history of independent existence as a separate state over a distinct territory for several centuries till they were conquered by the armed might of the European invaders and above all by their will to exist as a separate entity ruling themselves in their own territory, are a nation distinct and apart from Sinhalese and this Convention announces to the world that the Republican Constitution of 1972 has made the Tamils a slave nation ruled by the new colonial masters, the Sinhalese ,who are using the power they have wrongly usurped to deprive the Tamil Nation of its territory, language citizenship, economic life, opportunities of employment and education, thereby destroying all the attributes of nationhood of the Tamil people.

And, while taking note of the reservations in relation to its commitment to the setting up of a separated state of Tamil Eelam expressed by the Ceylon Workers Congress as a Trade Union of the Plantation Workers, the majority of whom live and work outside the Northern and Eastern areas,

This convention resolves that restoration and reconstitution of the Free, Sovereign, Secular, Socialist State of Tamil Eelam, based on the right of self determination inherent to every nation, has become inevitable in order to safeguard the very existence of the Tamil Nation in this Country.

This Convention further declares:

- That the State of Tamil Eelam shall consist of the people of the Northern and Eastern provinces and shall also ensure full and equal rights of citizenship of the State of Tamil Eelam to all Tamil speaking people living in any part of Ceylon and to Tamils of Eelam origin living in any part of the world who may opt for citizenship of Tamil Eelam.
- That the constitution of Tamil Eelam shall be based on the principle of democratic decentralization so as to ensure the non-domination of any religious or territorial community of Tamil Eelam by any other section.
- That in the state of Tamil Eelam caste shall be abolished and the observance of the pernicious practice of untouchability or inequality of any type based on birth shall be totally eradicated and its observance in any form punished by law.
- That Tamil Eelam shall be a secular state giving equal protection and assistance to all religions to which the people of the state may belong.
- That Tamil shall be the language of the State, but the rights of Sinhalese speaking minorities in Tamil Eelam to education and transaction of business in their language shall be protected on a reciprocal basis with the Tamil speaking minorities in the Sinhala State.
- That Tamil Eelam shall be a Socialist State wherein the exploitation of man by man shall be forbidden, the dignity of labor shall be recognized, the means of production and distribution shall be subject to public ownership and control while permitting private enterprise in these branches within limit prescribed by law, economic development shall be on the basis of socialist planning and there shall be a ceiling on the total wealth that any individual of family may acquire.

This Convention directs the Action Committee of the Tamil United Liberation Front to formulate a plan of action and launch without undue delay the struggle for winning the sovereignty and freedom of the Tamil Nation;

And this Convention calls upon the Tamil Nation in general and the Tamil youth in particular to come forward to throw themselves fully into the sacred fight for freedom and to flinch not till the goal of a sovereign state of Tamil Eelam is reached.

# Appendix 3

# Article 370 of the Constitution of India

{370. TEMPORARY PROVISIONS WITH respect of the State of Jammu and Kashmir}

1. Notwithstanding anything in this Constitution:
   a. the provisions of article 238 shall not apply in relation to the State of Jammu and Kashmir,
   b. the power of Parliament to make laws for the said State shall be limited to;
      i. those matters in the Union List and the Concurrent List which, in consultation with the Government of the State, are declared by the President to correspond to matters specified in the Instrument of Accession governing the accession of the State to the Dominion of India as the matters with respect to which the Dominion Legislature may make laws for that State; and
      ii. such other matters in the said Lists, as, with the concurrence of the Government of the State, the President may by order specify.

      Explanation—For the purpose of this article, the Government of the State means the person for the time being recognised by the President as the Maharaja of Jammu and Kashmir acting on the advice of the Council of Ministers for the time being in office under the Maharaja's Proclamation dated the fifth day of March, 1948;
   c. he provisions of article 1 and of this article shall apply in relation to this State;
   d. such of the other provisions of this Constitution shall apply in relation to that State subject to such exceptions and modifications as the President may by order specify

---

Reproduced with permission from *South Asia Terrorism Portal* http://www.satp.org/satporgtp/countries/india/states/jandk/documents/actsandordinances/article_370_constitution_india.htm

i. Provided that no such order which relates to the matters specified in the Instrument of Accession of the State referred to in paragraph (i) of sub-clause (b) shall be issued except in consultation with the Government of the State:
ii. Provided further that no such order which relates to matters other than those referred to in the last preceding proviso shall be issued except with the concurrence of the Government.

2. If the concurrence of the Government of the State referred to in paragraph (ii) of sub-clause (b) of clause (1) or in second proviso to sub-clause (d) of that clause be given before the Constituent Assembly for the purpose of framing the Constitution of the State is convened, it shall be placed before such Assembly for such decision as it may take thereon.
3. Notwithstanding anything in the foregoing provisions of the article, the President may, by public notification, declare that this article shall cease to be operative or shall be operative only with such exceptions and modifications and from such date as he may notify:

   Provided that the recommendation of the Constituent Assembly of the State referred to in clause (2) shall be necessary before the President issues such a notification.
4. In exercise of the powers conferred by this article the President, on the recommendation of the Constituent Assembly of the State of Jammu and Kashmir, declared that, as from the 17th day of November, 1952, the said art. 370 shall be operative with the modification that for the explanation in cl.(1) thereof the following Explanation is substituted namely:

   Explanation—For the purpose of this Article, the Government of the State means the person for the time being recognised by the President on the recommendation of the Legislative Assembly of the State as the *Sadar-I-Riyasat of Jammu and Kashmir, acting on the advice of Council of Ministers of the State for the time being in office.

# Appendix 4

# Anandpur Sahib Resolution

## THE RESOLUTION

Adopted, in the light of the Anandpur Sahib Resolution, at the open session of the 18th All India Akali Conference held at Ludhiana on 28–29 October, 1978 under the Presidentship of Jathedar Jagdev Singh Talwandi are as under:

(It was after the passing of these Resolutions that Shiromani Akali Dal started the struggle therefore).

## RESOLUTION NO. 1

Moved by S. Gurcharan Singh Tohra, President Shiromani Gurdwara Prabandhak Committee and endorsed by S. Prakash Singh Badal, Chief Minister, Punjab.

The Shiromani Akali Dal realizes that India is a federal and republican geographical entity of different languages, religions and cultures. To safeguard the fundamental rights of the religious and linguistic minorities, to fulfil the demands of the democratic traditions and to pave the way for economic progress it has become imperative that the Indian constitutional infrastructure should be given a real federal shape by redefining the Central and State relations and rights on the line of aforesaid principles and objectives.

---

Authenticated by Sant Harchand Singh Longowal. Reproduced with permission from *South Asia Terrorism Portal* http://www.satp.org/satporgtp/countries/india/states/punjab/document/papers/anantpur_sahib_resolution.htm

The concept of the total revolution given by Lok Naik Sh. Jaya Parkash Narain also based upon the progressive decentralization of powers. The climax of the process of centralization of powers of the states through repeated amendments of the Constitution during the Congress regime came before the countrymen in the form of the Emergency, when all fundamental rights of all citizens were usurped. It was then that the programme of decentralization of powers ever advocated by Shiromani Akali Dal was openly accepted and adopted by other political parties including Janata Party, C.P.I. (M), A.D.M.K. etc.

Shiromani Akali Dal has ever stood firm on this principle and that is why after very careful considerations it unanimously adopted a resolution to this effect first at all India Akali Conference, Batala, then at Shri Anandpur Sahib which has endorsed the principle of State autonomy in keeping with the concept of Federalism.

As such, the Shiromani Akali Dal emphatically urges upon the Janata Government to take cognizance of the different linguistic and cultural sections, religious minorities as also the voice of millions of people and recast the constitutional structure of the country on real and meaningful federal principles to obviate the possibility of any danger to National unity and the integrity of the Country and further, to enable the states to play a useful role for the progress and prosperity of the Indian people in their respective areas by the meaningful exercise of the powers.

## RESOLUTION NO. 2

The momentous meeting of the Shiromani Akali Dal calls upon the Government of India to examine the long tale of the excesses, wrongs illegal actions committed by the previous Congress government, more particularly during Emergency, and try to find an early solution to the following problems:

a. Chandigarh originally raised as a Capital for Punjab should be handed over to Punjab.
b. The long standing demand of the Shiromani Akali Dal for the merger in Punjab of the Punjabi speaking areas, to be identified by linguistic experts with village as an unit, should be conceded.
c. The control of Head Works should continue to be vested in Punjab and, if need be, the Reorganization Act should be amended.
d. The arbitrary and unjust Award given by Mrs. Indira Gandhi during the Emergency on the distribution of Ravi-Beas waters should be revised on the universally accepted norms and principles, thereby justice be done to Punjab.
e. Keeping in view the special aptitude and martial qualities of the Sikhs the present ratio of their strength in Army should be maintained.
f. The excess being committed on the settlers in the Terai region of UP in the name of Land Reforms should be vacated by making suitable amendments in the Ceiling Law on the Central guidelines.

## RESOLUTION NO. 3

(Economic Policy Resolution)

The chief sources of inspiration of the economic politics and programme of the Shiromani Akali Dal are the secular, democratic and socialistic concepts of Sri Guru Nanak Dev and Sri Guru Gobind Singh Ji. Our Economic programme is based on three basic principles.

a. Dignity of Labour.
b. An economic and social structure which provides for the uplift of the poor and depressed sections of society.
c. Unabated opposition to concentration of economic and political power in the hands of the capitalists.

While drafting its economic policies and programme, the Shiromani Akali Dal in its historic Anandpur Sahib Resolution had laid particular on the need to break the monopolistic hold of the capitalists foisted on the Indian economy by 30 years of Congress rule in India. This capitalistic hold enabled the central government to assume all powers in its hands after the manner of Mughal Imperialism. This was bound to thwart the economic progress of the states and injure the social and economic interests of the people. The Shiromani Akali Dal once again reiterates the Sikh way of life by resolving to fulfill the holy words of Guru Nank Dev:

"He alone realizes the True Path who labours honestly and shares the fruits of that Labour."

This way of life is based upon three basic principles:

i. Doing honest labour.
ii. Sharing the fruits of this labour, and
iii. Meditation on the Lord's Name.

The Shiromani Akali Dal calls upon the Central and the State Government to eradicate unemployment during the next ten years. While pursuing this aim special emphasis should be laid on ameliorating the lot of the weaker sections, Scheduled and depressed classes, workers, landless and poor farmers and urban poor. Minimum wages should be fixed for them all.

The Shiromani Akali Dal urges upon the Punjab Government to draw up such an economic plan for the State as would turn it into the leading province during the next ten years, by raising per capita income to Rs. 3,000 and by generating an economic growth rate of 7% per annum as against 4% at National level.

The Shiromani Akali Dal gives first priority to the redrafting of the taxation structure in such a way that the burden of taxation is shifted from the poor to the richer classes and an equitable distribution of National income is ensured.

The main plank of the economic programme of the Shiromani Akali Dal is enable the economically weaker sections of the Society to share the fruits of National income.

The Shiromani Akali Dal calls upon the Central Government to make an international air-field at Amritsar which should also enjoy the facilities of a dry port. Similarly a Stock Exchange should be opened at Ludhiana to accelerate the process of industrialisation and economic growth in the State. The Shiromani Akali Dal also desires that suitable amendments should be made in the Foreign Exchange rules for free exchange of foreign currencies and thereby removing the difficulties being faced by the Indian emigrants.

The Shiromani Akali Dal emphatically urges upon the Indian Government to bring a parity between the prices of the agricultural produce and that of the industrial raw materials so that the discrimination against such states which lack these materials may be removed.

The Shiromani Akali Dal demand that exploitation of the producers of the cash crops like cotton, sugarcane, oil seeds etc. at the hands of the traders should be stopped forthwith and for such a purpose arrangements for the purchase of these crops by the government, at remunerative prices should be made. Besides, effective steps should be taken by the government for the purchase of cotton through the Cotton Corporation.

The Shiromani Akali Dal strongly feels that most pressing National problem is the need to ameliorate the lot of millions of exploited persons belonging to the scheduled classes. For such a purpose the Shiromani Akali Dal calls upon the Central and State Governments to earmark special funds. Besides the State Governments should allot sufficient funds in their respective budgets for giving free residential plots both in the urban and rural areas to the Scheduled Castes.

The Shiromani Akali Dal also calls for the rapid diversification of farming. The shortcomings in the Land Reforms Laws should be removed, rapid industrialization of the State, ensured the credit facilities for the medium industries, expanded and unemployment allowance given to those who are unemployed. For remunerative farming perceptive reduction should be made in the prices of farm machinery like tractors, tubewells as also the inputs etc.

## RESOLUTION NO. 4

This huge session of the Shiromani Akali Dal regards the discrimination to which the Punjabi language is being subjected in the adjoining States of Himachal, Haryana, Delhi and Jammu and Kashmir etc. It is firm demand that in accordance with the Nehru Language Formula the neighbouring States of Punjab should give second language status to the Punjabi language because a fairly large sections of their respective population are Punjabi speaking.

## RESOLUTION NO. 5

The meeting regrets the claims of the refugees who had migrated to Jammu and Kashmir as a result of the partition of the country, no compensation has been provided to them even after such a long time and these unfortunate refugees are rotting in the camps ever since then.

The Akali Dal Session therefore forcefully demands that their claims should be soon settled and immediate steps should be taken to rehabilitate them even if it involves an amendment in Section 370.

## RESOLUTION NO. 6

The 18th session of the All India Conference takes strong exception to the discrimination to which the minorities in other states are being subjected and the way in which their interests are being ignored. As such, it demands that injustice against the Sikhs in other states should be stopped and proper representation should be accorded them in government service, local bodies, and state legislatures, through nominations, if need be.

## RESOLUTION NO. 7

The 18th session of the All India Conference notes with satisfaction that mechanization of farming in the country handled to increase in the farm yield and as a result the country is heading towards self-sufficiency.

However, the session feels that poor farmers are unable to take to mechanization because of the enormity of the cost involved.

As such, the Shiromani Akali Dal urges upon the Government of India to abolish the excise duty on tractors so that with the decrease in their prices the ordinary farmers may also be able to avail of farm machinery and contribute to the growth of gross agricultural produce of the country.

## RESOLUTION NO. 8

The meeting of the Shiromani Akali Dal appeals to the Central and State Government to pay particular attention to the poor and labouring classes and demands that besides making suitable amendments in the Minimum Wages Act, suitable legal steps should be taken to improve the economic lot of the labouring class to enable it to lead a respectable life and play a useful role in the rapid industrialization of the country.

## RESOLUTION NO. 9

This session seeks permission from the Government of India to install a broadcasting station at Golden Temple, Amritsar, for the relay of "Gurbani Kirtan" for the spiritual satisfaction of those Sikhs who are living in foreign lands.

The session wishes to make it clear that the entire cost of the proposed Broadcasting Project would be borne by the Khalsa Panth and its over-all control shall vest with the Indian Government. We have every hope that the government would have no hesitation in conceding this demand after the consideration.

## RESOLUTION NO. 10

The huge Session of the Shiromani Akali Dal strongly urges upon the Government of India to make necessary amendments in the following enactments for the benefit of the agricultural classes who have toiled hard for the larger national interests:

1. By suitable amendment in the relevant clause of the Hindu Succession Act, a women should be given rights of inheritance in the properties of her father-in-law instead of the father's.
2. The agricultural land of the farmers should be completely exempted from the Wealth Tax and the Estate Duty.

## RESOLUTION NO. 11

The vast Session of the Shiromani Akali Dal strongly impresses upon the Government of India that keeping in view the economic backwardness of the scheduled and non-scheduled castes provisions proportionate to population should be made in the budget for utilization for their welfare. A special ministry should be created at the Central as a practical measure to render justice to them on the basis of the reservation.

The Session also calls upon the government that in keeping with the settlement already no discrimination should be made between the Sikh and Hindu Harijans in any part of the country.

## RESOLUTION NO. 12

The Congress government is called upon to vacate the gross injustice discrimination done to Punjab in the distribution of Ravi-Beas waters. The Central Government must also give approval for the immediate establishment of six sugar and four textile mills in Punjab so that the state may be able to implement its agro-industrial policy.

## BASIC POSTULATES OF THE SHIROMANI AKALI DAL

As adopted by the working committee of the Shiromani Akali Dal at its meeting held at Sri Anandpur Sahib on 16–17 October, 1973.

### (A) Postulates

1. The Shiromani Akali Dal is the very embodiment of the hopes and aspirations of the Sikh Nation and as such is fully entitled to its representation. The basic postulates of this Organization are Human progress and ultimate unity of all human beings with the Spiritual Soul.
2. These postulates are based upon the three great principles of Guru Nanak Dev Ji, namely, a Meditation on God's Name, dignity of labour and sharing of fruits of this Labour.(Nam Japo, Kirat Karo, Wand Chhako)

### (B) Purposes

This Shiromani Akali Dal shall ever strive to achieve the following aims:

1. Reiteration of the unicity (Oneness) of God, meditation on His Name, recitation of Gurbani, renewal of faith on the ten Holy Sikh Gurus and the Holy Sri Guru Granth Sahib and other appropriate measures for such a purpose.
2. Grooming accomplished preachers, Ragis, Dhandis, and poets in the Sikhs Missionary College for a more effective propagation of Sikhism, Sikh Philosophy, belief in Sikh code of conduct and Kirtan etc. at home and abroad, in schools and colleges, in villages and in cities as indeed at every place.
3. Baptising the Sikhs (Amrit Prachar) on a vast scale, with particular emphasis on Schools and College of which the teachers and the taught shall be enthused through regular study circles.
4. Reinculcate the religious practice of "DASWAND" among the Sikhs. (Given one tenth of one's earnings for the welfare of the Community).
5. Generating feelings of respect for the Sikh intellectuals, writers, preachers, granthis, etc., who also in turn, would be enthused to improve upon their accomplishments while conforming to the basic Sikh tenets and traditions.
6. Streamlining the Gurdwara administration by giving better training to their workers. Appropriate steps would also be taken to maintain Gurdwara buildings in proper condition. For such a purpose, the party representatives in the Shiromani Gurdwara Prabandhak Committee and local Committees would be directed time to time to pull their weight.
7. Making appropriate arrangements for the error free publication of Gurbani; promoting research work in the ancient and modern Sikh history as also its publication; rendering Gurbani in other languages and producing first rate literature on Sikhism.
8. Taking appropriate steps for the enactment of an All India Gurdwara Act with a view to introduce improvements in the administration of the Gurdwaras throughout the country and to reintegrate the traditional preaching sects to Sikhism like Udasis and Nirmalas with the mainstream of Sikhism without in any way encroaching on the properties of the respective individuals "maths."

9. Taking such steps as may be necessary to bring the Sikh Gurdwaras all over the world under a single system of administration with a view to run them according to the basic Sikh norms and to pool their sources for the dissemination of Sikhism on a wider and more impressive scale.

Striving for free access to all those holy Sikh Shrines, including Nankana Sahib from which the Sikh Panth has been separated, for pilgrimage and proper upkeep.

## POLITICAL GOAL

The political goal of the Panth without doubt, is enshrined in the commandments of the Tenth Lord, in the pages of Sikh history and in the very heart of the Khalsa Panth, the ultimate objective of which is the pre-eminence of the Khalsa.

The fundamental policy of the Shiromani Akali Dal is to seek the realization of this birth right of the Khalsa through creation of congenial environment and a political set up.

For attainment of this aim

1. The Shiromani Akali Dal is determined to strive by all possible means to:
   a. Have, all those Punjabi speaking areas deliberately kept on: of Punjab, such as Dalhousie in Gurdaspur District; Chandigarh; Pinjore-Kalka and Ambala Saddar etc. in Ambala District; the entire Una tehsils of Hoshiarpur District; the "Desh" area of Nalagarh; Shahabad and Gulha blocks of Karnal District; Tohana Sub-Tehsil, Ratia block and Sirsa tehsil of Hissar District and six tehsil of Ganganagar District in Rajasthan; merged with Punjab to constitute a single administrative unit where the interests of the Sikhs and Sikhism are specifically protected.
   b. It this new Punjab and in other States the Centre's interference would be restricted to Defence, Foreign relations Currency and General Communication; all other departments would be in the jurisdiction of Punjab (and other states) which would be fully entitled to frame own laws on these subjects for administration. For the above departments of the Centre, Punjab and other States contribute in the proportion to representation in the Parliament.
   c. The Sikhs and other religious minorities living out of Punjab should be adequately protected against any kind of discrimination.
2. The Shiromani Akali Dal would also endeavour to have the Indian Constitution recast on real federal principles, with equal representation at the Centre for all the States.
3. The Shiromani Akali Dal strongly denounces the foreign policy of India framed by the Congress party. It is worthless, hopeless and highly detrimental to the interests of the country, the Nation and the mankind at large. Shiromani Akali Dal shall extend its support only to that foreign policy of India which is based on the principles of peace and national interests. It strongly advocates a policy of peace with all neighbouring countries, especially those inhabited by the Sikhs and their sacred shrines. The Akali Dal is of the firm view that our foreign policy should in no case play second fiddle to that of any other country.

4. The Shiromani Akali Dal shall raise its firm voice against any discrimination against any Sikh (or even other) employees of the Central or State Governments. The Shiromani Akali Dal shall also endeavour to maintain the traditional position of the Sikhs in all the wings of the defence departments and the Panth would pay particular attention to the needs of the Sikh Armymen. The Shiromani Akali Dal would also see that "kirpan" is accepted as an integral part of the Uniform of the Sikhs in Army.
5. It shall be the primary duty of the Shiromani Akali Dal to help rehabilitate the ex-servicemen of the Defence Departments in the civil life and or such a purpose it would extend them every help to enable them to organize themselves so that they are able to raise their voice in an effective way of giving adequate concessions and proper safeguards for a life of self-respect and dignity.
6. The Shiromani Akali Dal is of the firm opinion that all those persons males or females— who have not been convicted of any criminal offences by a court of law, should be at liberty to possess all types of small arms, like revolvers, guns, pistols, rifles, carbines etc., without any licence, the only obligation being their registration.
7. The Shiromani Akali Dal seeks ban on the sale of liquor and other intoxicants and shall press for prohibition on the consumption of intoxicants and smoking on public places.

## THE ECONOMIC POLICY AND PROGRAMME OF THE SHIROMANI AKALI DAL

As adopted by its Working Committee on 17th October, 1973 at its meeting held at Sri Anandpur Sahib:

Although the mainstay of the Indian economy is agriculture and all those political powers who claim to raise social structure on the basis of justice cannot afford to ignore this fact, yet this is a hard fact that the levers of economic powers, continue to be in the hands of big traders, capitalists and monopolists. Some marginal benefits might have accrued to other classes, but the benefits of economic growth have been reaped by these categories during the last 26 years after Independence. The political power has also been misappropriated by these classes which are wielding the same for their own benefits. As such, any peaceful attempt to usher in a new era of social justice would have to break the economic and political strongholds of these categories of the people.

The Shiromani Akali Dal strongly advocates that the growing gulf between the rich and the poor, in the urban and rural areas both, should be abridged but, it is of the firm opinion that, for such a purpose, the first assault would have to be made on the classes who have assumed all the reins of economic power in their hands. In rural areas, the Akali Dal determined to help the weaker classes, like the scheduled castes, backward classes, landless tenants, ordinary labourers, the poor and middle class farmers. For such a purpose, it stands for meaningful land reforms which envisage a ceiling of 30 standard acres and the distribution of excess land among the poor farmers.

The motto of the Shiromani Akali Dal is to provide employment for all, requisite food and clothing for all, a house to live in, suitable transport and to create means to fulfil all those necessities of a civilized life without which life appears incomplete.

As such, the economic policy of the Shiromani Akali Dal shall endeavour to achieve the following objectives:

## AGRICULTURE SECTOR

During recent years the agriculture sector has witnessed land reforms and green revolution. The Shiromani Akali Dal undertakes to enrich the green revolution by an increase in yield per acre. It shall also ensure perceptible improvement in the standard of living of all rural classes, more particularly of the poor and the middle class farmers, as also the landless labourers. For such a purpose it plans to work on the following lines:

a. Introducing land reforms and measures for increasing agricultural production with a view to remove the growing gap between the rich and the poor. For such a purpose the existing legislation on land ceiling would have to be revised and a firm ceiling of 30 standard acres per family would have to be enforced with proprietary rights to the actual tillers. The excess land would be distributed among the landless tenants and poor farmers, while the cultivable government land unused shall be distributed among the landless classes, especially the scheduled castes and tribes. While distributing such lands the interests of Harijans and landless labourers would be particularly taken care of. The Akali Dal would also consider the possibilities of allowing the tenants to service loans by mortgaging the land under their plough, as also prohibiting the scheduled castes/tribes and backward classes from mortgaging the land distributed among them.
b. The Shiromani Akali Dal shall work for the modernization of farming and would also try to enable the middle class and poor farmers to seek loans and inputs made available by different agencies.
c. The Shiromani Akali Dal shall try to fix the prices of the agricultural produce on the basis of the returns of the middle class farmers. Such prices would be notified well before the sowing seasons and only the State government would be empowered to fix such prices.
d. The Shiromani Akali Dal stands for complete nationalization of the wholesale trade in foodgrains through the establishment of State agencies.
e. The Shiromani Akali Dal strongly opposes the demarcation of food zones and the attendant restrictions on the movements of foodgrains. The whole country should be the single food zone.

The party shall make special efforts to bring the Thein Dam and the Bhatinda Thermal plants to a speedy completion so that increased and cheaper power and irrigation facilities are made available. Definite efforts would be made for the establishment of an Atomic power station in the state.

Co-operative societies would be set up in the rural areas. In all those areas where canal water is not available small irrigation projects would be taken in hand.

## INDUSTRIAL SECTOR

The Shiromani Akali Dal strongly advocates that all key industries should be under the public sector.

It is of the opinion that consumer industries should be immediately nationalized to stabilize the prices of the consumer goods and to save the poor consumer from exploitation at the hands of the industrialists and the middlemen.

The public sector industries should be established in such a way that the imbalance between different States is removed.

A planned effort to establish agro-industries in the rural areas should be made to relieve the growing population pressure in the urban areas. The industrial management should be democratized by enabling the workers to have a say in the management and by fair distribution of profits between the industrialists and the workers. The credit agencies, especially the nationalized banks, should be directed to invest a fixed ratio of their deposits in the rural areas. Every industrial unit beyond worth one crore assets should be brought under the public sector. The Akali Dal stands for progressive nationalization of Transport.

The Public Sector units should be fully autonomous and manned by competent young executives drawn from a central pool of talent.

### Economic Policy

The Shiromani Akali Dal demands that the whole tax structure be revised in such a way that the evasion of taxes and the flow of black money is completely eradicated. It stands for a straightforward system of taxation. The present infrastructure of taxation weighs heavily against the poor and enables the rich to bypass it. The party stands for a more realistic policy in this respect so that the black money running a parallel economy may be usefully employed.

### Workers, Middle Class Employees and Agricultural Labour.

For their benefits the Shiromani Akali Dal would try its best:

1. To fix need based wages for industrial workers.
2. To bring progressive improvement in the standard of living of government employees.
3. To re-assess the minimum wages of agricultural labour and to standard of living for them.
4. To take necessary steps to provide roofed accommodation for standard of living for them.
5. To take necessary steps to provide roofed accommodation for the rural and urban poor.

## UNEMPLOYMENT

The Shiromani Akali Dal stands for full employment in the country. For such a purpose it is of the firm opinion that the Govt. must provide immediate employment to the educated and trained persons, otherwise reasonable unemployment allowance should be paid to them. This amount should be shared by the centre and the state government. The minimum rates of such an allowance should be as under:

1. Matric and or trained hands
   50/- per month
2. B.A.
   70/- per month
3. M.A.
   100/- per month
4. Engineers and Doctors
   150/- per month
5. Other trained Labour
   50/- per month
6. All persons above the age of 65, should be given old-age pension.

## Weaker Section and Backward Classes

The Shiromani Akali Dal shall try to improve the economic conditions of the backward classes and weaker sections of Society by extending them facilities for education, employment and other concessions, to enable them to come at par with other sections of society. Foodgrains at cheaper rates would be made available to them.

## Educational and Cultural

The Shiromani Akali Dal aims at grooming the Sikhs into a strong and sturdy Nation highly educated, fully aware of its fundamental rights, very well versed in various arts and ever ready to honour the more outstanding of its sons. For such a purpose:

1. The Shiromani Akali Dal regards the educationalists, scientists, philosophers, poets, writers and artists of the Sikh Nation as its most prized asset.
2. The Shiromani Akali Dal stands for compulsory and free education upto matric standard.
3. To check the growing rate of unemployment, Shiromani Akali Dal would try to introduce such courses to study as would enable their students to get immediate employment on completion of a course.
4. The Shiromani Akali Dal shall make arrangements for the education of the rural and weaker Classes and would also make provision for the higher education of the more promising students among them.
5. Punjabi would be a compulsory subject for all students upto the matric standard.

6. Special attention would be paid to the science and technical field of education, with particular emphasis on the study of Nuclear physics and space science in the University.
7. The Shiromani Akali Dal shall try to improve the standard of games and bring them on level with international standards.

Sd/-
Giani Ajmer Singh
Secretary.
Dated: 1-8-1977
Shiromani Akali Dal.

# Notes

## Chapter 1

1. Although "international intervention" is often used broadly to include anything from humanitarian assistance to aiding and abetting to peacekeeping operations, I use it here in a narrower sense to refer to an external power using force, such as a military strike, to help insurgents obtain their goal of secession.

2. See Donald L. Horowitz, "Irredentas and Secession," in *Irredentism and International Politics,* ed. Naomi Chazan (Boulder, CO: Lynne Rienner, 1991), 9.

3. See Linda Bishai, "Altered States: Secession and the Problem of Liberal Theory," in *Theories of Secession,* ed. Percy B. Lehning (London: Routledge, 1998), 93.

4. See Abeysinghe M. Navaratna-Bandara, *The Management of Ethnic Secessionist Conflict: The Big Neighbor Syndrome* (Brookfield, VT: Dartmouth, 1995), 12.

5. Important works on neorealism include Kenneth Waltz's "Theory of International Relations," in *The Handbook of Political Science*, ed. Fred Greenstein and Nelson Polsby (Reading, MA: Addison-Wesley, 1975) and Kenneth Waltz's *Theory of International Politics* (Reading, MA: Addison-Wesley, 1979); Robert Gilpin, *War and Change in World Politics* (New York: Cambridge University Press, 1981). Also important are Stephen Walt, *The Origin of Alliances* (Ithaca, NY: Cornell University Press, 1987); Joseph Grieco, "Anarchy and the Limits of Cooperation: A Realist Critique of the Newest Liberal Institutionalism," *International Organization* 42 (Summer 1988), 485–507 and *Cooperation among Nations: Europe, America, and Non-Tariff Barriers to Trade* (Ithaca, NY: Cornell University Press, 1990).

6. Neorealism or structural realism emphasizes that states exist in an anarchic international system and, therefore, must provide for their own security in order to survive. This "self-help" system is responsible for balance of power between states in the international system. The emphasis is on systemic factors like power differences between states and is not on unit-level factors like ideology or pressures from inside the state. In Kenneth Waltz's own words, "state behavior varies more with differences of power than with differences

in ideology, in internal structure of property relations, or in governmental form. In self-help systems, the pressures of competition weigh more heavily than ideological preferences or internal political pressures." For more on this, see Waltz, "Reflections on *Theory of International Politics:* A Response to My Critics," in *Neorealism and Its Critics*, ed. Robert O. Keohane (New York: Columbia University Press, 1986) 329; and *Theory of International Politics*, 127–128.

7. Preventive wars refer to "those wars that are motivated by the fear that one's military power and potential are declining relative to that of a rising adversary." See Randall L. Schweller, "Democratic Structure and Preventive War: Are Democracies More Pacific?" *World Politics* 44 (January 1992), 235–269.

8. I distinguish between "alliance" and "international intervention in a secessionist war." For the purpose of this study, an alliance refers to an agreement between a secessionist group and an external power for the latter's help in military training, arms, and protection. In other words, when an external power agrees to provide the secessionist group with military training or monetary assistance, an alliance is formed.

9. See Herbert K. Tillema, "Foreign Overt Military Intervention in the Nuclear Age," *Journal of Peace Research* 26.2 (1989): 179.

10. Examples of these works include Michael E. Brown, ed., *The International Dimensions of Internal Conflict* (Cambridge, MA: MIT Press, 1996); George Modelski, "The International Relations of Internal War," in *International Aspects of Civil Strife*, ed. James N. Rosenau (Princeton, NJ: Princeton University Press, 1964), 14–44; Astri Suhrke and Lela Garner Noble, eds, *Ethnic Conflict in International Relations* (New York: Praeger, 1977); David A. Lake and Donald Rothchild, eds, *The International Spread of Ethnic Conflict: Fear, Diffusion, and Escalation* (Princeton, NJ: Princeton University Press, 1998); Ted Robert Gurr and Barbara Harff, eds, *Ethnic Conflict in World Politics* (Boulder and Oxford: Westview Press, 1994); Michael E. Brown, ed., *Ethnic Conflict and International Security* (Princeton, NJ: Princeton University Press, 1993); and Michael E. Brown, Owen R. Cote, Sean M. Lynn-Jones, and Steven E. Miller, eds, *Nationalism and Ethnic Conflict* (Cambridge, MA: MIT Press, 1997).

11. See Alex Heraclides, "Secessionist Minorities and External Involvement," *International Organization* 44.3 (Summer 1990): 341–379.

12. See Stephane Dion, "Why is Secession Difficult in Well-Established Democracies? Lessons from Quebec," *British Journal of Political Science* 26, no. 2 (April, 1996), 269–284.

13. See Michael Hechter, "The Dynamics of Secession," *Acta Sociologica* 35 (1992): 267–283.

14. Ibid.

15. See Ralph Premdas, "Secessionist Movements in Comparative Perspective," in *Secessionist Movements in Comparative Perspective,* ed. Ralph Premdas et al. (New York: John Wiley, 1990).

16. Ibid.

17. See John R. Wood, "Secession: A Comparative Analytical Framework," *Canadian Journal of Political Science* 16 (1981): 107–134.

18. See Rupen Cetinyan, "Ethnic Bargaining in the Shadow of Third-Party Intervention," *International Organization* 56.3 (Summer 2002): 645–677.

19. Examples of these include Colin H. Williams, ed., *National Separatism* (Cardiff: University of Wales Press, 1982); Alex Heraclides, *The Self-Determination of Minorities in*

*International Politics* (London: Frank Cass, 1991); Frederick L. Shiels, ed., *Ethnic Separatism and World Politics* (Lanham, MD: University Press of America, 1984); Ralph R. Premdas, S.W.R. de A. Samarasinghe, and Alan B. Anderson, eds, *Secessionist Movements in Comparative Perspective* (New York: St. Martin's Press, 1990); K.M. de Silva and R.J. May, eds, *Internationalization of Ethnic Conflict* (London: Pinter, 1991); Peter Janke, ed., *Ethnic and Religious Conflicts: Europe and Asia* (Brookfield, VT: Dartmouth, 1994); Metta Spencer, ed., *Separatism: Democracy and Disintegration* (Lanham, MD: Rowman & Littlefield, 1998); Rajat Ganguly, *Kin State Intervention in Ethnic Conflicts* (New Delhi: Sage, 1998).

20. See Stephen M. Walt, *The Origin of Alliances* (New York: Cornell University Press, 1987).

21. See Richard Ned Lebow, "Windows of Vulnerability. Do States Jump Through Them?" *International Security* 9 (Summer 1984), 147–186; Jack Levy, "Declining Power and the Preventive Motivation for War," *World Politics* 40 (1987): 82–107; Emerson M.S. Niou and Peter C. Odershook, "Preventive War and the Balance of Power," *Journal of Conflict Resolution* 31 (September 1987): 387–419; Randall L. Schweller, "Democratic Structure and Preventive War: Are Democracies More Pacific?" *World Politics* 44 (January 1992): 235–269; Stephen Van Evera, *Causes of War: Power and Roots of Conflict* (Ithaca, NY: Cornell University Press, 1999), chap. 5.

22. See Theda Skocpol, *States and Social Revolutions* (Cambridge, UK: Cambridge University Press, 1979), 36.

23. See Alexander L. George, "Case Studies and Theory Development: The Method of Structured, Focused Comparison," in *Diplomacy: New Approaches in History, Theory and Policy,* ed. Paul Gordon Laursen (New York: Free Press, 1979); Alexander L. George and Timothy J. McKeown, "Case Studies and Theories of Organizational Decisionmaking," in *Advances in Information Processing in Organizations,* vol. 2, ed. Robert F. Coulam and Richard A. Smith (Greenwich, CT: JA1Press, 1985).

24. See Alexander L. George and Richard Smoke, *Deterrence in American Foreign Policy: Theory and Practice* (New York: Columbia University Press), 96.

25. See Andrew Bennett and Alexander L. George, "Research Design Tasks in Case Study Methods," Paper presented at the McArthur Foundation Workshop on Case Study Methods, Belfer Center for Science and International Affairs (BCSIA), Harvard University (October 1997).

26. See Richard Smoke, *War: Controlling Escalation* (Cambridge, MA: Harvard University Press, 1977), 37.

27. Ibid.

28. Ibid.

29. See John Stuart Mill, "Two Methods of Comparison," in *Comparative Perspectives: Theories and Methods,* ed. Amitai Etzioni and Frederic L. Dubow (Boston: Little Brown, 1970). J.S. Mill's "method of difference" design corresponds to Przeworski's and Teune's "most similar systems" design. For an explanation, see David Collier's endnote 10 in "The Comparative Method" in *Political Science: The State of the Discipline II,* ed. Ada W. Finifter (Washington: American Political Science Association, 1993), where he says that whereas Przeworski's and Teune's labels of "similar" and "different" refer to whether the cases are matched, as opposed to contrasting, on a series of *background* variables, Mill's labels of "difference" and "agreement" refer to whether the cases are contrasting, as opposed to matched, on the *dependent* variable.

## Chapter 2

1. See Robert Gilpin, *War and Change in World Politics* (Cambridge, UK: Cambridge University Press, 1981), 18.

2. See Ernst Haas, *Beyond the Nation-State—Functionalism and International Organization* (Stanford, CA: Stanford University Press, 1964), 84.

3. See Naomi Chazan, "Approaches to the Study of Irredentism," in *Irredentism and International Politics,* ed. Naomi Chazan (Boulder, CO: Lynne Rienner, 1991), 1.

4. See Ishtiaq Ahmed, *State, Nation and Ethnicity in Contemporary South Asia* (London: Pinter, 1996), 27.

5. See John Herz, *Political Realism and Political Idealism* (Chicago: University of Chicago Press, 1951), 14.

6. Gilpin, *War and Change*, 85.

7. John Vasquez, *The War Puzzle* (Cambridge, UK: Cambridge University Press, 1993), 15.

8. Fred Frohock, *Normative Political Theory* (Englewood Cliffs, NJ: Prentice Hall, 1974), 56–60.

9. Vasquez, *The War Puzzle*, 15.

10. Gilpin, *War and Change*, 94.

11. See Hans Morgenthau, *Politics among Nations* (New York: Knopf, 1978).

12. Ibid., 173.

13. Dina Zinnes, "An Analytical Study of the Balance of Power Theories," *Journal of Peace Research* 4 (1967): 272.

14. Martin Wight, "The Balance of Power," in *Diplomatic Investigations,* ed. H. Butterfield and M. Wight (London: George, Allen, & Unwin,1966), 151. Here Wight lists nine distinct ways the concept has been used.

15. See Sheehan, *The Balance of Power: History and Theory* (New York: Routledge, 1996), 17.

16. Ibid.

17. Richard L. Merritt and Dina A. Zinnes, "Alternative Indexes of National Power," in *Power in World Politics,* ed. Richard J. Stoll and Michael D. Ward (Boulder and London: Lynne Rienner, 1989), 27. The authors maintain (and I quote them again from p. 27) "the attributes of the power concept are linked directly to arguments made within the theory."

18. Ted Robert Gurr, "War, Revolution, and the Growth of the Coercive State," *Comparative Political Studies*, 21.1 (1988): 46.

19. For earlier references to the concept of preventive war, see Thucydides' work *The Peloponnesian War,* trans. Rex Warner (New York: Penguin, 1954), v.23; also see Hans Morgenthau, *Politics among Nations*, 4th edn (New York: Knopf, 1967), 202–203; Gilpin, *War and Change*, 94; Michael Howard, *The Causes of War* (Cambridge, MA: Harvard University Press, 1983), 18. For the latest and most developed version of the idea of preventive war, see Dale Copeland, *The Origins of Major War* (Ithaca and London: Cornell University Press, 2000).

20. See Jack S. Levy, "Declining Power and the Preventive Motivation for War," *World Politics* 40 (October 1987): 87.

21. Randall L. Schweller, "Domestic Structure and Preventive War: Are Democracies More Pacific?" *World Politics* 44 (January 1992): 236.

22. Levy, "Declining Power," 82.

23. Ibid.

24. Ibid., 84.

25. John A. Vasquez, *The War Puzzle* (Cambridge, UK: Cambridge University Press, 1993), 75.

26. Paul F. Diehl, "Introduction: An Overview and Some Theoretical Guidelines," in *The Dynamics of Enduring Rivalries,* ed. Paul F. Diehl (Urbana and Chicago: University of Illinois Press, 1998), 4.

27. Ibid., 5

28. Zeev Maoz and Ben D. Mor, "Learning, Preference Change, and the Evolution of Enduring Rivalries," in *The Dynamics of Enduring Rivalries,* ed. Paul F. Diehl (Urbana and Chicago: University of Illinois Press, 1998), 129.

29. Ibid., 130.

30. Paul Diehl, "Arms Races to War: Testing Some Empirical Linkages," *Sociological Quarterly* 26.3 (1985): 334.

31. Frank Whelon Wayman and Daniel M. Jones, "Evolution of Conflict in Enduring Rivalries," Paper presented at the annual meeting of the International Studies Association, Vancouver, British Columbia, March 20–23, 1991.

32. See David A. Lake and Donald Rothchild, eds, "Spreading Fear: The Genesis of Transnational Ethnic Conflict," in *The International Spread of Ethnic Conflict* (Princeton: Princeton University Press, 1998), 4.

33. George Liska, *Nations in Alliance: The Limits of Interdependence* (Baltimore, MD: Johns Hopkins University Press, 1962), 3.

34. Stephen M. Walt, *The Origin of Alliances* (Ithaca, NY: Cornell University Press, 1987), 12.

35. Arnold Wolfers, "Alliances," in *International Encyclopedia of the Social Sciences,* ed. David L. Sills (New York: Macmillan, 1968), 268.

36. Oppenheim, L., "Peace," in *International Law: A Treatise,* vol. I, ed. H. Lauterpacht (London: Longmans, 1955), 305.

37. This term is used in the title *Military Intervention: From Gunboat Diplomacy to Humanitarian Intervention*, ed. Andrew M. Dorman and Thomas G. Otte (Brookfield, VT: Dartmouth, 1995).

38. Hedley Bull, ed., "Conclusion," in *Intervention in World Politics* (Oxford: Oxford University Press, 1984), 181.

39. Herbert K. Tillema, "Foreign Overt Military Intervention in the Nuclear Age: A Clarification," *Journal of Peace Research* 26.4 (1989): 419.

40. Linda Bishai, "Altered States: Secession and the Problems of Liberal Theory," in *Theories of Secession,* ed. Percy B. Lehning (London: Routledge, 1998), 92–110.

41. Frederick L. Shiels, "Introduction," in *Ethnic Separatism and World Politics,* ed. Frederick L. Shiels (Lanham, MD: University Press of America, 1984), 1.

42. John Breuilly, *Nationalism and the State* (Manchester: Manchester University Press, 1982), 1–2.

43. Ishtiaq Ahmed, *State, Nation and Ethnicity in Contemporary South Asia* (London: Pinter, 1996), 3.

44. Don MacIver, "Introduction: States and Ethnic Pluralism," in *The Politics of Multinational States,* ed. Don MacIver (Great Britain: Macmillan, 1999), 2.

45. Jack S. Levy, "Declining Power and the Preventive Motivation for War," *World Politics* 40 (1987): 82–107.

46. Gilpin, *War and Change*, 191.

47. James D. Fearon, "Rationalist Explanations for War," *International Organization* 49.3 (1995): 381.

48. For an excellent summary of James Fearon's explanations for war, see Lake and Rothchild, "Spreading Fear," 15.

49. See Hanspeter Kriesi, Ruud Koopmans, Jan Willem Dyvendak, and Marco G. Giugni, *New Social Movements in Western Europe* (Minneapolis: University of Minnesota Press, 1995), 84.

50. See Ruud Koopmans, *Democracy from Below: New Social Movements and the Political System in West Germany* (Boulder, CO: Westview Press, 1995).

51. Ahmed, *State, Nation and Ethnicity in Contemporary South Asia,* 64–65.

52. See Jack Goldstone, "Social Movements or Revolutions? On the Evolution and Outcomes of Collective Action," in *From Contention to Democracy,* eds. Marco G. Giugni, Doug McAdam and Charles Tilly (Lanham, MD: Rowman and Littlefield Publishers, 1998), 130. For an earlier analysis on how arbitrary repression radicalizes a movement, see Sabine Karstedt-Henke, "Theorien zur Erklarung terroristischer Bewegungen," in *Politikder inneren Sicherheit,* ed. E. Blankenburg (Frankfurt: Suhrkamp, 1980).

53. Sabine Karstedt-Henke, "Theorien zur Erklarung terroristischer Bewegungen," 213–217.

54. See Hans Morgenthau, *Politics among Nations* (New York: Alfred A. Knopf, 1967).

55. See Stephen M. Walt's "balance-of-threat" theory in *The Origin of Alliances* (Ithaca and London: Cornell University Press, 1987).

56. Ibid., 21.

57. John A. Vasquez, *The War Puzzle* (Great Britain: Cambridge University Press, 1993), 166.

58. Lake and Rothchild, "Spreading Fear," 11.

59. Will H. Moore and David R. Davis, "Transnational Ethnic Ties and Foreign Policy," in *The International Spread of Ethnic Conflict: Fear Diffusion and Escalation,* ed. David A. Lake and Donald Rothchild (Princeton, NJ: Princeton University Press, 1998), 89.

60. Ibid., 92.

61. John Herz first introduced the concept of the security dilemma in International Relations in 1950. See John Herz "Idealist Internationalism and the Security Dilemma," *World Politics* 2.2 (January 1950): 157–180. Basically it means that an increase in one state's security diminishes the security of other states, which in turn take steps to increase their own security. In Herz's words, "Since none can feel entirely secure in such a world of competing units, power competition ensues, and the vicious circle of security and power accumulation is on." Subsequently, the concept has been used by Robert Jervis in "Cooperation under the Security Dilemma," *World Politics* 30.2 (January 1978): 167–214. Barry Posen has applied this concept to ethnic conflict. See his "The Security Dilemma and Ethnic Conflict," *Survival* 35.1 (Spring 1993): 27–47.

62. Ibid., 193.

63. Edward Grey, *Twenty-Five Years,* vol. I (London: Hodder and Staughton, 1925), 92.

64. Robert H. Bates and Barry R. Weingast, "Rationality and Interpretation: The Politics of Transition," Paper presented at the annual meeting of the American Political Science Association, August 31–September 3, 1995.

65. Barry R. Weingast, "Constructing Trust: The Political and Economic Roots of Ethnic and Regional Conflict," in *Institutions and Social Order*, ed. Virginia Haufler, Karol Soltan, and Eric Uslaner (Ann Arbor: University of Michigan Press, 1998).

66. Lake and Rothchild, "Spreading Fear," 17.

67. See James D. Fearon, "Rationalist Explanations for War," 381.

68. Lake and Rothchild, "Spreading Fear," 12.

69. R.M. Siverson and J. King, "Alliances and the Expansion of War," in *To Augur Well: Early Warning Indicators in World Politics*, ed. J.D. Singer and M. Wallace (Beverly Hills: Sage, 1979), 37–49.

70. P. Huth and B. Russett, "What Makes Deterrence Work? Cases from 1900 to 1980." *World Politics* 36 (1984): 496–526.

71. G. Modelski, "The International Relations of Internal War," in *International Aspects of Civil Strife*, ed. J. Rosenau (Princeton, NJ: Princeton University Press, 1964).

72. C.R. Mitchell, "Civil Strife and the Involvement of External Parties," *International Studies Quarterly* 14 (June 1970): 166–194.

73. Karen Rasler, "Internationalized Civil War: A Dynamic Analysis of the Syrian Intervention in Lebanon," *The Journal of Conflict Resolution* 27.3 (September 1983): 449.

## Chapter 3

1. East Bengal became part of Pakistan at the time of the partition of the Indian subcontinent in 1947. West Bengal is part of India. In 1956, the Constitution of Pakistan renamed East Bengal as East Pakistan. Therefore, the names East Pakistan and East Bengal are often used interchangeably. The term "Bengalis" refers to the linguistic group from either East or West Bengal. It does not distinguish between Hindu and Muslim Bengalis. In this book, Bangla Desh and Bangladesh are used interchangeably. Originally referred to as Bangla Desh (land of the Bengalis), the country is now known as Bangladesh.

2. Census of Pakistan, 1951, vol. I, tables 7 and 7A (Karachi: Government of Pakistan, 1951), 7–3, 7–6, 7–8. The first census of Pakistan was taken in February 1951.

3. Ibid., vol. I, 35.

4. Ibid., vol. I, table 1, 1–2.

5. Anthony Mascarenhas, *The Rape of Bangladesh* (New Delhi: Vikas, 1971).

6. Ibid., 91.

7. For an excellent summary of the happenings in Pakistan till 1969, see Sisir Gupta, "From the Partition to Yahya Khan," in *The Challenge of Bangladesh: A Special Debate,* ed. Pran Chopra (New York: Humanities Press, 1971), 28.

8. See *Constituent Assembly of Pakistan Debates* (Karachi: Government of Pakistan Press, 1948), February 24, vol. II, 7.

9. See A. Rehman, *East and West Pakistan: A Problem in Political Economy of Regional Planning.* Occasional Paper No. 20, Harvard University Center for International Affairs, 1968.

10. See Mascarenhas, *The Rape of Bangladesh*, 16.

11. *Report of the Advisory Panels for Fourth Five-Year Plan* 1970–1975, vol. I; Planning Commission Government of Pakistan, July 1970, 25; table 2.

12. Ibid., 23.

13. These figures have been taken from a paper entitled "History of Economic and Political Domination of East Pakistan" by J. Lee Auspitz, Stephen A. Marglin, and Gustav F. Papenek. Printed in *Bangla Desh Documents* (New Delhi: Ministry of External Affairs, Government of India, 1971), 6. *Bangla Desh Documents* is a collection of documents that provides an excellent primary source of information on events leading to the East Pakistan crisis of 1971.

14. Ibid.

15. Ibid.

16. See *Report of the Advisory Panels for Fourth Five-Year Plan 1970–1975*, vol. I, 22, table 1.

17. Table taken from an article entitled "Why Bangladesh," written by a group of scholars in Vienna and printed in *Bangla Desh Documents,* 21.

18. See Mascarenhas, *The Rape of Bangladesh,* 22.

19. *Bangladesh: Contemporary Events and Documents* (External Publicity Division, Ministry of Foreign Affairs, Government of the People's Republic of Bangladesh, 1971).

20. See Mascarenhas, *The Rape of Bangladesh.*

21. Article written by a group of Scholars in Vienna, "Why Bangladesh," *Bangladesh Documents* (New Delhi: Government of India, Ministry of External Affairs, 1971), 19.

22. Subrata Roy Chowdhury, *The Genesis of Bangladesh* (New York: Asia, 1972), 12.

23. *Census of Pakistan*, 1951, vol. I, statement 4B, 71.

24. See G.P. Bhattacharjee, *Renaissance and Freedom Movement in Bangladesh* (Calcutta: The Minerva Associates), 58.

25. Ibid., 58.

26. See Constituent Assembly of Pakistan, Debates, vol. II, February 25, 1948, 17.

27. Ibid.

28. Mitra Das, *From Nation to Nation: A Case Study of Bengali Independence* (Columbia, MO: South Asia Books, 1981), 107.

29. See Sisir Gupta, "From the Partition to Yahya," 29.

30. See Bhattacharjee, *Renaissance and Freedom Movement in Bangladesh*, 59.

31. Chowdhury, *The Genesis of Bangladesh*, 24.

32. Bhattacharjee, *Renaissance and Freedom Movement in Bangladesh,* 69.

33. See Charles Peter O'Donnell, *Bangladesh: Biography of a Muslim Nation* (Boulder and London: Westview Press, 1984), 71.

34. Edward S. Mason, Robert Dorfman, Stephen A. Marglin, "Conflict in East Pakistan: Background and Prospects," in *Bangla Desh Documents* (New Delhi: Ministry of External Affairs, Government of India, 1971), 13.

35. For a full description of the plan, see Sheikh Mujibur Rehman, *Bangladesh, My Bangladesh* (New Delhi: Orient Longman, 1972), 125.

36. See O'Donnell, *Bangladesh*, 71.

37. On March 23, 1966, Sheikh Mujibur Rahman issued a booklet entitled, "6-Point Formula—Our Right to Live," in which he explained in detail every point of his plan. Reprinted in *Bangla Desh Documents.*

38. Statement issued by Sheikh Mujibur Rahman at a press conference in Dacca on November 26, 1970. Reported in *Morning News,* Karachi and Dacca, November 27, 1970.

39. Confidential telegram sent from the American Embassy in Rawalpindi, Pakistan to U.S. Department of State in Washington on May 22, 1970. Taken from a compilation of declassified secret and confidential documents from 1965 to 1973 by Roedad Khan (Oxford: Oxford University Press, 1999), 358.

40. For a summary of the events in Pakistan between 1969 and 1971, see Mohammed Ayoob, "From Martial Law to Bangla Desh," in *The Challenge of Bangla Desh: A Special Debate,* ed. Pran Chopra (New York: Humanities Press, 1971), 41.

41. This is a statement from President Yahya Khan's address to the nation on December 3, 1970. Reported in *The Dawn,* Karachi, December 4, 1970.

42. *Bangla Desh Documents*, 130.

43. Ibid., 130.

44. *Morning News*, Karachi and Dacca, November 28, 1970. The article in this newspaper reports on President Yahya Khan's statement at a press conference in Dacca on November 27, 1970.

45. Mujib's words as reported in an article entitled "Constitution Has to Be Based on Six-Points," *The Dawn*, Karachi, December 20, 1970.

46. Ibid.

47. Sheikh Mujib's statement in Dacca on January 3, 1971, as reported in *The Pakistan Observer*, January 4, 1971.

48. See *Bangla Desh Documents*, 6.

49. Mr. Bhutto's statement in Karachi on February 17, 1971, as reported in *The Dawn*, February 18, 1971.

50. Mr. Bhutto's declaration in Peshawar on February 15, 1971, as reported in *The Dawn*, Karachi, February 16, 1971.

51. Taken from Yahya Khan's statement on March 1, 1971. *Morning News*, Karachi and Dacca, March 2, 1971.

52. See *Bangla Desh Documents*, 672.

53. Ibid., 3.

54. Simon Dring, *Daily Telegraph*, London, March 30, 1971. In an effort to prevent the world from hearing about the atrocities being committed in the region, 35 foreign journalists were forced to leave Dacca on Saturday, March 27, 1971. These journalists witnessed the events of March 25 and 26 and sent their reports to different newspapers as soon as they were out of Dacca.

55. Anthony Mascarenhas, *Sunday Times*, London, June 13, 1971. During the crisis in East Pakistan, Mascarenhas worked as senior assistant editor, *Morning News* of Karachi and the Karachi correspondent of the London *Sunday Times*. In April 1971, he was one of the few Pakistani journalists who were invited by the Pakistan Ministry of Information to Dacca to report favorably on the events taking place there. In other words, he was mandated by the Government of Pakistan to falsely report that conditions in East Pakistan had returned to normal. During his 10-day visit and after seeing the genocide that was being launched on the Bengalis by the Pakistan army, Mascarenhas decided to defect to London at the end of May to tell the world about the atrocities that were taking place in East Pakistan.

56. For several eyewitness accounts on how the Pakistan army terrorized the Bengali population, see Chowdhury, *The Genesis of Bangladesh*, 97.

57. *Newsweek*, December 6, 1971.

58. Mascarenhas, *Sunday Times*, June 13, 1971.

59. Dring, *Daily Telegraph*, London, March 30, 1971.

60. East Pakistani Rifles (EPR) was a Bengali paramilitary force that was formed to focus on border patrol.

61. John E. Rhode, letter written to Senator William B. Saxbe, April 17, 1971. This extract from Record of the U.S. Senate is printed in *Bangla Desh Documents*, 350.

62. Mrs. Edward Sammel wrote this letter to the *Denver Post*, April 18, 1971. This extract from Record of U.S. House is printed in *Bangla Desh Documents*, 356.

63. Simon Dring of the *Daily Telegraph*, London sent this report to the *Washington Post*, March 30, 1971. Dring was one of the 35 foreign newsmen evacuated from Dacca on Saturday, March 27, 1971.

64. Ibid.

65. Press statement issued by Prime Minister Tajuddin Ahmed after the inauguration of the People's Republic of Bangladesh on April 17, 1971.

66. These were Indira Gandhi's words during a debate in the Lok Sabha (Lower House of Parliament) in New Delhi on March 27, 1971.

67. Anthony Mascarenhas, article titled "Genocide," *Sunday Times,* London, June 13, 1971.

68. U.S. Senate, *Congressional Record,* May 18, 1971, S7128–S7129.

69. Text of editorial entitled "The Slaughter in East Pakistan," *The Times*, London, April 3, 1971.

70. The *Mukti Fauj* came to be called the *Mukti Bahini* after the force changed from a land force to an all-services force. See Major General D.K. Palit (Retd.), *The Lightning Campaign* (New Delhi: Thomson Press, 1972), 58.

71. For more information on the *Mukti Fauj*, see B.P. Saha, *Liberation Struggle and After* (New Delhi: Vikas, 1985), 13–16 and Palit, *The Lightning Campaign*, 56.

72. Mr. Tajuddin Ahmed, general secretary of the Awami League became prime minister of the new State of Bangladesh on April 13, 1971.

73. See note 60.

74. The Pakistani government created the Ansars and the Mujahids as auxiliary forces in the early 1950s. They were trained to handle basic guns and rifles. During the East Pakistani crisis, the Ansars and the Mujahids made up the Razakars who were the main supporters of the Pakistanis throughout the genocide. See Talukder Maniruzzaman, *The Bangladesh Revolution and Its Aftermath* (Dacca: Bangladesh Books, 1980), 106; Palit, *The Lightning Campaign*, 52.

75. This is part of a statement that Tajuddin Ahmed made to the nation on April 11, 1971. For the full text, see *Bangladesh Documents,* 282–286.

76. Saha, *Liberation Struggle and After* (New Delhi: Vikas, 1985), 13.

77. Mujibur Rehman's remarks made at a press conference in Dacca, November 26, 1970. Reported in *Morning News*, Karachi and Dacca, November 27, 1970.

78. Ibid.

79. See "Why Bangladesh," Paper written by a group of scholars in Vienna in *Bangla Desh Documents,* 15.

80. *Daily Telegraph,* March 29, 1971.

81. For an interesting account of the Indo-Pakistani war of 1971, see Palit's *The Lightning Campaign*, 50.

82. For the full text of the resolution moved by the prime minister of India in Parliament on March 31, 1971, see *Bangla Desh Documents*, 672.

83. For the text of the Declaration of Independence, see *Bangla Desh Documents*, 281–282.

84. See Palit, *The Lightning Campaign*, 49.

85. See *Amrita Bazaar Patrika*, Calcutta, April 2, 1971.

86. See *Daily Telegraph,* London, April 14, 1971.

87. *New York Times*, April 29, 1971.

88. *Times of London*, May 22, 1971.

89. Reuters News Agency, London, May 7, 1971. Taken from a collection of newspaper reports printed in *India and "Bangla Desh": Testimony from the Foreign and Indian Press* (New York: Pakistan-American Friends Association, 1971), 10.

90. *Daily Observer,* London, June 20, 1971.

91. For an account of the events leading to the Indo-Pak war of December 1971, see Robert Jackson, *South Asian Crisis* (London: Chatto and Windus, 1975), 77.

92. *The Times of India*, August 21, 1971; *Indian Express,* August 12, 1971.

93. See Saha, *Liberation Struggle and After*, p. 40.

94. See Richard Sisson and Leo E. Rose, *War and Secession: Pakistan, India and the Creation of Bangladesh* (Berkeley and Los Angeles: University of California Press, 1990), 38.

95. See J.N. Dixit, *Anatomy of a Flawed Inheritance* (New Delhi: Konark, 1995), 23–24.

96. President Yahya Khan's broadcast to his nation, June 28, 1971, *Pakistan Horizon,* vol. XXIV, no. 3, 111–112.

97. President Yahya Khan's broadcast to the nation, October 12, 1971; Reported in *Pakistan Times*, October 13, 1971.

98. Peter Kann, The *Wall Street Journal*, May 12, 1971.

99. Parts of President Yahya Khan's address to the nation on June 28, 1971 are reproduced in *India and "Bangla Desh": Testimony from the Foreign and Indian Press.*

100. U. Thant's memorandum to the president of the Security Council, July 19, 1971, *Pakistan Horizon,* vol. XXIV, no. 3, 127–30.

101. Statement made by Brigadier Mohammed Yusuf, deputy sub-martial law administrator on September 29, 1971; *Jang*, Karachi, September 30, 1971. Reprinted in *Bangladesh Documents*, vol. II (New Delhi: Ministry of Information and Broadcasting, 1971), 137.

102. Statement made by Mr. Akhtaruddin Ahmad, minister for Trade, Industry and Parliamentary Affairs in Dacca on October 2, 1971; *Jang*, Karachi, October 3, 1971. Reprinted in *Bangladesh Documents*, vol. II, 137.

103. Statement made by Mr. Mahmud Ali, leader of the Pakistani Delegation at the UN on October 6, 1971; *Pakistan Times,* Lahore, October 7, 1971.

104. Media reports pertaining to the war fever appeared in *Washington Post*, October 17, 1971, and *Newsweek*, November 8, 1971.

105. *Realities Cambodgiennes*, Phnom Penh, October 22, 1971.

106. *The New York Times,* October 20, 1971.

107. See *Bangladesh Documents,* vol. II, 141.

108. For an excellent account of India-Pakistan military tactics before the 1971 war, see Sisson and Rose, *War and Secession*, 213.

109. See Swaran Singh's statement in the Lok Sabha on December 3, 1971. This statement and a collection of primary documents on South Asia can be found in *U.S.-South Asian Relations 1947–1982,* vol. 3, ed. Rajendra K. Jain (New Jersey: Humanities Press, 1983), 26.

110. See O'Donnell, *Bangladesh*, 103.

111. Indira Gandhi addressed Parliament soon after the Pakistani forces surrendered to India on December 16, 1971. Text of her speech is printed in Vinod Gupta, *Anderson Papers: A Study of Nixon's Blackmail of India* (New Delhi: ISSD, 1972).

## Chapter 4

1. See this study's definition of intervention in chapter 2.

2. The word "Eelam" is the Tamil name for Ceylon or Sri Lanka.

3. See *World Development Report 1999/2000: Entering the 21st Century* (New York: Oxford University Press for the World Bank), 231, table 1. According to this report, Sri Lanka had an annual GDP of $810 and ranked 144th out of 210 economies ranked by the World Bank in 1998.

4. Sumantra Bose, *States, Nations, Sovereignty* (New Delhi: Sage, 1994), 108.

5. The name Ceylon was officially changed to the Sinhalese name Sri Lanka, meaning "resplendent island," on May 22, 1972.

6. I include figures for 1981 since most of this case study covers the late 1970s and early 1980s.

7. The 2001 census figures are somewhat distorted because the census could not be conducted in Jaffna, Mullaitivu, and Kilinochchi. All of these areas are inhabited by the Sri Lankan Tamils. That is why the 2001 figure of the Sri Lankan Tamils is so low—730,200 as compared to 1,886,900 in 1981. The census was only partially conducted in Mannar, Vavuniya, Batticalo, and Trincomalee. The "Indian Tamils" figure also appears lower than it should be because the census was not conducted in several Tamil areas.

8. See James Manor, "Introduction," in *Sri Lanka in Change and Crisis*, ed. James Manor (London and Sydney: Croom Helm, 1984), 5.

9. Ibid., 6.

10. K.M. de Silva, *Managing Ethnic Tensions in Multi-Ethnic Societies: Sri Lanka 1880–1985* (Lanham, MD: University Press of America, 1986), 2.

11. For a comprehensive analysis of the interethnic competition in Sri Lanka, see Jagath P. Senaratne, *Political Violence in Sri Lanka, 1977–1990* (Amsterdam: VU University Press, 1997), 20–31.

12. See Alan J. Bullion, *India, Sri Lanka and the Tamil Crisis 1976 –1994* (London and New York: Pinter), 15.

13. Ibid., 16.

14. Manor, "Introduction," 2.

15. Robert C. Oberst, "Youth Militancy and the Rise of Sri Lanka: Tamil Nationalism," in *Subnational Movements in South Asia*, ed. Subrata K. Mitra and R. Alison Lewis (Boulder, CO: Westview Press, 1996), 143.

16. "Tamils Fight for National Freedom," A memorandum submitted by the Liberation Tigers to the Seventh Summit Meeting of Non-Aligned Nations held in New Delhi, India, March 7–15, 1983. See Satchi Ponnambalam, *Sri Lanka: National Conflict and the Tamil Liberation Struggle* (London: Zed Books, 1983), appendix 8, 260.

17. Bose, *States, Nations, Sovereignty*, 54.

18. See Jonathan Spencer, "Introduction: The Power of the Past," in *Sri Lanka: History and Roots of Conflict*, ed. Jonathan Spencer (London and New York: Routledge, 1990), 2.

19. Ponnambalam, *Sri Lanka,* 5

20. Ibid.

21. Cited in Bose, *States, Nations, Sovereignty,* 68, footnote 16.

22. Ibid., 57.

23. For a comprehensive account of the roots of the Sri Lankan conflict, see P. Saravanamuttu, "Instability in Sri Lanka," *Survival,* 32.5 (1990): 457.

24. Ceylon House of Representatives *Debates*, vol. 56, col. 247.

25. Ibid., vol. 28, col. 120.

26. Ibid., vol. 33, col. I695

27. Ibid., vol. 56, col. 727.

28. Bose, *States, Nations, Sovereignty,* 58.

29. Ibid., 67–68.

30. See Bullion, *India, Sri Lanka and the Tamil Crisis,* 23.

31. See A. Jeyaratnam Wilson, *The Break-up of Sri Lanka* (London: C. Hurst and Company, 1988), 131.

32. See V. Nithiyanandan, "An Analysis of Economic Factors behind the Origin and Development of Tamil Nationalism in Sri Lanka," in *Facets of Ethnicity in Sri Lanka,* ed. Abeysekera and Gunasinghe (Colombo: Social Scientists' Association, 1987).

33. Walter Schwarz, *The Tamils of Sri Lanka* (London: Minority Rights Group, 1988).

34. See D. Hellmann-Rajanayagam, "The Tamil Tigers in Northern Sri Lanka: Origins, Factions, Programmes," *Internationales Asienforum,* 17.1/2 (May 1986): 67.

35. Ibid.

36. The South Asia Terrorism Portal (www.satp.org).

37. Chandra Richard de Silva, "Sinhala-Tamil Relations and Education in Sri Lanka: The University Admissions Issue—The First Phase, 1971–7," in *From Independence to Statehood: Managing Ethnic Conflict in Five African and Asian States,* ed. Robert B. Goldmann and A. Jeyaratnam Wilson (London: Frances Pinter, 1984), 133–134.

38. Denzil Peiris, "Colombo Rides the Tiger," *South* (March 1985): 15.

39. Ibid.

40. Rohan Gunaratna, *Indian Intervention in Sri Lanka* (Colombo: South Asian Network on Conflict Research, 1993), 81.

41. Ponnambalam, *Sri Lanka,* 200.

42. Ibid., 192.

43. Ibid., 194.

44. Senaratne, *Political Violence in Sri Lanka,* 63.

45. Ponnambalam, *Sri Lanka,* 191.

46. Ibid., 201.

47. Ibid., 197.

48. Amnesty International Report 1980, 234.

49. Ibid. Cited in Ponnambalam, *Sri Lanka,* 204.

50. Brian Eads, *The Observer,* London, September 20, 1981.

51. Amnesty International Report, 1982.

52. See S.J. Tambiah, *Sri Lanka: Ethnic Fratricide and the Dismantling of Democracy* (Chicago and London: The University of Chicago Press, 1986), 21.

53. *The Hindu,* September 3, 1983.

54. Ibid.

55. *The Times,* London, August 8, 1983.

56. *India Today,* New Delhi, August 31, 1983.

57. Shiva Naipaul, *Unfinished Journey* (London: Hamish Hamilton, 1986).

58. *The Times,* London, August 5, 1983.

59. *The Hindu,* September 3, 1983.

60. See L. Piyadasa, *Sri Lanka: The Holocaust and After* (London: Marram Books, 1984), 90.

61. Ibid., 99.

62. Taken from *Country Reports on Human Rights Practices for 1983: Report Submitted to the Committee on Foreign Affairs U.S. House of Representatives and the Committee on Foreign Relations U.S. Senate by the Department of State* (Washington, DC: U.S. Government Printing Office: 1984), 1418, 1419.

63. *Diary of a Survivor,* July 27, 1983, http://tamiltigers.net/history/his1983news01.htm

64. *The Hindu,* August 14, 1984, 1.

65. Ibid.

66. *The Hindu,* August 17, 1984.

67. Memorandum presented to President Jayewardene in September 1982 by members of Ceylon Institute of National and Tamil Affairs (CINTA). See *Tribune*, Colombo, September 25, 1982.

68. Ponnambalam, *Sri Lanka,* 205.

69. Senaratne, *Political Violence in Sri Lanka,* 69.

70. See Bose, *States, Nations, Sovereignty*, 74.

71. See William McGowan, *Only Man Is Vile* (New York: Farrar, Straus and Giroux, 1992), 182.

72. Senaratne, *Political Violence in Sri Lanka,* 73.

73. See Tom Marks, "'Peoples War' in Sri Lanka: Insurgency and Counterinsurgency," *Issues and Studies,* 22.8 (1986): 63–100.

74. *India Today,* March 31, 1984, 89.

75. Tambiah, *Sri Lanka,* 124.

76. Bose, *States, Nations, Sovereignty,* 96.

77. R.L. Stirrat, "The Riots and the Roman Catholic Church in Historical Perspective," in *Sri Lanka in Change and Crisis,* ed. James Manor (New York: St. Martin's Press, 1984), 203.

78. See Shelton U. Kodikara, "Introduction," in *South Asian Strategic Issues*, ed. Shelton U. Kodikara (New Delhi, Newbury Park, and London: Sage, 1990), 18.

79. Bose, *States, Nations, Sovereignty,* 139.

80. Cited in A. Sivarajah, "Indo-Sri Lanka Relations and Sri Lanka's Ethnic Crisis: The Tamil Nadu Factor," in *South Asian Strategic Issues,* ed. Shelton U. Kodikara (New Delhi, Newbury Park, and London: Sage, 1990), 140.

81. Bose, *States, Nations, Sovereignty,* 139.

82. Ibid., 141.

83. See Shelton Kodikara, "Internationalization of Sri Lanka's Ethnic Conflict: The Tamil Nadu Factor," in *Internationalization of Ethnic Conflict,* ed. K.M. de Silva and R.J. May (London: Pinter), 110.

84. Ahsan Ali Khan, "The Tamil Question in Historical Perspective: Its Impact on Indo-Sri Lankan Relations," *Pakistan Horizon,* 37. 2 (1984): 58.

85. K.M. de Silva, "Indo-Sri Lankan Relations, 1975–89: A Study in the Internationalization of Ethnic Conflict," in *Internationalization of Ethnic Conflict,* ed. K.M. de Silva and R.J. May (London: Pinter, 1991), 80.

86. *The Island,* January 25, 1987.

87. A. Sivarajah, "Indo-Sri Lankan Relations and Sri Lanka's Ethnic Crisis: The Tamil Nadu Factor," 140.

88. See Munro R. "Sri Lanka: Case Study of a Disaster," *Time,* New York, April 3, 1989, 14–15.

89. R.N. Kao established India's External Intelligence Agency, RAW, in 1968 under the instructions of the then prime minister, Indira Gandhi. RAW is a top secret intelligence gathering organization.

90. For copious details on India's covert assistance to the Sri Lankan Tamils, see Gunaratna, *Indian Intervention in Sri Lanka,* 341–402.

91. Ibid., 5.

92. Ibid., 7.

93. Munro, "Sri Lanka," 14.

94. Ibid.

95. Ibid.

96. See Manoj Joshi, "A Base for All Seasons," *Frontline,* August 3–16, 1991, 21–22.

97. "The Tamil Nadu Coast," *Frontline,* June 22–July 5, 1991, 28.

98. "Ominous Presence in Tamil Nadu," *India Today*, March 31, 1984, 88.

99. See Rajesh Kadian, *India's Sri Lanka Fiasco: Peacekeepers at War* (New Delhi and Bombay: Vision Books, 1990), 141–142.

100. Rajeev K. Bajaj, *Surya*, September 1984.

101. See Bertram E.S.J. Bastiampillai, "Ethnic Conflicts in South Asia and Inter-State Relations Especially in Relation to Sri Lanka," in *South Asian Strategic Issues,* ed. Shelton Kodikara (New Delhi: Sage, 1990), 96.

102. *South*, March 1985, 14.

103. Marguerite Johnson, "Island at War," *Lanka Guardian,* 9, 5–9.

104. *South*, March 1985, 14.

105. See Shelton U. Kodikara, "Internationalization of Sri Lanka's Ethnic Conflict," 112.

106. See Rohan Gunaratna, *International and Regional Security Implications of the Sri Lankan Tamil Insurgency* (Colombo: Bandaranaike Centre for International Studies, 1997), 11, 17–19.

107. See Shelton U. Kodikara, *Indo-Ceylon Relations since Independence* (Colombo: Ceylon Institute of World Affairs, 1965), 32–35.

108. These words of a retired Commander of the Indian Navy are cited in Ravi Kaul, "The Indian Ocean: A Strategic Posture for India," in T.T. Poulose, ed., *Indian Ocean Power Rivalry* (New Delhi: International Publications Service, 1974), 66.

109. Shelton U. Kodikara, "Introduction," in *South Asian Strategic Issues: Sri Lankan Perspectives,* ed. Shelton U. Kodikara (New Delhi: Sage, 1990), 13.

110. A. Sivarajah, "Indo-Sri Lanka Relations and Sri Lanka's Ethnic Crisis: The Tamil Nadu Factor," in *South Asian Strategic Issues,* ed. Shelton U. Kodikara (New Delhi, Newbury Park, and London: Sage, 1990), 136.

111. Ahsan Ali Khan, "The Tamil Question in Historical Perspective: Its Impact on Indo-Sri Lankan Relations," *Pakistan Horizon*, 37. 2 (1984): 58.

112. Telegram sent to Indira Gandhi from four TULF leaders, August 11, 1984.

113. K.G. Reddy, "India Cannot Be Silent on Sri Lanka: PM", *The Hindu,* August 16, 1984.

114. See Shelton U. Kodikara, "Internationalization of Sri Lanka's Ethnic Conflict," 109.

115. See K.M. de Silva, "Indo-Sri Lankan Relations," 77–78.

116. Kadian, *India's Sri Lanka Fiasco,* 85.

117. Once again, see my definition of "intervention" in chapter 2. India, too, refused to use the word "intervention" for her role in Sri Lanka from 1987 to 1990. The Indian High Commissioner in the United Kingdom, M. Ragostra stated, "Intervention is hardly the word for our going to the succour of the legitimate governments of two of our friendly neighbours, Sri Lanka and the Maldives—one facing a violent threat to the unity and integrity of its country, the other confronted with a coup engineered by a bunch of terrorist adventurers. Indian forces went there at the request of those governments." This statement appeared in an article by M. Ragostra entitled, "India and Her Neighbours," *The Independent,* London, April 15, 1989, 15.

118. "The Sri Lankan Conflict on Indian Perception," *Lanka Guardian,* 10.4 (June 15, 1987): 17.

119. Bose, *States, Nations, Sovereignty,* 150.

120. *The Island,* June 3, 1987.

121. Ibid.

122. Bastiampillai, "Ethnic Conflicts in South Asia," 91.

123. *India Today,* "Tackling the Tigers," June 30, 1987, 18.

124. Ibid.

125. Ibid.

126. See Rajat Ganguly, *Kin State Intervention in Ethnic Conflicts: Lessons from South Asia* (New Delhi: Sage, 1998), 203.

127. Bose, *States, Nations, Sovereignty*, 135.

128. Ibid.

129. See Peter Chalk, "The Liberation Tigers of Tamil Eelam Insurgency in Sri Lanka," in *Ethnic Conflict and Secessionism in South and Southeast Asia,* eds. Rajat Ganguly and Ian Mcduff (New Delhi: Sage Publications, 2003), 134.

## Chapter 5

1. The state of Jammu and Kashmir is simply referred to as Kashmir in this chapter.

2. Victoria Schofield, *Kashmir in Conflict: India, Pakistan and the Unending War* (London and New York: I.B. Taurus, 2003), xii.

3. For a good background to the Kashmir dispute, see Louis D. Hayes, *The Impact of U.S. Policy on the Kashmir Conflict* (Tucson: University of Arizona Press, 1971), 11–31.

4. Ibid., 15.

5. J.K. Banerji, *I Report on Kashmir* (Calcutta: Republic, 1948), 8.

6. For details on the early history of Kashmir from 1846, see Alastair Lamb, *Kashmir: A Disputed Legacy 1846–1990* (Hertfordshire: Roxford Books, 1991), 121, 154.

7. Hayes, *The Impact of U.S. Policy on the Kashmir Conflict,* 17.

8. Sumit Ganguly, *The Crisis in Kashmir* (Cambridge: Cambridge University Press; Washington, DC: The Woodrow Wilson Center Press, 1997), 10.

9. Ibid.

10. See note 3.

11. *The Dawn,* October 31, 1947.

12. For more on Kashmir's special status, see Victoria Schofield, *Kashmir in the Crossfire* (London: I.B. Tauris, 1996), 165.

13. Clause 7 of the Instrument of Accession as reproduced in M.J. Akbar, *Kashmir: behind the Vale* (New Delhi: Viking, 1991), 135.

14. See Clause 8 of the Instrument of Accession in Akbar, *Kashmir,* 135.

15. See Suranjan Das, *Kashmir and Sindh* (London: Anthem Press, 2001), 28.

16. See Rajat Ganguly, *Kin State Intervention in Ethnic Conflicts* (New Delhi: Sage, 1998), 49.

17. Ibid. 50.

18. See A.G. Noorani, "The Betrayal of Kashmir," in *Perspectives on Kashmir: The Roots of Conflict in South Asia,* ed. Raju G.C. Thomas (Boulder, CO: Westview Press, 1992), 272.

19. Ibid.

20. See Ganguly, *The Crisis in Kashmir,* 87.

21. See Mir Qasim, *My Life and Times* (New Delhi: Allied, 1992), 162.

22. Schofield, *Kashmir in the Crossfire*, 228.

23. See George Fernandes, "India's Policies in Kashmir: An Assessment and Discourse," in *Perspectives on Kashmir: The Roots of Conflict in South Asia,* ed. Raju G.C. Thomas (Boulder, CO: Westview Press, 1992), 287.

24. See Sumit Ganguly, "The Prospects of War and Peace in Kashmir," in *Perspectives on Kashmir: The Roots of Conflict in South Asia,* ed. Raju G.C. Thomas (Boulder CO: Westview Press, 1992), 357.

25. A.G. Noorani, "The Betrayal of Kashmir," 272.

26. Tavleen Singh, *Kashmir: A Tragedy of Errors* (New Delhi: Viking, 1995), 102.

27. Sumit Ganguly, *The Crisis in Kashmir*, 92.

28. See Inderjit Badhwar, "A Tarnished Triumph," *India Today,* April 15, 1987, 40–42.

29. Ibid.

30. A.G. Noorani, "The Betrayal of Kashmir," 273.

31. Saifuddin Soz, "An Ostrich-Like Attitude towards Kashmir Won't Do," *The Times of India*, September 3, 1990.

32. See Edward W. Desmond, "At War with Itself," *Time,* December 24, 1990, 9

33. Tavleen Singh, *Tragedy of Errors*, 103.

34. See Shekhar Gupta, "Kashmir Valley: Militant Siege, "*India Today,* January 31, 1990, 35.

35. Ajit Bhattacharjea, *Kashmir: The Wounded Valley* (New Delhi: UBSPD, 1994), 253.

36. See Rajesh Kadian, *The Kashmir Tangle* (Boulder, CO: Westview Press, 1993), 16.

37. See Ganguly, "The Prospects of War and Peace in Kashmir," 358.

38. Ibid.

39. For a list of these groups, see Jagmohan, *My Frozen Turbulence in Kashmir* (New Delhi: Allied, 1991), 677.

40. See Iffat Malik, *Ethnic Conflict International Dispute* (Oxford: Oxford University Press, 2002), 155.

41. Ganguly, "The Prospects of War and Peace in Kashmir," 357.

42. For a comprehensive analysis of "Exercise Brasstacks," see Kanti Bajpai, P.R. Chari, Pervaiz Iqbal Cheema, Stephen P. Cohen, and Sumit Ganguly, *Brasstacks and Beyond: Perception and Management of Crisis in South Asia* (New Delhi: Manohar, 1995).

43. For an excellent account on the domestic situation in India in the 1980s, see Ganguly, *The Crisis in Kashmir*, 99.

44. See Mustapha Kamal Pasha, "Beyond the Two-Nation Divide: Kashmir and Resurgent Islam," in *Perspectives on Kashmir: The Roots of Conflict in South Asia,* ed. Raju G.C. Thomas (Boulder CO: Westview Press, 1992), 377.

45. See Kanhya L. Kaul and M.K. Teng, "Human Rights Violations of Kashmiri Hindus," in *Perspectives on Kashmir: The Roots of Conflict in South Asia,* ed. Raju G.C. Thomas (Boulder CO: Westview Press, 1992), 180.

46. See Pasha, "Beyond the Two-Nation Divide: Kashmir and Resurgent Islam," 374.

47. See Jagmohan, *My Frozen Turbulence in Kashmir*, 122.

48. Ibid. 125

49. *Patriot*, October 24, 1989.

50. Sanjeev Miglani, *The Stateman*, November 6, 1989.

51. *The Times of India*, November 23, 1989.

52. *Hindustan Times,* December 17, 1989.

53. *Nation,* December 1989. Cited in Jagmohan, *My Frozen Turbulence in Kashmir*, 340.

54. Ibid.

55. See Jagmohan, *My Frozen Turbulence in Kashmir*, 119.

56. Sumit Ganguly, *Conflict Unending* (New York: Columbia University Press, 2001), 91.

57. See *The Human Rights Crisis in Kashmir: A Pattern of Impunity* (New York: Asia Watch: A Division of Human Rights Watch, 1993), 1.

58. See Mushahid Hussain, "The Kashmir Issue: Its New International Dimensions," in *Perspectives on Kashmir: The Roots of Conflict in South Asia,* ed. Raju G.C. Thomas (Boulder, CO: Westview Press, 1992), 346.

59. Asia Watch (a part of Human Rights Watch) was established in 1985 to monitor the observance of human rights in Asia.

60. *Kashmir under Siege: Human Rights in India*, An Asia Watch Report (New York: Human Rights Watch, 1991), 15.

61. Ibid., 2

62. See Tavleen Singh, *A Tragedy of Errors,* 135–136.

63. *Human Rights Crisis in Kashmir: A Pattern of Impunity*, 38.

64. Ibid., 2.

65. Andy Messing Jr., "Hidden Conflict in Kashmir," *The Washington Times*, February 5, 1992.

66. *Human Rights Crisis in Kashmir: A Pattern of Impunity*, 23.

67. *Physicians for Human Rights* is an organization of physicians founded in 1989 for the prevention of human rights violations.

68. *Human Rights in Kashmir: A Pattern of Impunity*, 13

69. See *India: Torture, Rape and Deaths in Custody* (New York: Amnesty International, 1992), 124.

70. *Surya India,* January 1990. Cited in Suranjan Das, 71.

71. "India's Kashmir War," Report of the Committee for Initiative on Kashmir, March 1990. See Tapan Bose, Dinesh Mohan, Gautam Navlakha, and Sumanto Banerjee, "India's Kashmir War," in *Secular Crown on Fire,* ed. Asghar Ali Engineer (New Delhi: Ajanta, 1991), 225.

72. *Indian Express* New Delhi, August 15, 1990

73. *Indian Express*, New Delhi, October 21, 1990.

74. Girish Srinivasan, "Kashmir and Punjab: Fundamental Differences," *The Independent*, May 2, 1990.

75. *The New York Times,* January 15, 1990.

76. Report of the Committee for Initiative on Kashmir, March 1990. See Bose et al., "India's Kashmir War," 225.

77. *India Today*, April 30, 1990.

78. *Insight,* August 20, 1990.

79. See V.M. Tarkunde, Balraj Puri, Sulochana Shikhre, and N.D. Pancholi, *Report on Human Rights Situation in the Kashmir Valley*, May 20–25, 1992 (New Delhi: Coordination Committee on Kashmir, 1992), 15.

80. See Schofield, *Kashmir in Conflict*, 154.

81. Barbara Crossette, "Protesters in Pakistan Vow to Free Kashmiris in India," *The New York Times International*, January 27, 1990, 8.

82. K. Subramanyam, "Kashmir," *Strategic Analysis*, vol. III, no. 2, May 1990. Also see L.E. Rose, "Indian Foreign Relations: Reassessing Basic Policies," in *India Briefing 1990,* ed. Marshall M. Bouton and Philip Oldenburg (Boulder: Westview Press, 1990), 73.

83. David Housego, *The Financial Times,* June 6, 1990.

84. "Conspiracy Theory," *The Economist,* July 13, 1991.

85. Jagmohan, *My Frozen Turbulence in Kashmir*, 404.

86. Cited in *Peace Initiatives,* vol. III, no. V, September–October 1997, 5.

87. Ibid.

88. See "Human Rights Watch on Arms Project Report," *India: Arms and Abuses in Indian Punjab and Kashmir*, September 1994, vol. VI, no. 10.

89. "Exporting Terror," *India Today*, May 15, 1994.

90. Cited in Schofield, *Kashmir in Conflict*, 176. This is part of Victoria Schofield's interview with former governor Saxena.

91. John Ward Anderson, "Pakistan Aiding Rebels in Kashmir," *The Washington Post*, May 16, 1994.

92. *The Proxy War Still Continues*, Government of India, 1999, 28–29.

93. See Roger Howard, "Wrath of Islam: The HUA Analysed," in *Jane's Intelligence Review*, vols 9 and 10, October 1997.

94. Cited in Schofield, *Kashmir in Conflict*, 177.

95. Ibid.

96. Robert G. Wirsing, *India, Pakistan, and the Kashmir Dispute* (New York: St. Martin's Press, 1994), 134.

97. See Richard Sisson and Leo Rose, *War and Secession: Pakistan, India, and the Creation of Bangladesh* (Berkeley and Los Angeles: University of California Press, 1990), 43.

98. Ibid., 54.

99. *The Hindu*, August 24, 1950.

100. Sumit Ganguly has called the Kargil conflict a war because it had "at least 1000 battle deaths." See Ganguly, *Conflict Unending,* 11, footnote 1.

101. After an attack by Kashmir secessionists, aided by Pakistan, on the Indian Parliament in New Delhi, India and Pakistan came very close to war.

102. See Robert G. Wirsing, *Kashmir in the Shadow of War* (New York: M.E. Sharpe, 2003), 243.

103. See Partha S. Ghose, "Kashmir Tangle and Indo-Pak Relations: Some Suggestions," in *Secular Crown on Fire,* ed. Asghar Ali Engineer (New Delhi: Ajanta, 1991), 97.

104. Gen. Shankar Roy-Chowdhury (Retd.), former chief of the Army Staff, in *Times of India*, June 20, 1999.

105. Rajat Ganguly, *Kin State Intervention in Ethnic Conflicts*, 75.

106. Ibid., 81.

107. Ibid.

108. Cited in Jagmohan, *My Frozen Turbulence in Kashmir*, 401.

109. Sumantra Bose, *The Challenge in Kashmir: Democracy, Self-Determination and a Just Peace* (New Delhi: Sage, 1997), 85.

110. P.M. Benazir Bhutto's words in an address to a joint session of the Pakistan Parliament on February 10, 1990.

111. Barbara Crossette, "Protesters in Pakistan Vow to Free Kashmiris in India," *The New York Times International,* January 27, 1990, 8.

112. Sanjoy Hazarika, "India Says Pakistan Is Stirring Up Kashmir Unrest," *The New York Times International*, February 1, 1990.

113. Ibid.

114. Ganguly, *Conflict Unending*, 95.

115. See Rodney W. Jones and Mark G. McDonough, *Tracking Nuclear Proliferation: A Guide in Maps and Charts, 1998* (Washington, DC: Carnegie Endowment for International Peace, 1998), 138.

116. Wirsing, *Kashmir in the Shadow of War*, 13.

117. "Pakistan's Words: 'To Restore the Strategic Balance,'" *New York Times* Web Service, May 29, 1998.

118. Wirsing, *Kashmir in the Shadow of War*, 13.

119. See Ganguly, *Kin State Intervention in Ethnic Conflicts,* 76.

120. Jim Garamone, "Intelligence Chief Details Threats Facing America," *Defense Link* (American Forces Information Service) Web Service, February 22, 2001.

121. For an excellent account of the Kargil war, see Ganguly, *Conflict Unending,* 114–129.

122. See *From Surprise to Reckoning: The Kargil Review Committee Report* (New Delhi: Sage, 1999), 21.

123. See *From Surprise to Reckoning: The Kargil Review Committee Report* (New Delhi: Sage, 1999), 16. This report is authentic and unedited.

124. Ganguly, *Conflict Unending*, 7.

125. Ibid., 7.

126. Ibid., 88

127. Ibid., 122.

128. *Proliferation: Threat and Response* (Washington, DC: Department of Defense Report, January 2001), 30.

129. See Ganguly, *Conflict Unending*, 142.

## Chapter 6

1. See K.P.S. Gill, "Endgame in Punjab: 1988–1993," *Faultlines*, vol. 1, May 1999.

2. Evidence suggests that Pakistan is trying to revive the secessionist movement by supporting the Babbar Khalsa International, a secessionist group that still exists and is active in some parts of Europe, the United States, Canada, and Pakistan. See "Babbar Khalsa International," *South Asia Terrorism Portal* http://www.satp.org/satporgtp/countries/india/states/punjab/terrorist_outfits/BKI.

3. The word Punjab means the "land of five rivers." The five rivers—Jhelum, Chenab, Ravi, Sutlej, and Beas—are responsible for the fertile Punjab plains. Punjab is located northwest of New Delhi and borders Pakistan. It is a prosperous agricultural state.

4. S. Ganga Singh Dhillon's address at the 54th All India Sikh Educational Conference held in Chandigarh, India, March 13–15, 1981.

5. See Ishtiaq Ahmed, *State, Nation and Ethnicity in Contemporary South Asia* (London and New York: Pinter), 1996, 121.

6. Khushwant Singh, "Genesis of the Hindu-Sikh Divide," in *The Punjab Story* (New Delhi: Roli Books, 1985), 1.

7. See Khushwant Singh, *My Bleeding Punjab* (New Delhi: UBSPD, 1992), 38.

8. See Khushwant Singh, *A History of the Sikhs*, vol. II, 293. For more on the history of the Sikhs, see among others, Gurmit Singh, *History of the Sikh Struggle*, vols I–III (New Delhi: Atlantic, 1991); Joyce J.M. Pettigrew, *The Sikhs of the Punjab* (London and New Jersey: Zed Books, 1995); Mark Tully and Satish Jacob, *Amritsar: Mrs. Gandhi's Last Battle* (London: Jonathan Cape, 1985); Kuldip Nayar and Khushwant Singh, *Tragedy of Punjab* (New Delhi: Vision Books, 1984).

9. See *Constituent Assembly Debates: Official Report*, vol. XI (New Delhi: Lok Sabha Secretariat, 1949), 752.

10. See K.P.S. Gill, *Punjab: The Knights of Falsehood* (New Delhi: Har-Anand, 1997), 14.

11. See Nayar and Singh, *Tragedy of Punjab*, 21.

12. The Akali Dal, formed in 1920, consisted mainly of the Jat Sikhs—a powerful agrarian caste.

13. See V.D. Chopra, R.K. Mishra, and Nirmal Singh, *Agony of Punjab* (New Delhi: Patriot Publishers, 1984), 102.

14. See Gurmit Singh, *History of Sikh Struggles*, vol. II (New Delhi: Atlantic, 1991), 2

15. See Gurharpal Singh, *Ethnic Conflict in India* (New York: St. Martin's Press, 2000), 104.

16. Khushwant Singh, *My Bleeding Punjab*, 39.

17. Ibid., 40.

18. See Ahmed, *State, Nation and Ethnicity*, 127.

19. Ibid.

20. Ibid.

21. Gurharpal Singh, *Ethnic Conflict in India*, 105.

22. See Tavleen Singh, "Terrorists in the Temple," in *The Punjab Story* (New Delhi: Roli Books, 1985), 33.

23. Harji Malik, "The Politics of Alienation," in *Punjab: The Fatal Miscalculation,* ed. Patwant Singh and Harji Malik (New Delhi: Patwant Singh, 1985), 37.

24. Rajni Kothari, "Electoral Politics and the Rise of Communalism," in *Punjab: The Fatal Miscalculation,* ed. Patwant Singh and Harji Malik (New Delhi: Patwant Singh, 1985), 78.

25. Lt. Gen. Jagjit Singh Aurora, "Assault on the Golden Temple Complex 5–6 June 1984," in *The Punjab Story* (New Delhi: Roli Books, 1985), 92.

26. See Pettigrew, *The Sikhs of the Punjab*, 33.

27. Khushwant Singh, *History of the Sikhs*, vol. II, 329.

28. Sarab Jit Singh, *Operation Black Thunder: An Eyewitness Account of Terrorism in Punjab* (New Delhi: Sage, 2002), 46.

29. Ibid., 46.

30. Ahmed, *State, Nation and Ethnicity*, 129.

31. See *White Paper on the Punjab Agitation: A Summary* (New Delhi: Government of India, 1984), 13.

32. Gill, *Punjab: The Knights of Falsehood*, 80.

33. Nayar and Singh, *Tragedy of Punjab*, 178.

34. Amarjit Kaur, "Akali Dal: The Enemy Within," in *The Punjab Story* (New Delhi: Roli Books, 1985), 21.

35. *White Paper on the Punjab Agitation*, 1.

36. Brar, *Operation Blue Star: The True Story* (New Delhi: UBSPD, 1993), 27.

37. Tully and Jacob, *Amritsar*, 94–95.

38. Khushwant Singh, *My Bleeding Punjab*, 54.

39. Manoj Joshi, "Combating Terrorism in Punjab," in *Ethnic and Religious Conflicts*, ed. Peter Janke (Aldershot, England: Dartmouth, 1994), 229.

40. Under Article 356 of the Indian Constitution, the central government has the power to dismiss a state legislature if the governor of that state feels that "governance of the state cannot be carried out in accordance with the provisions of the constitution." The president's rule has often been arbitrarily imposed on various states in India.

41. Tully and Jacob, *Amritsar*, 105.

42. The Akal Takht is the Supreme temporal seat of the Sikh religious order. It literally means the "throne of the Timeless One."

43. Gill, *Punjab: The Knights of Falsehood*, 90.

44. For a detailed description of *Operation Bluestar,* see Brar, *Operation Blue Star*, 26.

45. Ibid., 27.

46. Ibid., 28.

47. Ibid., 6.

48. John Dayal, "A Fortnight of Anguish," in *The Punjab Crisis: Challenge and Response,* ed. Abida Samiuddin (New Delhi: Mittal, 1985), 189.

49. See *White Paper on the Punjab Agitation*, 3.

50. Brar, *Operation Blue Star*, 36.

51. Ibid., 41.

52. Ibid., 44.

53. See *White Paper on the Punjab Agitation*, 33–34.

54. Gurmit Singh, *History of Sikh Struggles*, vol. III, 2.

55. See *White Paper on the Punjab Agitation,* 20.

56. Estimates of the dead vary. The *White Paper on the Punjab Agitation* lists the number of civilians/terrorists dead as 493 and the number of the army casualties as 83. Tully and Jacob contend that this low estimate leaves around 1,600 people unaccounted for. An *Asia Watch Report* claims that thousands were killed. See *Punjab in Crisis: Human Rights in India* (New York: Human Rights Watch, 1991), 1. Other estimates concede that 2,000 men, women, and children were killed. See Malik, "The Politics of Alienation," 43.

57. Brar, *Operation Blue Star,* 140.

58. Tully and Jacob, *Amritsar,* 155.

59. A soldier later recounted that after suffering several casualties from the rocket-propelled grenades used by the secessionists, the Indian Army decided to use tanks to crush the secessionists. See Gurmit Singh, *History of Sikh Struggles*, vol. III, 5.

60. Tully and Jacob, *Amritsar,* 159.

61. Brar, *Operation Blue Star*, 44.

62. Maj. Gen. Brar, "It was a Difficult Task," in *The Punjab Crisis: Challenge and Response,* ed. Abida Samiuddin (New Delhi: Mittal, 1985), 162.

63. Tully and Jacob, *Amritsar,* 159.

64. A soldier of the Kumaon Regiment told this story. Reported in *Probe India*, August 1984.

65. See *Oppression in Punjab,* A Citizen's for Democracy Report to the Nation (Bombay: Hind Mazdoor Kisan Panchayat, 1985), 76.

66. See Tavleen Singh, *Kashmir: A Tragedy of Errors* (New Delhi: Viking, 1995), 64.

67. Brar, *Operation Blue Star*, 36.

68. Ibid., 48.

69. Nayar and Singh, *Tragedy of Punjab*, 172.

70. Gurharpal Singh, "The Punjab Crisis since 1984: A Reassessment," in *Subnational Movements in South Asia,* ed. Subrata K. Lewis and R. Allison Lewis (Boulder CO: Westview Press, 1996), 113.

71. *Patka* is a small piece of cloth used by a male Sikh to cover the topknot into which the hair is tied on the top of his head.

72. Cited in Pettigrew, *The Sikhs of the Punjab*, 36.

73. Joyce Pettigrew explains, "TADA allows confessions extracted under torture to be admissible as evidence.... Under TADA a statement made before a Superintendent of Police (SP) has evidential value. TADA shifts the burden of proof onto the accused, who is presumed guilty." See *The Sikhs of Punjab,* 13.

74. The "NSA provides for detention without trial for a two-year period and continued detention beyond the two-year period on the production of fresh detention orders. Trial is *in camera* and without legal representation." See *The Sikhs of the Punjab*, 13.

75. Ibid.

76. Gurharpal Singh, *Ethnic Conflict in India*, 134.

77. See *Economic and Political Weekly,* April 23, 1988.

78. See Cynthia Keppley Mahmood, *Fighting for Faith and Nation: Dialogues with Sikh Militants* (Philadelphia: University of Pennsylvania Press, 1996), 99.

79. See *Punjab in Crisis: An Asia Watch Report* (New York: Human Rights Watch, 1991), 4.

80. *India: Torture, Rape and Deaths in Custody* (New York: Amnesty International USA, 1992), 161–166.

81. Words of Wassan Singh Zaffarwal, leader of the KCF in an interview recorded for Joyce J.M. Pettigrew. Cited in Pettigrew, *The Sikhs of the Punjab*, 149.

82. Khushwant Singh, *My Bleeding Punjab,* 71.

83. Statement made by an Akali minister. Cited in Pettigrew, *The Sikhs of the Punjab*, 36.

84. Cited in Mahmood, *Fighting for Faith and Nation*, 105.

85. Director-General of Police Julio Ribeiro later acknowledged that terrorism could not be fought with repressive antiterrorist strategies, but rather, it needed a "political solution." See Gurharpal Singh, *Ethnic Conflict in India*, 134.

86. Gurharpal Singh, *Ethnic Conflict in India,* 134.

87. Gurmit Singh, *History of Sikh Struggles*, vol. III, 17.

88. Pettigrew, *The Sikhs of the Punjab*, 13

89. Ibid., 139.

90. Shekhar Gupta, *India Today*, January 15, 1991.

91. *The Sunday Times of India*, February 10, 1991.

92. "Punjab's Winter of Despair," *Frontline,* December 8–21, 1990, 9.

93. See Gurharpal Singh, *Ethnic Conflict in India*, 150, 151.

94. See Joshi, "Combating Terrorism in Punjab," 229.

95. For more on Pakistan's role, see Sharda Jain, *Politics of Terrorism in India: The Case of Punjab* (New Delhi: Deep and Deep, 1995), 255.

96. Prakash Singh, *Kohima to Kashmir: On the Terrorist Trail* (New Delhi: Rupa, 2001), 116.

97. Ibid.

98. See Shekhar Gupta, "Arms for the Asking," *India Today*, July 31, 1989, 58–63.

99. Ibid.

100. *From Surprise to Reckoning: The Kargil Review Committee Report* (New Delhi: Sage, 1999), 70.

101. Joint Intelligence Report Paper No. 8/94 on *Anti-India Activities of the ISI on the Indian Sub-Continent*, 16.

102. Ibid.

103. Manoj Joshi, "The Pakistan Connection," *Frontline*, May 28–June10, 1988, 14.

104. Ibid.

105. Ibid.

106. Interview by Joyce J.M. Pettigrew with Hardeep Singh Dhillon. Cited in *The Sikhs of the Punjab*, 105.

107. Manoj Joshi, "The Pakistan Connection," *Frontline*, May 28–June 10, 1988, 14.

108. See Chopra et al., *Agony of Punjab*, 10.

109. Ibid.

110. Ibid.

111. During the partition of India in 1947, Punjab was divided between India and Pakistan. Hindus and Sikhs from the western part of Punjab moved into the eastern part of Punjab (part of India) and Muslims from the latter moved into the former. People from both parts of Punjab are called Punjabis.

112. See Chris Smith, *The Diffusion of Small Arms and Light Weapons in Pakistan and Northern India*, The Center for Defense Studies (London: Brassey's, 1993), 27.

113. Cited in Robin Jeffrey, *What's Happening to India?* (New York: Holmes and Meier, 1994), 53.

114. Ibid.

115. Ibid., 51–52.

116. See Joshi, "Combating Terrorism in Punjab," 231.

117. See Pettigrew, *The Sikhs of the Punjab*, 106.

118. Interview of Sarabjit Singh, a former DC of Amritsar, by Joyce J.M. Pettigrew. Cited in Pettigrew, *The Sikhs of the Punjab*, 106.

119. Ibid.

## Chapter 7

1. See Herbert K. Tillema, "Foreign Overt Military Intervention in the Nuclear Age," *Journal of Peace Research* 26.2 (1989): 179.

2. For more on Kashmir's special status, see chapter 5, 70.

# Bibliography


Ahmed, Ishtiaq, *State, Nation and Ethnicity in Contemporary South Asia* (London: Pinter, 1996).

Akbar, M.J., *Kashmir: Behind the Vale* (New Delhi: Viking, 1991).

*Amrita Bazaar Patrika*, Calcutta, April 2, 1971, reprinted in *India and "Bangla Desh": Testimony from the Foreign and Indian Press* (New York: Pakistan-American Friends Association, 1971), 5.

Anderson, John Ward, "Pakistan Aiding Rebels in Kashmir," *The Washington Post*, May 16, 1994, A1.

Aurora, Jagjit Singh, "Assault on the Golden Temple Complex 5–6 June 1984," in *The Punjab Story* (New Delhi: Roli Books International, 1985), 92.

Auspitz, J. Lee, Stephen A. Marglin, and Gustav F. Papenek, "History of Economic and Political Domination of East Pakistan," in *Bangla Desh Documents*, vol. I (New Delhi: Ministry of External Affairs, Government of India, 1971).

Ayoob, Mohammed, "From Martial Law to Bangla Desh," in Pran Chopra (ed.), *The Challenge of Bangla Desh: A Special Debate* (New York: Humanities Press, 1971), 41.

Badhwar, Inderjit, "A Tarnished Triumph," *India Today*, April 15, 1987, 40–42.

Bajaj, Rajeev K., "Dead Men Tell No Tales," *Surya*, September 1984, 8–15.

Bajpai, Kanti, P.R. Chari, Pervaiz Iqbal Cheema, Stephen P. Cohen, and Sumit Ganguly, *Brasstacks and Beyond: Perception and Management of Crisis in South Asia* (New Delhi: Manohar, 1995).

Banerji, J.K., *I Report on Kashmir* (Calcutta: Republic, 1948).

*Bangladesh: Contemporary Events and Documents* (External Publicity Division, Ministry of Foreign Affairs, Government of the People's Republic of Bangladesh, 1971).

*Bangla Desh Documents*, vol. I (New Delhi: Ministry of External Affairs, Government of India, 1971).

*Bangla Desh Documents*, vol. II (New Delhi: Ministry of Information and Broadcasting, 1971).

Banyal, S. S., "Behind the rise of J & K militants," *Hindustan Times*, December 17, 1989, 24.

Bastiampillai, Bertram E.S.J., "Ethnic Conflicts in South Asia and Inter-State Relations Especially in Relation to Sri Lanka," in Shelton Kodikara (ed.), *South Asian Strategic Issues* (New Delhi: Sage, 1990), 96.

Bates, Robert H. and Barry R. Weingast, "Rationality and Interpretation: The Politics of Transition." Paper presented at the annual meeting of the American Political Science Association, August 31–September 3, 1995.

Bennett, Andrew and Alexander L. George, "Research Design Tasks in Case Study Methods," Paper presented at the McArthur Foundation Workshop on Case Study Methods, Belfer Center for Science and International Affairs (BCSIA), Harvard University, October 1997.

Bhattacharjea, Ajit, *Kashmir: The Wounded Valley* (New Delhi: UBSPD, 1994).

Bhattacharjee, G.P., *Renaissance and Freedom Movement in Bangladesh* (Calcutta: Minerva Associates).

Bishai, Linda, "Altered States: Secession and the Problem of Liberal Theory," in Percy B. Lehning (ed.), *Theories of Secession* (London: Routledge, 1998).

Bose, Sumantra, *States, Nations, Sovereignty* (New Delhi: Sage, 1994).

Bose, Tapan, Dinesh Mohan, Gautam Navlakha, and Sumanto Banerjee, "India's Kashmir War," in Asghar Ali Engineer (ed.), *Secular Crown on Fire* (New Delhi: Ajanta, 1991), 224.

Brar, K.S., *Operation Blue Star: The True Story* (New Delhi: UBSPD, 1993).

———, "It Was a Difficult Task," in Abida Samiuddin (ed.), *The Punjab Crisis: Challenge and Response* (New Delhi: Mittal, 1985), 162.

Breuilly, John, *Nationalism and the State* (Manchester: Manchester University Press, 1982).

Brown, Michael E., ed., *Ethnic Conflict and International Security* (Princeton, NJ: Princeton University Press, 1993).

———, *The International Dimensions of Internal Conflict* (Cambridge, MA: MIT Press, 1996).

Brown, Michael E., Owen R. Cote, Sean M. Lynn-Jones, and Steven E. Miller, eds, *Nationalism and Ethnic Conflict* (Cambridge, MA: MIT Press, 1997).

Bull, Hedley, ed., "Conclusion," in *Intervention in World Politics* (Oxford: Oxford University Press, 1984), 181.

Bullion, Alan J., *India, Sri Lanka and the Tamil Crisis 1976–1994* (London and New York: Pinter).

Census of Pakistan, vol. I (Karachi: Government of Pakistan, 1951).

Cetinyan, Rupen, "Ethnic Bargaining in the Shadow of Third-Party Intervention," *International Organization* 56.3 (Summer 2002): 645–677.

Ceylon House of Representatives *Debates*, vol. 56, col. 247.

———, vol. 28, col. 120.

———, vol. 33, col. I695.

———, vol. 56, col. 727.

Chalk, Peter, "The Liberation Tigers of Tamil Eelam Insurgency in Sri Lanka," in Rajat Ganguly and Ian Mcduff (eds), *Ethnic Conflict and Secessionism in South and South-east Asia* (New Delhi: Sage, 2003), 134.

Chazan, Naomi, "Approaches to the Study of Irredentism," in Naomi Chazan (ed.), *Irredentism and International Politics* (Boulder, CO: Lynne Rienner, 1991), 1.

Chopra, V.D. *Genesis of Indo-Pakistan Conflict on Kashmir* (New Delhi: Patriot, 1990).

Chopra, V.D., R.K. Mishra, and Nirmal Singh, *Agony of Punjab* (New Delhi: Patriot, 1984), 102.

Chowdhury, Subrata Roy, *The Genesis of Bangladesh* (New York: Asia, 1972).

Collier, David, "The Comparative Method," in Ada Finifter (ed.), *Political Science: The State of the Discipline II* (Washington: American Political Science Association, 1993).

*Constituent Assembly of India Debates*, vol. XI, 752 (New Delhi: Government of India).

*Constituent Assembly of Pakistan Debates*, vol. II, February 24 (Karachi: Government of Pakistan Press, 1948).

Copeland, Dale, *The Origins of Major War* (Ithaca and London: Cornell University Press, 2000).

*Country Reports on Human Rights Practices for 1983*, Report submitted to the Committee on Foreign Affairs U.S. House of Representatives and the Committee on Foreign Relations U.S. Senate by the Department of State (Washington: U.S. Government Printing Office, 1984), 1418, 1419.

Crossette, Barbara, "Protesters in Pakistan Vow to Free Kashmiris in India," *The New York Times International*, January 27, 1990, 8.

*Daily Observer*, London, June 20, 1971, reprinted in *India and "Bangla Desh": Testimony from the Foreign and Indian Press* (New York: Pakistan-American Friends Association, 1971), 13.

*Daily Telegraph*, "Divide or Rule," London, March 29, 1971, 16.

*Daily Telegraph*, "Armed Resistance Crumbles before Pakistan Army," London, April 14, 1971, reprinted in *India and "Bangla Desh": Testimony from the Foreign and Indian Press* (New York: Pakistan-American Friends Association, 1971), 5.

Das, Mitra, *From Nation to Nation: A Case Study of Bengali Independence* (Columbia, Mo: South Asia Books, 1981).

Das, Suranjan, *Kashmir and Sindh* (London: Anthem Press, 2001).

Dayal, John, "A Fortnight of Anguish," in Abida Samiuddin (ed.), *The Punjab Crisis: Challenge and Response* (New Delhi: Mittal, 1985), 189.

Desmond, Edward W., "At War with Itself," *Time*, December 24, 1990, 9.

de Silva, Chandra Richard, "Sinhala—Tamil Relations and Education in Sri Lanka: The University Admissions Issue—The First Phase, 1971–7," in Robert B. Goldmann and A. Jeyaratnam Wilson (eds), *From Independence to Statehood: Managing Ethnic Conflict in Five African and Asian States* (London: Frances Pinter, 1984), 133–134.

de Silva, K.M., *Managing Ethnic Tensions in Multi-Ethnic Societies: Sri Lanka 1880–1985* (Lanham, MD: University Press of America, 1986).

———, "Indo-Sri Lankan Relations, 1975–1989: A Study in the Internationalization of Ethnic Conflict," in K.M. de Silva and R.J. May (eds), *Internationalization of Ethnic Conflict* (London: Pinter, 1991), 77–78.

de Silva K.M. and R.J. May, eds, *Internationalization of Ethnic Conflict* (London: Pinter, 1991).

*Diary of a Survivor*, July 27, 1983, http://tamiltigers.net/history/his1983news01.htm (accessed June 28, 2007).

Diehl, Paul, "Arms Races to War: Testing Some Empirical Linkages," *Sociological Quarterly* 26.3 (1985): 334.

———, "Introduction: An Overview and Some Theoretical Guidelines," in Paul F. Diehl (ed.), *The Dynamics of Enduring Rivalries* (Urbana and Chicago: University of Illinois Press, 1998), 4.

Dion, Stephane, "Why Is Secession Difficult in Well-Established Democracies? Lessons from Quebec," *British Journal of Political Science* 26.2 (April 1996): 269–284.

Dixit, J.N., *Anatomy of a Flawed Inheritance* (New Delhi: Konark, 1995).

Dorman, Andrew M. and Thomas G. Otte, eds, *Military Intervention: From Gunboat Diplomacy to Humanitarian Intervention* (Brookfield, VT: Dartmouth, 1995).

Dring, Simon, "Dacca Eyewitness: Bloodbath, Inferno," *The Washington Post*, March 30, 1971, A1.

———, "Tanks Crush Revolt in Pakistan," *Daily Telegraph*, London, March 30, 1971, 30.

Eads, Brian, "Sri Lanka Tries to Cover Up Riot Orgy," *The Observer*, London, September 20, 1981, 405-413.

*Economic and Political Weekly*, "Punjab: Tiwana Commission's Findings," April 23, 1988, 813.

Fearon, James D., "Rationalist Explanations for War," *International Organization* 49.3 (1995): 381.

Fernandes, George, "India's Policies in Kashmir: An Assessment and Discourse," in Raju G.C. Thomas (ed.), *Perspectives on Kashmir* (Boulder, CO: Westview Press, 1992), 287.

Frohock, Fred, *Normative Political Theory* (Englewood Cliffs, NJ: Prentice Hall, 1974).

*From Surprise to Reckoning: The Kargil Review Committee Report* (New Delhi: Sage, 1999), 70.

*Frontline*, "Punjab's Winter of Despair," December 8–21, 1990, 9.

*Frontline*, "The Tamil Nadu Coast," June 22–July 5, 1991, 28.

Ganguly, Rajat, *Kin State Intervention in Ethnic Conflicts* (New Delhi: Sage, 1998).

Ganguly, Sumit, "The Prospects of War and Peace in Kashmir," in Raju G.C. Thomas (ed.), *Perspectives on Kashmir* (Boulder CO: Westview Press, 1992), 357.

———, *The Crisis in Kashmir* (Cambridge, UK: Cambridge University Press; Washington, DC: The Woodrow Wilson Center Press, 1997).

———, *Conflict Unending* (New York: Columbia University Press, 2001).

Garamone, Jim, "Intelligence Chief Details Threats Facing America," *Defense Link* (American Forces Information Service) Web Service, February 22, 2001.

George, Alexander L., "Case Studies and Theory Development: The Method of Structured, Focused Comparison," in Paul Gordon Laursen (ed.), *Diplomacy: New Approaches in History, Theory and Policy* (New York: Free Press, 1979).

George, Alexander L. and Timothy J. McKeown, "Case Studies and Theories of Organizational Decisionmaking," in Robert F. Coulam and Richard A. Smith (eds), *Advances in Information Processing in Organizations*, vol. 2 (Greenwich, CT: JA1Press, 1985).

George, Alexander L. and Richard Smoke, *Deterrence in American Foreign Policy: Theory and Practice* (New York: Columbia University Press).

Gill, K.P.S., "Endgame in Punjab: 1988–1993," *Faultlines*, vol. 1, May 1999, 1–72.

———, *Punjab: The Knights of Falsehood* (New Delhi: Har-Anand, 1997), 14.

Gilpin, Robert, *War and Change in World Politics* (New York: Cambridge University Press, 1981).

Ghose, Partha S., "Kashmir Tangle and Indo-Pak Relations: Some Suggestions," in Asghar Ali Engineer (ed.), *Secular Crown on Fire* (New Delhi: Ajanta, 1991), 97.

Goldstone, Jack, "Social Movements or Revolutions? On the Evolution and Outcomes of Collective Action," in Marco G. Giugni, Doug McAdam and Charles Tilly (eds.), *From Contention to Democracy* (Lanham, MD: Rowman & Littlefield, 1998), 130.

Grey, Edward, *Twenty-Five Years*, vol. I (London: Hodder and Staughton, 1925).

Grieco, Joseph, "Anarchy and the Limits of Cooperation: A Realist Critique of the Newest Liberal Institutionalism," *International Organization* 42 (Summer 1988), 485–507.
———, *Cooperation among Nations: Europe, America, and Non-Tariff Barriers to Trade* (Ithaca: Cornell University Press, 1990).
Gunaratna, Rohan, *Indian Intervention in Sri Lanka* (Colombo: South Asian Network on Conflict Research, 1993).
Gupta, Shekhar, "Arms for the Asking," *India Today*, July 31, 1989, 58–63.
———, "Kashmir Valley: Militant Siege," *India Today*, January 31, 1990, 35.
———, "Ominous Presence in Tamil Nadu," *India Today*, March 31, 1984, 88.
Gupta, Shekhar, "Exporting Terror," *India Today*, May 15, 1994, 25–45.
Gupta, Sisir, "From the Partition to Yahya Khan," in Pran Chopra (ed.), *The Challenge of Bangladesh: A Special Debate* (New York: Humanities Press, 1971).
Gupta, Vinod, *Anderson Papers: A Study of Nixon's Blackmail of India* (New Delhi: ISSD, 1972).
Gurr, Ted Robert, "War, Revolution, and the Growth of the Coercive State," *Comparative Political Studies* 21.1 (1988): 45–65.
Gurr, Ted Robert and Barbara Harff, eds, *Ethnic Conflict in World Politics* (Boulder and Oxford: Westview Press, 1994).
Haas, Ernst, *Beyond the Nation-State—Functionalism and International Organization* (Stanford, CA: Stanford University Press, 1964).
Hayes, Louis D., *The Impact of U.S. Policy on the Kashmir Conflict* (Tucson: The University of Arizona Press, 1971).
Hazarika, Sanjoy, "India Says Pakistan Is Stirring Up Kashmir Unrest," *The New York Times International*, February 1, 1990, A5.
Hechter, Michael, "The Dynamics of Secession," *Acta Sociologica* 35 (1992): 267–283.
Hellmann-Rajanayagam, D., "The Tamil Tigers in Northern Sri Lanka: Origins, Factions, Programmes," *Internationales Asienforum* 17.1/2 (May 1986): 67.
Heraclides, Alex, "Secessionist Minorities and External Involvement," *International Organization* 44.3 (Summer 1990): 341–379.
———, *The Self-Determination of Minorities in International Politics* (London: Frank Cass, 1991).
Herz, John, "Idealist Internationalism and the Security Dilemma," *World Politics* 2.2 (January 1950): 157–180.
———, *Political Realism and Political Idealism* (Chicago: University of Chicago Press, 1951).
Hewitt, Vernon, "India: The State, Ethnicity and Nationalism," in Don MacIver (ed.), *The Politics of Multinational States* (New York: St. Martin's Press, 1999), 54.
Horowitz, Donald L., "Irredentas and Secession," in Naomi Chazan (ed.), *Irredentism and International Politics* (Boulder, CO: Lynne Rienner, 1991).
Housego, David, "In Kashmir, One Man's Refugee is another Man's Guerrilla," *The Financial Times*, June 6, 1990.
Howard, Michael, *The Causes of War* (Cambridge, MA: Harvard University Press, 1983).
Howard, Roger, "Wrath of Islam: The HUA Analysed," in *Jane's Intelligence Review*, 9. 10 (October 1997): 466-468.
Hussain, Mushahid, "The Kashmir Issue: Its New International Dimensions," in Raju G.C. Thomas (ed.), *Perspectives on Kashmir: The Roots of Conflict in South Asia* (Boulder, CO: Westview Press, 1992), 346.

Huth, Paul and Bruce Russett, "What Makes Deterrence Work? Cases from 1900 to 1980," *World Politics* 36 (1984): 496–526.

*India and "Bangla Desh": Testimony from the Foreign and Indian Press* (New York: Pakistan-American Friends Association, 1971).

*India: Arms and Abuses in Indian Punjab and Kashmir*, "Watch on Arms Project Report," vol. VI, no. 10, September 1994, 2.

*India Today*, "The Tamil Tragedy," New Delhi, August 31, 1983, 17.

*India Today*, "Tackling the Tigers," New Delhi, June 30, 1987, 18.

*India: Torture, Rape and Deaths in Custody* (New York: Amnesty International, 1992), 124.

*Indian Express*, "Bahini Controls 300 Border Posts," New Delhi, August 12, 1971, 1.

*Indian Express*, New Delhi, August 15, 1990.

*Indian Express*, New Delhi, October 21, 1990.

*Insight*, August 20, 1990.

Jackson, Robert, *South Asian Crisis* (London: Chatto and Windus, 1975).

Jagmohan, *My Frozen Turbulence in Kashmir* (New Delhi: Allied, 1991).

Jain, Rajendra K., *U.S–South Asian Relations 1947–1982*, vol. 3 (New Jersey: Humanities Press, 1983).

Jain, Sharda, *Politics of Terrorism in India: The Case of Punjab* (New Delhi: Deep and Deep, 1995), 255.

*Jang*, "Statement by Brig. Mohammed Yusuf," Karachi, September 30, 1971, reprinted in *Bangla Desh Documents*, vol. II (New Delhi: Ministry of Information and Broadcasting, 1971), 137.

*Jang*, "Statement by Mr. Akhtaruddin Ahmed," Karachi, October 3, 1971, reprinted in *Bangla Desh Documents*, vol. II (New Delhi: Ministry of Information and Broadcasting, 1971), 137.

Janke, Peter, ed., *Ethnic and Religious Conflicts: Europe and Asia* (Brookfield, VT: Dartmouth, 1994).

Jeffrey, Robin, *What's Happening to India?* (New York: Holmes and Meier, 1994).

Jervis, Robert, "Cooperation under the Security Dilemma," *World Politics* 30.2 (January 1978), 167–214.

Johnson, Marguerite, "Island at War," *Lanka Guardian*, vol. 9, 5–9.

Joint Intelligence Report Paper No. 8/94 on *Anti-India Activities of the ISI on the Indian Sub-Continent*, 16.

Jones, Rodney W. and Mark G. McDonough, *Tracking Nuclear Proliferation: A Guide in Maps and Charts, 1998* (Washington DC: Carnegie Endowment for International Peace, 1998).

Joshi, Manoj, "The Pakistan Connection," *Frontline*, May 28–June 10, 1988, 14.

———, "A Base for all Seasons," *Frontline*, August 3–16, 1991, 21–22.

———, "Combating Terrorism in Punjab," in Peter Janke (ed.), *Ethnic and Religious Conflicts* (Aldershot, England: Dartmouth, 1994), 229.

Kadian, Rajesh, *India's Sri Lanka Fiasco: Peacekeepers at War* (New Delhi and Bombay: Vision Books, 1990).

———, *The Kashmir Tangle* (Boulder, CO: Westview Press, 1993).

Kann, Peter, "Bangla Desh: A Pragmatic Silence," *The Wall Street Journal*, May 12, 1971, 16.

Karstedt-Henke, Sabine, "Theorien zur Erklarung terroristischer Bewegungen," in E. Blankenburg (ed.), *Politikder inneren Sicherheit* (Frankfurt: Suhrkamp, 1980).

*Kashmir under Siege: Human Rights in India*, An Asia Watch Report (New York: Human Rights Watch, 1991), 1–127.

Kaul, Kanhya L. and M.K. Teng, "Human Rights Violations of Kashmiri Hindus," in Raju G.C. Thomas (ed.), *Perspectives on Kashmir: The Roots of Conflict in South Asia* (Boulder, CO: Westview Press), 180.

Kaul, Ravi, "The Indian Ocean: A Strategic Posture for India," in T.T. Poulose (ed.), *Indian Ocean Power Rivalry* (New Delhi: International Publications Service, 1974), 66.

Kaur, Amarjit, "Akali Dal: The Enemy Within," in *The Punjab Story* (New Delhi: Roli Books, 1985), 21.

Khan, Ahsan Ali, "The Tamil Question in Historical Perspective: Its Impact on Indo-Sri Lankan Relations," *Pakistan Horizon*, vol. 37, no. 2 (1984): 58.

Khan, Roedad, *The American Papers* (Oxford: Oxford University Press, 1999).

Kodikara, Shelton U., *Indo-Ceylon Relations since Independence* (Colombo: Ceylon Institute of World Affairs, 1965).

———, "Internationalization of Sri Lanka's Ethnic Conflict: The Tamil Nadu Factor," in K.M. de Silva and R.J. May (eds), *Internationalization of Ethnic Conflict* (London: Pinter, 1991), 112.

———, "Introduction," in Shelton U. Kodikara (ed.), *South Asian Strategic Issues: Sri Lankan Perspectives* (New Delhi: Sage, 1990), 13.

Koopmans, Ruud, *Democracy from Below: New Social Movements and the Political System in West Germany* (Boulder, CO: Westview Press, 1995).

Kothari, Rajni, "Electoral Politics and the Rise of Communalism," in Patwant Singh and Harji Malik (eds), *Punjab: The Fatal Miscalculation* (New Delhi: Patwant Singh, 1985), 78.

Kriesi, Hanspeter, Ruud Koopmans, Jan Willem Dyvendak, and Marco G. Giugni, *New Social Movements in Western Europe* (Minneapolis: University of Minnesota Press, 1995), 84.

Lake, David A. and Donald Rothchild, "Spreading Fear: The Genesis of Transnational Ethnic Conflict," in David A. Lake and Donald Rothchild (eds), *The International Spread of Ethnic Conflict* (Princeton, NJ: Princeton University Press, 1998), 4.

Lamb, Alastair, *Kashmir: A Disputed Legacy 1846–1990* (Hertfordshire: Roxford Books, 1991).

*Lanka Guardian*, "The Sri Lankan Conflict on Indian Perception," vol. 10, no. 4, June 15, 1987, 17.

Lebow, Richard Ned, "Windows of Vulnerability. Do States Jump through Them?" *International Security* 9 (Summer 1984): 147–186.

Levy, Jack, "Declining Power and the Preventive Motivation for War," *World Politics* 40 (1987): 82–107.

Liska, George, *Nations in Alliance: The Limits of Interdependence* (Baltimore, MD: Johns Hopkins University Press, 1962).

MacIver, Don, "Introduction: States and Ethnic Pluralism," in Don MacIver (ed.), *The Politics of Multinational States* (Great Britain: Macmillan, 1999), 2.

Mahmood, Cynthia Keppley, *Fighting for Faith and Nation: Dialogues with Sikh Militants* (Philadelphia: University of Pennsylvania Press, 1996).

Malhotra, Inder, "Kashmir's Unending Agony," *The Times of India*, November 23, 1989, 6.

Malik, Harji, "The Politics of Alienation," in Patwant Singh and Harji Malik (eds), *Punjab: The Fatal Miscalculation* (New Delhi: Patwant Singh, 1985), 37.

Malik, Iffat, *Ethnic Conflict International Dispute* (Oxford: Oxford University Press, 2002), 155.

Maniruzzaman, Talukder, *The Bangladesh Revolution and Its Aftermath* (Dacca: Bangladesh Books, 1980), 106.

Manor, James, "Introduction," in James Manor (ed.), *Sri Lanka in Change and Crisis* (London and Sydney: Croom Helm, 1984), 5.

Maoz, Zeev and Ben D. Mor, "Learning, Preference Change, and the Evolution of Enduring Rivalries," in Paul F. Diehl (ed.), *The Dynamics of Enduring Rivalries* (Urbana and Chicago: University of Illinois Press, 1998), 129.

Marks, Tom, "'Peoples War' in Sri Lanka: Insurgency and Counterinsurgency," *Issues and Studies*, 22.8 (1986): 63–100.

Mascarenhas, Anthony, *The Rape of Bangladesh* (New Delhi: Vikas, 1971).

———, "The Slaughter in East Pakistan," *The Times*, London, April 3, 1971, 15.

———, "Genocide," *Sunday Times*, June 13, 1971, 12–14.

———, "Tamil Fighters Prepare for War," *The Sunday Times*, London, April 1, 1984, 9.

McGowan, William, *Only Man Is Vile* (New York: Farrar, Straus & Giroux, 1992).

Merritt, Richard L. and Dina A. Zinnes, "Alternative Indexes of National Power," in Richard J. Stoll and Michael D. Ward (eds), *Power in World Politics* (Boulder and London: Lynne Rienner, 1989), 27.

Messing, Andy Jr., "Hidden Conflict in Kashmir," *The Washington Times*, February 5, 1992, F3.

Miglani, Sanjeev, *The Statesman*, November 6, 1989.

Mill, John Stuart, "Two Methods of Comparison," in Amitai Etzioni and Frederic L. Dubow (eds), *Comparative Perspectives: Theories and Methods* (Boston: Little Brown, 1970), 205–213.

*Ministry of Home Affairs, Agenda: National Integration Council Meeting*, December 31, 1991 (New Delhi: Government of India Press, 1991), Annexure 1.

Mitchell, C.R., "Civil Strife and the Involvement of External Parties," *International Studies Quarterly* 14 (June 1970): 166–194.

Modelski, George, "The International Relations of Internal War," in James N. Rosenau (ed.), *International Aspects of Civil Strife* (Princeton, NJ: Princeton University Press, 1964), 14–44.

Moore, Will H. and David R. Davis, "Transnational Ethnic Ties and Foreign Policy," in David A. Lake and Donald Rothchild (eds), *The International Spread of Ethnic Conflict: Fear Diffusion and Escalation* (Princeton, NJ: Princeton University Press, 1998), 89.

Morgenthau, Hans, *Politics among Nations* (New York: Knopf, 1978).

*Morning News*, "Mujib Deplores Apathy Towards Cyclone Victims," November 27, 1970, Karachi and Dacca, reprinted in *Bangla Desh Documents*, vol. I (New Delhi: Ministry of External Affairs, Government of India, 1971), 123.

*Morning News*, "Elections on Schedule. Maximum Autonomy to E. Wing," November 29, 1970, Karachi and Dacca.

*Morning News*, "Yahya puts off National Assembly Session," March 2, 1971, Karachi and Dacca, 1.

Munro, R., "Sri Lanka: Case Study of a Disaster," *Time*, New York, April 3, 1989, 14–15.

Naipaul, Shiva, *Unfinished Journey* (London: Hamish Hamilton, 1986).

*Nation*, December 1989.

Navaratna-Bandara, Abeysinghe M., *The Management of Ethnic Secessionist Conflict: The Big Neighbor Syndrome* (Brookfield, VT: Dartmouth, 1995).

Nayar, Kuldip and Khushwant Singh, *Tragedy of Punjab* (New Delhi: Vision Books, 1984).

*Newsweek*, "A Talk with Pakistan's President Yahya Khan," November 8, 1971, 53.

*Newsweek*, "The Battle for Bengal," December 6, 1971, 30–37.

Niou, Emerson M.S. and Peter C. Odershook, "Preventive War and the Balance of Power," *Journal of Conflict Resolution* 31 (September 1987): 387–419.

Nithiyanandan, V., "An Analysis of Economic Factors behind the Origin and Development of Tamil Nationalism in Sri Lanka," in C. Abeysekara and N. Gunasinghe (eds), *Facets of Ethnicity in Sri Lanka* (Colombo: Social Scientists' Association, 1987).

Noorani, A.G., "The Betrayal of Kashmir: Pakistan's Duplicity and India's Complicity," in Raju G.C. Thomas (ed.), *Perspectives on Kashmir: The Roots of Conflict in South Asia* (Boulder, CO: Westview Press, 1992), 272.

O'Ballance, Edgar, *The Cyanide War: Tamil Insurrection in Sri Lanka* 1973–88 (London: Brassey's, 1989).

Oberst, Robert C., "Youth Militancy and the Rise of Sri Lanka: Tamil Nationalism," in Subrata K. Mitra and R. Alison Lewis (eds), *Subnational Movements in South Asia*, (Boulder, CO: Westview Press, 1996), 143.

O'Donnell, Charles Peter, *Bangladesh: Biography of a Muslim Nation* (Boulder and London: Westview Press, 1984).

Oppenheim, L., "Peace," in H. Lauterpacht (ed.), *International Law: A Treatise*, vol. I (London: Longmans, 1955), 305.

*Oppression in Punjab*, A Citizen's for Democracy Report to the Nation (Bombay: Hind Mazdoor Kisan Panchayat, 1985).

*Pakistan Horizon*, "President Yahya Khan's Broadcast to His Nation," vol. XXIV, no. 3, June 28, 1971, 111–112, 127–130.

*Pakistan Times*, "World War if India not Checked: Appeal to U.N. to Act," Lahore, October 7, 1971, reprinted in *Bangla Desh Documents*, vol. II (New Delhi: Ministry of Information and Broadcasting, 1971), 7.

*Pakistan Times*, "India on Lookout to Destroy Pakistan," Lahore, October 13, 1971, reprinted in *Bangla Desh Documents*, vol. II (New Delhi: Ministry of Information and Broadcasting, 1971), 5.

Palit, D.K., *The Lightning Campaign* (New Delhi: Thomson Press, 1972).

Pasha, Mustapha Kamal, "Beyond the Two-Nation Divide: Kashmir and Resurgent Islam," in Raju G.C. Thomas (ed.), *Perspectives on Kashmir: The Roots of Conflict in South Asia* (Boulder, CO: Westview Press, 1992), 377.

*Patriot*, "Incipient Insurgency in Kashmir," October 24, 1989, 4.

*Peace Initiatives*, "Radical Islam, Mercenaries and the Proxy War," vol. III, no. V, September–October 1997, 5.

Peiris, Denzil, "Colombo Rides the Tiger," *South*, March 1985, 13–15.

Pettigrew, Joyce M., *The Sikhs of the Punjab* (London and New Jersey: Zed Books, 1995).

Piyadasa, L., *Sri Lanka: The Holocaust and After* (London: Marram Books, 1984).

Ponnambalam, Satchi, *Sri Lanka: National Conflict and the Tamil Liberation Struggle* (London: Zed Books, 1983).

Posen, Barry, "The Security Dilemma and Ethnic Conflict," *Survival* 35.1 (Spring 1993): 27–47.

Premdas, Ralph R., S.W.R. de A. Samarasinghe, and Alan B. Anderson, eds, *Secessionist Movements in Comparative Perspective* (New York: St. Martin's Press, 1990).

*Probe India*, August 1984.

*Proliferation: Threat and Response*, "NBC Proliferation Challenges: South Asia," (Washington, DC: Department of Defense Report, January 2001), 30.

*Punjab in Crisis: Human Rights in India*, an Asia Watch Report (New York: Human Rights Watch, 1991), 1–167.

Qasim, Mir, *My Life and Times* (New Delhi: Allied, 1992).

Ragostra, M., "India and Her Neighbours," *The Independent*, London, April 15, 1989, 15.

Rasler, Karen, "Internationalized Civil War: A Dynamic Analysis of the Syrian Intervention in Lebanon," *The Journal of Conflict Resolution*, 27.3 (September 1983): 449.

*Realities Cambodgiennes*, Phnom Penh, October 22, 1971.

Reddy, K.G., "India Cannot Be silent on Sri Lanka: PM," *The Hindu*, August 16, 1984.

Rehman, A., *East and West Pakistan: A Problem in Political Economy of Regional Planning*. Occasional paper no. 20, Harvard University Center for International Affairs, 1968.

Rehman, Sheikh Mujibur, *Bangladesh, My Bangladesh* (New Delhi: Orient Longman, 1972).

*Report of the Advisory Panels for Fourth Five-Year Plan* 1970–1975, vol. I; Planning Commission Government of Pakistan, July 1970, p. 25; table 2.

*Reuters News Agency*, London, May 7, 1971, reprinted in *India and "Bangla Desh": Testimony from the Foreign and Indian Press* (New York: Pakistan-American Friends Association, 1971), 10.

Rose, L.E. "Indian Foreign Relations: Reassessing Basic Policies," in M.M. Bouton and P. Oldenburg (eds), *India Briefing* (Boulder, CO: Westview Press, 1990), 73.

Roy-Chowdhury, Shankar, *Times of India*, June 20, 1999.

Saha, B.P., *Liberation Struggle and After* (New Delhi: Vikas, 1985), 13–16.

Saravanamuttu, P., "Instability in Sri Lanka," *Survival*, 32.5 (1990): 457.

Schanberg, Sydney H., "A Diplomatic Tightrope for India," *The New York Times*, April 29, 1971, 12.

———, "India and Pakistani Armies Confront Each Other Along Borders," *The New York Times*, October 20, 1971, 6.

Schofield, Victoria, *Kashmir in Conflict* (London and New York: I.B. Tauris, 2000).

———, *Kashmir in the Crossfire* (London: I.B. Tauris, 1996).

Schwarz, Walter, *The Tamils of Sri Lanka* (London: Minority Rights Group, 1988).

Schweller, Randall L., "Democratic Structure and Preventive War: Are Democracies More Pacific?" *World Politics* 44 (January 1992): 235–269.

Senaratne, Jagath P., *Political Violence in Sri Lanka, 1977–1990* (Amsterdam: VU University Press, 1997).

Sheehan, Michael, *The Balance of Power: History and Theory* (New York: Routledge, 1996).

Shiels, Frederick L., ed., *Ethnic Separatism and World Politics* (Lanham, MD: University Press of America, 1984).

Singh, Gurharpal, *Ethnic Conflict in India* (New York: St. Martin's Press, 2000).

———, "The Punjab Crisis since 1984: A Reassessment," in Subrata K. Lewis and R. Alison Lewis (eds), *Subnational Movements in South Asia* (Boulder, CO: Westview Press, 1996), 113.

Singh, Gurmit, *History of the Sikh Struggle*, vols I–III (New Delhi: Atlantic, 1991).

Singh, Khushwant, *A History of the Sikhs*, vol. II (Princeton, NJ: Princeton University Press, 1966).

———, "Genesis of the Hindu-Sikh Divide," in *The Punjab Story* (New Delhi: Roli Books, 1985), 1.

———, *My Bleeding Punjab* (New Delhi: UBSPD, 1992).

Singh, Prakash, *Kohima to Kashmir: On the Terrorist Trail* (New Delhi: Rupa, 2001), 116.

Singh, Sarab Jit, *Operation Black Thunder: An Eyewitness Account of Terrorism in Punjab* (New Delhi: Sage, 2002), 46.

Singh, Tavleen, *Kashmir: A Tragedy of Errors* (New Delhi: Viking, 1995), 135–136.

———, "Terrorists in the Temple," in *The Punjab Story* (New Delhi: Roli Books, 1985), 33.

Sisson, Richard and Leo E. Rose, *War and Secession: Pakistan, India and the Creation of Bangladesh* (Berkeley and Los Angeles: University of California Press, 1990).

Sivarajah, A., "Indo-Sri Lanka Relations and Sri Lanka's Ethnic Crisis: The Tamil Nadu Factor," in Shelton U. Kodikara (ed.), *South Asian Strategic Issues* (New Delhi and Newbury Park and London: Sage, 1990), 136.

Siverson R.M. and J. King, "Alliances and the Expansion of War," in J.D. Singer and M. Wallace (eds), *To Augur Well: Early Warning Indicators in World Politics* (Beverly Hills: Sage, 1979), 37–49.

Skocpol, Theda, *States and Social Revolutions* (Cambridge, UK: Cambridge University Press, 1979).

Smith, Chris, *The Diffusion of Small Arms and Light Weapons in Pakistan and Northern India*, The Center for Defense Studies (London: Brassey's, 1993).

Smoke, Richard, *War: Controlling Escalation* (Cambridge, MA: Harvard University Press, 1977).

South Asia Terrorism Portal, "Babbar Khalsa International," www.satp.org (accessed June 29, 2007).

Soz, Saifuddin, "An Ostrich-Like Attitude towards Kashmir Won't Do," *The Times of India*, September 3, 1990.

Spencer, Jonathan, "Introduction: The Power of the Past," in Jonathan Spencer (ed.), *Sri Lanka: History and Roots of Conflict* (London and New York: Routledge, 1990), 2.

Spencer, Metta, ed., *Separatism: Democracy and Disintegration* (Lanham, MD: Rowman & Littlefield, 1998).

Srinivasan, Girish, "Kashmir and Punjab: Fundamental Differences," *The Independent*, May 2, 1990.

Stirrat, R.L., "The Riots and the Roman Catholic Church in Historical Perspective," in James Manor (ed.), *Sri Lanka in Change and Crisis* (New York: St. Martin's Press, 1984), 203.

Subramanyam, K. "Kashmir," *Strategic Analysis* 3.2 (May 1990): 111–198.

Suhrke, Astri and Lela Garner Noble, eds, *Ethnic Conflict in International Relations* (New York: Praeger, 1977).

*Surya India*, "1990s: The Dawn of Terror," January 1990, 8-25.

Tambiah, S.J., *Sri Lanka: Ethnic Fratricide and the Dismantling of Democracy* (Chicago and London: University of Chicago Press, 1986).

Tarkunde, V.M., Balraj Puri, Sulochana Shikhre, and N.D. Pancholi, *Report on Human Rights Situation in the Kashmir Valley*, May 20–25 (New Delhi: Coordination Committee on Kashmir, 1992), 15.

*The Dawn*, October 31, 1947.

*The Dawn*, "Yahya Urges Calm During Polls," Karachi, December 4, 1970, 1.

*The Dawn*, "Constitution Has to Be Based on Six-Points," Karachi, December 20, 1970, 1.

*The Dawn*, "Mr. A. A. Bhutto's Declaration in Peshawar," Karachi, February 16, 1971, reprinted in *Bangla Desh Documents*, vol. I (New Delhi: Ministry of External Affairs, Government of India, 1971), 156.

*The Dawn*, "Pakistan Peoples's Party Not Going to Endorse a 'Dictated' Constitution," Karachi, February 18, 1971, reprinted in *Bangla Desh Documents*, vol. I (New Delhi: Ministry of External Affairs, Government of India, 1971), 164–165.

*The Economist*, "Kashmir: Conspiracy Theory," July 13, 1991, 35.

*The Hindu*, August 24, 1950.

*The Hindu*, September 3, 1983.

*The Hindu*, "Arson in Mannar, 36 Tamil Extremists Shot," August 14, 1984, 1.

*The Hindu*, "India Cannot be Silent on Sri Lanka: PM," August 16, 1984, 9.

*The Hindu*, "Concern Over Killings Conveyed to Colombo," August 17, 1984.

*The Human Rights Crisis in Kashmir: A Pattern of Impunity* (New York: Asia Watch: A Division of Human Rights Watch, 1993).

*The Island*, January 25, 1987.

*The Island*, June 3, 1987.

*The New York Times*, January 15, 1990.

*The New York Times* Web Service, "Pakistan's Words: 'To Restore the Strategic Balance,'" May 29, 1998, A8.

*The Pakistan Observer*, "Constitution based on Six and Eleven Points will be Framed: Mujib Confident," January 4, 1971, 1, 12.

*The Times*, "The Tragedy of India and Pakistan," London, May 22, 1971, 13.

*The Times*, "Colombo debates Separatist Ban," London, August 5, 1983, 4.

*The Times*, "Jayewardene Claims He Has Thwarted Scheme to Set Up Dictatorship," London, August 8, 1983, 5.

*The Times of India*, "Mukti Fauj Damages Pak Ships," August 21, 1971, 1.

*The Washington Post*, "India, Pakistan Build up Border Military Strength,: October 17, 1971, A1, A5.

Tillema, Herbert K., "Foreign Overt Military Intervention in the Nuclear Age: A Clarification," *Journal of Peace Research*, 26.4 (1989): 419.

*Tribune*, "The Preventions of Terrorism," Colombo, September 25, 1982, 15–16.

Thucydides, *The Peloponnesian War*, trans. Rex Warner (New York: Penguin, 1954), v.23

Tully, Mark and Satish Jacob, *Amritsar: Mrs. Gandhi's Last Battle* (London: Jonathan Cape, 1985).

U.S. Senate, *Congressional Record*, May 18, 1971, S7128–S7129.

Van Evera, Stephen, *Causes of War: Power and Roots of Conflict* (Ithaca, NY: Cornell University Press, 1999).

Vasquez, John, *The War Puzzle* (Cambridge,UK: Cambridge University Press, 1993).

Walt, Stephen M., *The Origin of Alliances* (New York: Cornell University Press, 1987).

Waltz, Kenneth, "Reflections on *Theory of International Politics*: A Response to My Critics," in Robert O. Keohane (ed.), *Neorealism and Its Critics* (New York: Columbia University Press, 1986), 322–345.

———, *Theory of International Politics* (Reading, MA: Addison-Wesley, 1979).

———, "Theory of International Relations," in Fred Greenstein and Nelson Polsby (eds), *The Handbook of Political Science* (Reading, MA: Addison-Wesley, 1975).

Wayman, Frank Whelon and Daniel M. Jones, "Evolution of Conflict in Enduring Rivalries," Paper presented at the annual meeting of the International Studies Association, Vancouver, British Columbia, March 20–23, 1991.

Weingast, Barry R., "Constructing Trust: The Political and Economic Roots of Ethnic and Regional Conflict," in Karol Soltan, Eric Uslaner, and V. Haufler (eds), *Institutions and Social Order* (Ann Arbor: University of Michigan Press, 1998), 163–200.

*White Paper on the Punjab Agitation* (New Delhi: Government of India, 1984).

Wight, Martin, "The Balance of Power," in H. Butterfield and M. Wight (eds), *Diplomatic Investigations* (London: George, Allen, & Unwin, 1966), 151.

Williams, Colin H., ed., *National Separatism* (Cardiff: University of Wales Press, 1982).

Wilson, A. Jeyaratnam, *The Break-up of Sri Lanka* (London: C. Hurst, 1988).

Wirsing, Robert G., *India, Pakistan, and the Kashmir Dispute* (New York: St. Martin's Press, 1994).

———, *Kashmir in the Shadow of War* (New York: M.E. Sharpe, 2003).

Wolfers, Arnold, "Alliances," in David L. Sills (ed.), *International Encyclopedia of the Social Sciences* (New York: Macmillan, 1968), 268.

Wood, John R., "Secession: A Comparative Analytical Framework," *Canadian Journal of Political Science* 16 (1981): 107–134.

*World Development Report 1999/2000: Entering the 21st Century* (New York: Oxford University Press for the World Bank), 231, table 1.

Zinnes, Dina, "An Analytical Study of the Balance of Power Theories," *Journal of Peace Research* 4 (1967): 272.

# Index

# About the Author

**ANNE NORONHA DOS SANTOS** is a lecturer in Political Science at California State University, Fullerton. She holds a PhD in Political Science, with a major in International Relations, from the University of California, Riverside.

www.ingramcontent.com/pod-product-compliance
Ingram Content Group UK Ltd.
Pitfield, Milton Keynes, MK11 3LW, UK
UKHW020815290926
15470UKWH00003B/1173